PRESIDENTIAL ★ ★ PAYOLA

Text © 2011 Thomas J. Craughwell

First published in the USA in 2011 by
Fair Winds Press, a member of
Quayside Publishing Group
100 Cummings Center
Suite 406-L
Beverly, MA 01915-6101
www.fairwindspress.com

15 14 13 12 11   1 2 3 4 5

ISBN-13: 978-1-59233-451-3
ISBN-10: 1-59233-451-2

Digital edition published in 2011
eISBN: 978-1-61058-049-6

Library of Congress Cataloging-in-Publication Data
Craughwell, Thomas J. 1956-
 Presidential payola : the true stories of monetary scandals in the Oval Office that robbed tax payers to grease palms, stuff pockets, and pay for undue influence from Teapot Dome to Halliburton / Thomas J. Craughwell.
    p. cm.
 Includes bibliographical references and index.
 ISBN-13: 978-1-59233-451-3
 ISBN-10: 1-59233-451-2
 1. Presidents--United States--History--Anecdotes. 2. Presidents--United States--Biography--Anecdotes. 3. Scandals--United States--History--Anecdotes. 4. Political corruption--United States--History--Anecdotes. 5. United States--Politics and government--Anecdotes. I. Title.

E176.C79 2011
973.09'9--dc22

                                                            2010047044

Cover design by Peter Long
Book design by Sheila Hart Design, Inc.

Printed and bound in Singapore

PRESIDENTIAL ★ PAYOLA ★

**THE TRUE STORIES OF MONETARY SCANDALS IN THE OVAL OFFICE
THAT ROBBED TAXPAYERS TO GREASE PALMS, STUFF POCKETS,
AND PAY FOR UNDUE INFLUENCE FROM TEAPOT DOME TO HALLIBURTON**

THOMAS J. CRAUGHWELL
AUTHOR OF *FAILURES OF THE PRESIDENTS*

FAIR WINDS
PRESS
BEVERLY, MASSACHUSETTS

CONTENTS

★ ★ ★

INTRODUCTION

★ ★ ★

It takes money to run a presidential campaign. To support the election campaigns of other members of your political party. And to gear up for your reelection campaign. And to build your presidential library after you leave office. Although the contributions of the ordinary party faithful are always welcome, the big bucks, the contributions that make a significant difference, come from corporations, trade unions, advocacy groups, and wealthy individuals. In exchange for their contributions, these donors may expect a government job or contract, or some favorable legislation. This kind of horse trading is as old as politics itself, but when the trading crosses the line into the realm of corruption, then we have a scandal.

Perhaps presidential scandals are inevitable. The federal government is so enormous and so complex that no one can monitor the activities of all of its employees. And the government has become so powerful that the opportunities for influence-peddling, payoffs, and old-fashioned graft are probably endless. Add to this a sense of arrogance, entitlement, and invulnerability that seem to come with the job.

Interestingly, it is hard to find a financial scandal involving the president from the administrations of George Washington through that of James Buchanan. It is difficult to pin down exactly why this is the case, but it may have to do with the political and business climate of those days. The federal government was much smaller than it is today, which would have made it more difficult to conceal illegal and unethical activities. Business was virtually unregulated so there was no need to go to Washington to convince some agency to look the other way as a factory dumped untreated chemicals into a river, or underpaid its employees, or sold shoddy goods to consumers. Although nearly all of those early presidents complained of being swarmed by office seekers, there is no record of a president soliciting or receiving a bribe in exchange for giving a political supporter a job.

The Civil War changed all that. The size of the federal government and the military exploded overnight. There were new government jobs, and new opportunities for lucrative government and military contracts. It was early in the war when the first recorded financial scandal took place in the White House—and it involved First Lady Mary Todd Lincoln. After Abraham Lincoln's election she had let it be known that she would be active in her husband's administration. Ambitious men took to calling upon Mrs. Lincoln to ask for her help in securing government posts. As a token of their esteem and appreciation, these gentlemen presented Mary Lincoln with gifts—one such office seeker gave her diamond jewelry.

In the accounts of presidential financial scandals that follow, readers will find that there are varying degrees of culpability. The presidency of Ulysses S. Grant was torn apart by scandal, but the president himself was incorruptible. It was his associates, his friends, even members of his family who were on the take. Grant had so much faith in the people he considered part of his inner circle, that, in some cases, even when the evidence of their guilt was glaring, he could not bring himself to believe it.

At the opposite end of the spectrum from the naïve Grant is Bill Clinton who offered donors a night in the White House's Lincoln Bedroom in exchange for a contribution of $100,000 to the Democratic National Committee, and the no-bid sweetheart deal the Bush-Cheney Administration awarded to Halliburton to supply food and water to U.S. troops in Iraq and Afghanistan, and operate mini shopping malls on military bases overseas. And then there is the story of John F. Kennedy, joking after his victory in the West Virginia primary that his father had been happy to funnel large sums of cash to the Kennedy campaign, but he reached his limit when he had spent about $2.5 million. "Don't buy another vote," he cabled his son. "I won't pay for a landslide."

This book is a collection of stories of fraud, bribery, double-dealing, money laundering, and a host of other illegal activities linked to the Oval Office. That said, I did not want to present any of the presidents associated with these scandals—whether Republican or Democrat—as monsters or morons. There are reasons why presidents "bend" the law, tolerate crooked associates, and approve sweetheart deals for supporters; and for me at least it is always much more interesting to explore motivations and examine an individual's character than to demonize him.

We see Abraham Lincoln, for example, responding in various ways to his wife Mary's acceptance of bribes from would-be office seekers and obliging merchants, as well as her profligate, budget-busting shopping sprees to redecorate the White House. When a group of New York merchants presented Mary with a handsome carriage and four matching carriage horses, Lincoln accepted the gift/bribe and rode in it—people in political office expected to receive such "tokens." When Mary overspent her redecoration budget by thousands of dollars, friendly members of Congress agreed to cover the additional costs with an appropriations bill. But Lincoln, because these funds were coming out of the taxpayers' pockets and because Mary's redecoration campaign would appear excessive and frivolous in a time of war, swore that he would not sign the bill. Ultimately, for his wife's sake, he relented, signed the bill, and the shortfall was covered.

THE WHITE HOUSE

WASHINGTON

August 9, 1974

Dear Mr. Secretary:

I hereby resign the Office of President of the
United States.

Sincerely,

Richard Nixon

11.35 AM

HK

The Honorable Henry A. Kissinger
The Secretary of State
Washington, D.C. 20520

THE RESIGNATION OF RICHARD NIXON, THE FIRST FOR A U.S. PRESIDENT, BECAME EFFECTIVE ON

11:35 A.M. ON AUGUST 9, 1974, AFTER SECRETARY OF STATE HENRY KISSINGER INITIALED THE LETTER OF

RESIGNATION, SHOWN HERE. NIXON'S INVOLVEMENT IN THE WATERGATE SCANDAL, WHICH OVERSHADOWED

HIS ACCOMPLISHMENTS WHILE IN OFFICE, MAKES HIM THE KING OF PRESIDENTIAL PAYOLA.

NATIONAL ARCHIVES

———— ★ ————

Whether it is keeping the price of gold artificially high, accepting bribes from oilmen, or pardoning a fugitive from justice, a president's actions have long-term consequences. A scandal-prone president may see the voters turn against him and his political party at the polls, or he may find his credibility and prestige affected overseas. All U.S. presidents are concerned about their legacies, how they will be remembered by the U.S. people, and how their administrations will be assessed by historians, and scandal can overwhelm even the most impressive achievements.

Richard Nixon's visit to Chairman Mao's China was an act of political courage and first-rate statesmanship, but it was overwhelmed by the Watergate scandal that forced the president to resign. At the other end of the spectrum is Ronald Reagan, who as president had no interest in the Department of Housing and Urban Development (HUD) and so let it spin wildly out of control and into scandal. An investigation of HUD uncovered flagrant examples of fraud and influence-peddling in twenty-eight HUD programs that involved 94 percent of HUD's budget. Of course, HUD was funded by the taxpayers, who had every right to howl like furies over such waste and hold President Reagan accountable. But the taxpayers didn't do that.

In spite of the HUD and Iran-Contra scandals, Ronald Reagan left office beloved by a majority of the U.S. people, and he is still loved and admired to this day. The reasons for Reagan's high standing are a mix of the significant and the sentimental: His policies helped bring down the Soviet Empire and liberate Eastern Europe from Communism; as president he projected an image that was warm, friendly, straightforward, and approachable—the qualities Americans like to believe we possess. Part of Reagan's appeal is that he was a great man who acted like an ordinary guy.

These days, scarcely a month goes by when the news media does not report on members of Congress blowing through millions of taxpayer dollars on travel, meals, and entertainment. But rarely have such scandals had significant effect at the polls. Typically bigger issues drive elections—war, the state of the economy, and the country's mood regarding the outgoing administration.

Most U.S. presidents were men of humble backgrounds. By grit, determination, ambition, and shrewd political horse trading they rose to high office, arguably today the most powerful office in the world. So it is fascinating to explore why a president would let himself be drawn, sometimes unwittingly, into a scheme that would undermine his effectiveness, ruin his reputation, and put him in danger of being listed among America's scoundrels rather than America's heroes. And that is what you will discover in this book.

---★---

CHAPTER I

Abraham Lincoln:

MARY TODD LINCOLN'S "FLAGRANT FRAUDS OF THE PUBLIC TREASURY"

---★---

In February 1861 the president-elect was late for an appointment. The gentlemen who were waiting for him, Norman B. Judd, a member of the Illinois Senate, and Herman Kreismann, a prominent Illinois Republican who had campaigned for Lincoln among German-speaking voters, were surprised—in general, Lincoln was a punctual man. As time went by and Lincoln still did not appear, Kreismann volunteered to walk over to the hotel where the Lincolns were staying to see what the cause of the delay was.

He entered the Lincolns' room to find Mary Todd Lincoln in the throes of a shrieking tantrum. Kreismann was shocked by Mrs. Lincoln's conduct and embarrassed to have walked in on such a disturbing family scene. Lincoln tried to explain, "She will not let me go until I promise her an office for one of her friends."

The acquaintance who was the cause of Mary Lincoln's fit of temper was Isaac Henderson, publisher of the *New York Evening Post*. Henderson and Mary scarcely knew each other, but there were rumors circulating among office seekers that Mrs. Lincoln was taking an active role in selecting who should have government jobs in the Lincoln Administration. Through newspaper stories about the new first lady it was already well known that Mrs. Lincoln had expensive tastes, and that gifts delighted her. Isaac Henderson wanted a post in the New York Customs House, so he wrote to Mary Lincoln, asking her to put in a good word for him with her husband. As a token of his esteem, he sent along some diamond jewelry.

Lincoln gave in to his wife; he appointed Henderson to the Customs House. It was not one of his best appointments: In 1864 Henderson was arrested and tried for corruption. He was charged with demanding kickbacks from contractors, and that one such payment totaled $70,000. In the months leading up to his trial there were rumors in New York City that Henderson had tried to buy members of the grand jury, prospective witnesses, even the district attorney. Henderson's acquittal proved to many people in government that he had corrupted the court just as he had once corrupted First Lady Mary Lincoln.

The Henderson matter was among the first instances of Mary Lincoln demanding that her husband give government jobs to men who, in one way or another, had won her good opinion. Her intentions may have been good—she did want to be one of Lincoln's trusted political advisors—but her susceptibility to bribery made her a political liability.

THE EDUCATION OF MARY TODD

The future Mrs. Lincoln was born Mary Ann Todd on December 13, 1818, in Lexington, Kentucky. She was the fourth child of Eliza Parker and Robert Todd, who were second cousins. Parkers and Todds had fought for American independence, and then fought Native Americans to carve towns out of the Kentucky wilderness. They prospered in the new land, and became prominent, respected members of the emerging Kentucky society. The

THIS PHOTO OF LINCOLN, TAKEN DURING THE PRESIDENTIAL CAMPAIGN OF 1860, REVEALS HIS GAUNT, RAW-BONED APPEARANCE, IN STARK CONTRAST TO HIS PLUMP AND STYLISH WIFE. AS MARY TOLD A FAMILY FRIEND, LINCOLN "IS TO BE PRESIDENT OF THE UNITED STATES SOME DAY; IF I HAD NOT THOUGHT SO I NEVER WOULD HAVE MARRIED HIM, FOR YOU CAN SEE HE IS NOT PRETTY."

Todds, for example, were among the founders of Lexington and of the town's Transylvania University; pride in the college inspired the citizens of Lexington to call their town "the Athens of the West."

Mary grew up in a handsome 14-room brick house, built in the elegant Georgian style. Robert Todd owned several slaves, including Mammy Sally, who cared for the Todd children.

At age six Mary suffered the first of the many tragedies that would haunt her life: Her mother died after giving birth to her sixth child, Mary's brother George. Seventeen months later Robert Todd married a woman from Frankfort, Kentucky, named Elizabeth Humphreys. Almost from the start animosity sprang up between the Todd children and their stepmother. Robert and Elizabeth had nine children together, and although for the most part the half-brothers and half-sisters got along amicably, Eliza's children never warmed up to Elizabeth Humphreys. Years later Mary would describe her childhood after the death of her mother as "desolate."

Her refuge was school. After attending elementary school, Mary's father enrolled her in Mentelle's for Young Ladies, an academy operated by French emigrants, Paris-born Augustus Waldemare Mentelle and his wife, Charlotte Victorie Leclere Mentelle. The academy was only a mile and a half (2.4 km) from the Todd house, and the family's driver, Nelson, could have taken Mary back and forth in a carriage every day, but Mary boarded at Mentelle's. It was her escape from an unhappy home life.

Thanks to Madame Mentelle, she became fluent in French, which Mary spoke with a Parisian accent. She read widely in literature and history. Theatricals were part of life at the school, and Mary performed in several plays—she was dramatic by nature. Furthermore Madame Mentelle passed along to Mary her outlook on life, particularly an admiration for aristocrats and women of an independent frame of mind. Robert Todd approved of well-educated, spirited women (Mary remained in school years longer than most of her friends), and he encouraged Mary to express herself. She was especially interested in politics and on several occasions she discussed the issues of the day with one of her father's friends, Senator Henry Clay.

As she approached her late teens Mary Todd developed into a well-educated, sophisticated, well-read young woman, who was not afraid to express her opinion on any subject.

THE BELLE OF SPRINGFIELD

In 1836, 17-year-old Mary graduated from Mentelle's and announced that she was leaving Lexington to live with her older sister Elizabeth and her brother-in-law Ninian Edwards in Springfield, Illinois. Her father was not terribly sorry to see her go, as it meant an end to the violent quarrels between Mary and her stepmother.

The Mary Todd who arrived in Springfield stood five-feet-two-inches tall (1.57 m). She possessed lively blue eyes and a lovely complexion. She was a bit plump, and her chin was a touch prominent, but she had a sharp wit, a good mind, and a degree of cultivation that was rare in a rawboned prairie town like Springfield.

If Mary had come husband-hunting, Springfield was the place to be. In 1836, there were 24 percent more men than women in Sangamon County (where Springfield was located). Furthermore, the Edwards's house was the center of Springfield's high society, where Mary would meet gentlemen from the best families as well as up-and-coming young men such as her cousin John Todd Stuart's law partner, the gangly, socially awkward 27-year-old Abraham Lincoln.

Mary and Abraham were both Kentuckians, but the similarity ended there. She grew up in luxury, he was born in a dirt-floored log cabin. As a child she had every comfort and security; he spent his boyhood doing strenuous physical labor and pinching pennies. She had attended a French-style academy, he was almost entirely self-educated.

They shared a love of literature, particularly poetry. And they were both intensely interested in politics. Mary had come to Springfield to start a new life, Abraham had come there to make something of himself.

Mary had plenty of suitors, at least one of whom was a good friend of Lincoln's. At a party William Herndon asked Mary to dance; as he led her around the floor, he made what he thought was a clever remark—that Mary "seemed to glide through the waltz with the ease of a serpent." Mary Todd stopped dancing, declared that she didn't like such a comparison, then walked off, leaving Herndon alone and embarrassed on the dance floor.

In addition to all her assets, Mary possessed a serious liability—a Springfield neighbor said that Mary was "subject to…spells of mental depression." Mary's mood swings could be violent and unpredictable—one moment she was laughing and vivacious, the next sunk in deep depression. Emotionally she was, as a saying of the time put it, always either in the garret or in the cellar.

In 1840 it became clear to Elizabeth Todd Edwards that Mary preferred Lincoln above all her other suitors. Elizabeth was not convinced that Lincoln was a suitable match for her sister. She described him as "a mighty rough man…dull in society…careless of his personal appearance…awkward and shy." No letters or other documents survive to tell us the details of Lincoln's courtship of Mary Todd, all we know is that sometime in 1840 they became engaged. Then, late in 1840, for unknown reasons, Lincoln broke off the engagement. But in 1842 they were reconciled and during the first few days of November 1842 they surprised their family and friends by announcing that they planned to marry on November 4. The ceremony took place before a handful of guests in the parlor of the Edwards's house.

MARY LINCOLN ADORED FLOWERS AND ESPECIALLY ENJOYED WEARING ELABORATE ARRANGEMENTS
IN HER HAIR AND ON HER GOWN ON FORMAL OCCASIONS. SHE WORE THIS FLORAL CROWN DURING THE
CELEBRATIONS OF HER HUSBAND'S INAUGURATION AS PRESIDENT.

———★———

"WE HAVE WON!"

In later years Lincoln's friends concluded that his marriage to Mary Todd was the making of him. By nature he lacked energy and drive, but Mary recognized his gifts and as Elizabeth Todd Edwards said, "pushed him along and upward—made him struggle and seize his opportunities." Lincoln's best friend, Joshua Speed, recalled, "Lincoln needed driving—(well, he got that)." And in the late 1840s Mary stated candidly to Ward Hill Lamon, a friend of the Lincoln family, that her husband "is to be president of the United States some day; if I had not thought so I never would have married him, for you can see he is not pretty."

Mary became Lincoln's most zealous political supporter. She even cut off friends if they disagreed with her political views. If Lincoln suffered a setback he took it in stride as part of the give-and-take of politics, but Mary could not exercise such restraint: she denounced Lincoln's political rivals as "dirty dogs… connivers… dirty abolitionists." Her confidence in her husband's political career never flagged. Once, when Lincoln was depressed about his prospects for national office, he lamented, "Nobody knows me." Mary replied, "They soon will." Even William Herndon, Lincoln's law partner whom Mary had shamed on the dance floor twenty years earlier, showed grudging respect for Mrs. Lincoln's tireless advancement of her husband's career, although Herndon put it in a nasty way. Mary Lincoln, he said, was "like a toothache, keeping her husband awake to politics night and day."

In 1859 and 1860 when Lincoln was campaigning for the Republican Party's nomination as president, Mary found herself courted by political power brokers. To her delight, newspapers published articles about her. A reporter from the *New York Tribune* praised Mary as "amiable and accomplished…vivacious and graceful…a sparkling talker."

Mary blossomed in the spotlight. She welcomed journalists into her home where she spoon-fed them lively, colorful copy, including the story of her friendly wager with her neighbor, Mrs. Bradford: if Lincoln won the presidency, Mrs. Bradford would present Mary with a pair of new shoes, and Mary would do the same if the Democrats' candidate, Stephen A. Douglas, won the White House. When Republican operatives called at the Lincoln home, Mary sat with them, assessing candidly the chances of office seekers who even before Election Day were jockeying for posts in the Lincoln Administration.

On November 6, 1860, Lincoln spent the evening in the Springfield telegraph office waiting for the election returns. When the wire carried word of his victory, he hurried home, crying, "Mary! Mary! We have won!"

"MAKING AND UNMAKING POLITICAL FORTUNES"

Mary had settled ideas about herself as first lady. She would entertain in her own right. She would equal if not surpass the most fashionable ladies of Washington. She would be her husband's political partner. And she would expect special favors to be granted her as first lady (a title invented for her by a reporter from the *Times* of London). When Mary went on a train trip, for example, most railway officials waived the customary fare. But when one railway asked her to purchase a ticket just like any other passenger, Mary bristled. She insisted that her eldest son, Robert, speak to the railway agents, which he did: "The Old Lady," he said, "is raising hell about her passes."

Nonetheless, once she arrived in Washington, D.C., Mary tried to assert that she was a conventional wife of a public figure, unwilling to step into the spotlight. "My character is wholly domestic," she declared to James Gordon Bennett, editor of the *New York Herald*. But a reporter for the *New York Times* revealed her real character: "Mrs. Lincoln is making and unmaking the political fortunes of men and is similar to Queen Elizabeth in her statesmanlike tastes."

And it was not just office seekers who sought Mary Lincoln's good opinion: In 1861 several New York store owners presented the first lady with a gleaming black barouche and four matching black carriage horses, with a note that the horses could be exchanged "if Mrs. Lincoln preferred another color." The unspoken message of the gift was that the merchants hoped when Mary shopped in New York City—and she adored shopping in New York City— she would patronize their stores. That President Lincoln knew about the carriage, who had sent it, and why they had sent it, clashes with our image of "Honest Abe." Mary Lincoln biographer Jean Baker assures her readers, "Accepting the barouche was hardly a conflict of interest, at least not as understood by freewheeling nineteenth-century politicians."

Of course, Lincoln had his limits. When the king of Siam sent magnificent gifts that included diamonds and elephants, he assumed he was presenting them to Lincoln personally, as a fellow sovereign. Lincoln did not know what to do with the elephants and would not dream of pocketing the diamonds, so in his thank-you note to the king he expressed his gratitude but also explained, "Our laws forbid the President from receiving these rich presents as personal treasures. They are therefore accepted in accordance with your Majesty's desire as tokens of goodwill and friendship in the name of the American People." Mary Lincoln had no such scruples.

In spring 1861 George Denison, a New York lawyer connected to the Lincolns' banker in Springfield, Robert Irwin, petitioned Mary to help him secure the post of naval officer in charge under the collector of customs of the port of New York. To guarantee Mary's help he sent her a carriage and opened for her a credit line of $5,000, which she could use in New York on her next shopping excursion. Mary, keeping up her end of the bargain, pressured Lincoln to give the appointment to Denison. Lincoln felt uneasy about this appointment because he knew nothing about the man. He wrote to his friend Irwin, "I am scared about your friend Denison. The [place] is so fiercely sought by, and for, others, while, except what has come through you, his name is not mentioned at all, that I fear appointing him will appear too arbitrary on my part."

IN 1875 ROBERT TODD LINCOLN, CONVINCED THAT HIS MOTHER WAS NOT SOUND IN MIND, HAD HER COMMITTED TO A PRIVATE SANITARIUM IN ILLINOIS. AFTER FOUR MONTHS, MARY WAS PRONOUNCED SANE AND RELEASED. SOON THEREAFTER SHE PURCHASED A GUN AND WAITED FOR HER SOLE SURVIVING CHILD TO COME VISIT HER.

ASSOCIATED PRESS

———— ★ ————

Ultimately, Lincoln granted Denison the appointment, but his hunch about Denison's character proved correct. As an official of the Customs House, Denison engaged in extortion, graft, and even seized ships without any legal justification. When Senator Preston King exposed Denison's malfeasance to Lincoln, he complained that such a rogue would never have been appointed had it not been for the expensive bribes Denison had given to Mrs. Lincoln.

"A VERY BAD MAN"

In the case of another office seeker, William S. Wood, Mary came very close to destroying her reputation. Wood was a railroad official who had arranged the Lincolns's journey from Springfield to Washington in 1861. During the trip he won Mary's good opinion by being especially solicitous. In March, shortly after the inauguration, Wood presented Mary with a gift of thoroughbred horses. Soon thereafter Mary began lobbying her husband as well as various influential senators to grant Wood the post of commissioner of public buildings. Unknown to Mary, Wood had earned a reputation as a seducer of other men's wives. By permitting Wood to serve as her escort on shopping trips north, Mary was exposing herself to the worst kind of gossip. According to Congressman Schuyler Colfax, when Wood's true character was made known to Lincoln, he confronted Mary about him, which led to such a falling-out between husband and wife that they "scarcely spoke…for several days." By being seen in public with Wood Mary had risked her reputation, but there is no evidence that she had an affair with Wood.

Wood only held office for a few months. His corruption was exposed during a Congressional hearing on suppliers of material for the war who were defrauding the government. One of the witnesses, Stephen A. Hopkins, had applied to Wood to do engraving work for the government. With complete candor Wood told Hopkins, "I want to tell you, as a friend, that [t]here is no use at all [in] trying; that the work will be given to the American Bank Note Company and the National Bank Note Company." When Hopkins said his firm would do the work better and cheaper than his competitors, Wood said it made no difference, because he owned shares in the American Bank Note Company and his friend George Denison owned shares in the National Bank Note Company.

A more damning story was told by Supreme Court Justice David Davis. He was a longtime friend of Abraham Lincoln; when they were both young lawyers, they had traveled together on the circuit. After Lincoln's assassination, Justice Davis served as the executor of his friend's estate. Simeon Draper was a wealthy real estate investor in New York and active in Republican politics. In 1864 he asked Mary to help him secure the position of collector of customs of the Port of New York. Justice Davis claimed that Mary agreed to use her influence in exchange for a payment of $20,000. Draper handed over the money, and on September 7, 1864, he received the post.

The year 1864 proved to be a very lucky one for Simeon Draper—in December he was granted the lucrative assignment of selling all the cotton that General William Tecumseh Sherman had seized when he captured Savannah.

In 1866, after Draper died, Mary appears to have tried to quash rumors of her dealings with the man. In a letter she wrote, "I never saw [Simeon Draper]—but two or three times, in my life[.] I never saw one of his family, in my life—I never received a line from him or a cent in my life."

THE FIRST SHOPPING TRIPS

As first lady, Mary had access to two lines of credit established by Congress for the maintenance of the White House: annual appropriations of $6,000 for repairs and $5,000 for furnishing and decorating the Executive Mansion. In spring 1861 when the Lincolns moved in, the White House was in sad shape. Mary's cousin, Elizabeth Todd Grimsley, described it as "seedy and dilapidated." William Stoddard, a White House secretary, said it reminded him "of an old and unsuccessful hotel." Carpets and curtains were threadbare, the china was mismatched, paper was peeling off the walls, and the roof on the north side of the house leaked. Mary was eager to begin refurbishing the White House, but the outbreak of the Civil War intervened.

In April twelve artillery batteries in Charleston, South Carolina, fired upon Fort Sumter in the harbor. Five days later Virginia seceded from the Union, which meant that now the Confederacy lay just across the Potomac River from Washington. Overnight, ordinary vistas became unsettling. The mansion of Robert E. Lee, commander of the Army of Northern Virginia, could be seen plainly just across the river in Arlington. Anyone who climbed a church steeple or to a high rooftop and looked south toward Alexandria, Virginia, would see a Confederate flag flying above Marshall's Tavern. Meanwhile, in Maryland, Confederate saboteurs were damaging or destroying railroad tracks and railway bridges.

There were some troops in Washington, as well as some militia who were assigned to protect the president and his family—these were quartered in the East Room of the White House, but they were insufficient to repulse a Confederate attack on the capital city. General Winfield Scott, the senior commander of the Union Army, urged Mary to take her sons back to Springfield for safety. Mary refused to go.

On April 20, the Sixth Massachusetts Regiment arrived in Washington, and in the days that followed more troops came to protect the city. Now that her family and Washington were secure, Mary decided to travel north to Philadelphia and New York to begin shopping for the White House. She brought along the commissioner of public buildings, William Wood, and her cousin Lizzie Grimsley. In Philadelphia she could not

SIMEON DRAPER, PICTURED HERE AROUND 1860–65, WAS ONE OF THE MOST PROMINENT
AND ACTIVE REPUBLICANS IN NEW YORK CITY AND GAVE MARY TODD LINCOLN
$20,000 TO SECURE FOR HIM THE LUCRATIVE POST OF COLLECTOR OF THE PORT OF NEW YORK,
ACCORDING TO SUPREME COURT JUSTICE DAVID DAVIS, ABRAHAM LINCOLN'S LONG-TIME FRIEND
AND COLLEAGUE IN THE LAW. MARY LATER DENIED EVER ACCEPTING MONEY FROM HIM.

LIBRARY OF CONGRESS

find the wallpaper she wanted, so she sent a dealer to Paris to purchase it for her. In New York the department store magnate, Alexander T. Stewart, held a dinner party in Mary's honor; the next day she visited his store and ordered $2,000 worth of carpets and curtains. Two weeks later she returned to the White House where she began supervising the repairs and redecoration of the staterooms as well as the private rooms she and her family used on the second floor of the house.

In the fall Mary returned to New York, this time accompanied by James Watt, the White House gardener (William Wood had been dismissed in disgrace). She was shopping for china, and she selected a 190-piece set described on the invoice as "fine porcelain dining service decorated with royal purple and double gilt…with the arms of the United States on each piece." Mary loved her choice so much she ordered a duplicate set in Limoges for the private use of the Lincoln family—although her initials, ML, replaced the U.S. coat of arms. The cost of the two sets of china was $3,195.

———★———

IN A MATTER OF MONTHS MARY LINCOLN WENT THROUGH THE ENTIRE $6,000 DESIGNATED FOR WHITE HOUSE REPAIRS AND SPENT MORE THAN $27,000 ON FURNISHINGS AND REDECORATION.

———★———

By now the Paris wallpaper had arrived, and the price of the paper, with installation, came to $6,800. After the militia moved out of the East Room, Mary replaced the ruined carpet with a new custom-made one for $2,500. She bought new furniture and damask draperies for the staterooms; she renovated the family's living quarters; she purchased for her bedroom a massive mahogany-and-rosewood canopy bed. In a matter of months she went through the entire $6,000 designated for White House repairs and spent more than $27,000 on furnishings and redecoration.

"FLAGRANT FRAUDS OF THE PUBLIC TREASURY"

To cover her expenses Mary tried to bamboozle the federal government through creative bookkeeping and by padding her bills. On one occasion she ordered a $500 chandelier from a New York merchant, but suggested that he bill the government for $1,000. When he was paid, she explained, he should pass along the extra $500 to her. The chandelier merchant refused to cooperate in the scheme.

During Prince Napoléon's visit to Washington the president and the first lady gave him a dinner at the White House. The cost of the meal was $300, but Mary needed more cash—she submitted a bill to the Department of the Interior for $900. The amount made Secretary of the Interior Caleb Smith suspicious, and he consulted Secretary of State William Seward. As it happened, Seward had also given a dinner for the prince, inviting the same number of guests as had been to the White House, serving the same menu, and even using the same caterer. When the secretary of the interior realized what Mary was doing, he refused to pay the bill.

But Mary was not defeated. She had James Watt, the White House gardener, submit a bill of $900 for plants and other gardening expenses; this bill was paid and Watt gave Mary the extra $600. Watt became her new partner in crime.

Their scheming did not end there. In fact, in July, August, and September of 1861, there were a flurry of garden-related bills—$700.75 for flowers, $107.50 for manure, $33.75 for a gardener's helper, and many more such invoices, totaling more than $1,000. The bills were all a scam—no flowers or cartloads of manure had ever been delivered to the White House, nor were any extra helpers hired to work in the garden. But the secretary of the interior didn't know that; he reimbursed Watt, who passed the money along to Mary Lincoln.

Somehow, perhaps through gossip among the White House servants, word of these fraudulent payments leaked out. In October 1861, James H. Upperman, the White House gatekeeper, brought the scam to the attention of Secretary of the Interior Smith, charging that the first lady and James Watt were involved in "deliberate collusion" involving "sundry petit, but flagrant frauds on the public treasury."

Mary was embarrassed, humiliated, and afraid to confront her husband about the matter. Fortunately, Secretary Smith was sympathetic; he offered to tell the president about the fraudulent bills. Watt weighed in, too, assuring Smith that the scheme had been put in place by the disgraced William Wood before he had been forced to resign as commissioner of public buildings. Smith and the new commissioner, Benjamin Brown French, covered up the scandal, and President Lincoln wrote a check to reimburse the Treasury for "accounts erroneously paid."

But the scandal was not over. By early March 1862, James Watt and Mary Lincoln had had a falling-out; he threatened to publish three incriminating letters written by Mary in which she discussed their plan to submit false bills to the government. Once again the Department of the Interior came to Mary's rescue—Isaac Newton, head of the agriculture division, sent Watt to Europe to shop around for new varieties of seeds that would be useful to U.S. farmers.

"FLUB DUDS FOR THE DAMNED OLD HOUSE"

As much as she had savored redecorating the White House, the arrival of a bill for $7,000, from a man named Carryl who had supplied a great deal of the new furnishings, sent Mary

into a panic. For help she turned to Benjamin Brown French. "I have sent for you to get me out of trouble," she told French during a private meeting at the White House. She confessed that she had overspent what Congress had appropriated for the repair and redecoration of the White House, and she dreaded admitting what she had done to Lincoln. "I want you to see him and tell him that it is common to overrun appropriations," she said. "Tell him how much it costs to refurnish; he does not know much about it." Then Mary made a promise, "If you will do it, I will never get into such difficulty again."

French did take up the matter with Lincoln, who became furious when he reviewed the bills. When French suggested that it would be a simple matter to pass an appropriation bill to cover the extra $7,000, Lincoln rejected the idea. "It never can have my approval," he said. "It would stink in the nostrils of the American people to have it said that the president of the United States had approved a bill overrunning an appropriation of $20,000 for flub dubs for the damned old house, when the poor freezing soldiers cannot have blankets!"

Nonetheless, in February 1862, Congress passed an appropriations bill for $14,000 to cover all of Mary's expenses in the White House. And Lincoln signed it.

Throughout the Lincolns's four-year occupancy of the White House, Mary continued her influence-peddling and extravagant shopping. At the time of her husband's assassination on April 14, 1865, she was deeply in debt to merchants in New York, Philadelphia, and elsewhere for jewelry, clothing, and household furnishings and decorative items. The exact amount is unknown, but it has been estimated that Mary owed perhaps as much as $70,000, including $27,000 to Alexander T. Stewart's department store in New York.

Lincoln's estate of cash, real estate, and bonds totaled more than $100,000 and was divided equally among Mary and her two surviving sons, Robert and Thomas (Tad). The inheritance generated only about $1,200 per year for each of the Lincolns—not enough for them to afford a comfortable house. They still owned the family home in Springfield, Illinois, but Mary refused to return there, saying it would be too painful to live in the house without her husband. And so it was rented out to tenants.

While public subscriptions were raised to purchase homes for Union generals, or to give them substantial sums of cash to do with as they pleased, President Lincoln's widow

----------★----------

PREVIOUS SPREAD: MARY TODD'S GOWNS ARE EXHIBITED IN NEW YORK IN THIS 1867 SKETCH BY STANLEY FOX, PUBLISHED IN *HARPER'S WEEKLY*. AFTER HER HUSBAND'S ASSASSINATION, MARY LINCOLN TRIED TO RAISE MONEY IN NEW YORK VIA A PRIVATE SALE OF SOME OF HER FORMAL GOWNS FROM HER YEARS IN THE WHITE HOUSE. SOMEONE LEAKED TO THE PRESS WHOSE GOWNS THEY WERE, AND MARY WAS VILIFIED AS AN AVARICIOUS WIDOW WHO WAS SULLYING THE MEMORY OF HER LATE HUSBAND.
LIBRARY OF CONGRESS

and sons were living in hotels. The contrast made Mary bitter, and she used what influence she still had to petition—some might describe it as pester—her friends in Washington to urge Congress to confer upon her $100,000, which would have been her late husband's full salary for the years 1864–68. Congress granted Mary only one year's salary.

To raise more money she attempted to sell anonymously some of her formal gowns at a special sale in New York. The identity of the gown's owner was leaked to the press and Mary was excoriated as grasping and unladylike.

For the rest of her life she was consumed with what she always regarded as her precarious financial situation, yet at the same time she found great comfort in compulsive shopping. On one occasion she purchased draperies, although she had no house in which to hang them.

The press, the American public, and Mary's relatives, friends, and acquaintances alternately pitied and censured her for her erratic behavior, but no blame was assigned to Abraham Lincoln, either for his first lady's intrigues with office seekers or her spendthrift shopping sprees during the Civil War.

Lincoln's assassination elevated him almost overnight to secular sainthood. Furthermore, Lincoln's old law partner and Mary's nemesis, William Herndon, was consciously shaping the American public's notion of the Lincoln marriage. In 1866, Herndon toured the country delivering a lecture on the relationship between Abraham Lincoln and Ann Rutledge, a New Salem tavern keeper's daughter whom Lincoln had courted as a young man. Ann had died during the courtship, and Herndon presented her not only as the great love of Lincoln's life, but the only woman he ever loved. Twenty-three years later, in 1889, Herndon published *Herndon's Lincoln: The True Story of a Great Life*, in which he characterized Mary as a harpy who made Lincoln's life miserable.

Herndon expected his audience to draw the conclusion that when it came to his wife, Abraham Lincoln tended to be too patient, too tolerant, too forgiving, too long-suffering. As for Mary Todd Lincoln, Herndon portrayed her as a shrewish wife and a scheming first lady who in spite of the many tragedies in her life deserved no pity.

THE MADNESS OF MARY LINCOLN

During her lifetime, some of Mary Todd Lincoln's friends, enemies, and even members of her family considered her insane. Today the issue is one of the most contentious among Lincoln scholars—both professionals and the armchair variety.

Mary's behavior could be erratic. She suffered from violent mood swings; her tragic life—the loss of her mother and three of her four sons, and the murder of her husband as she sat beside him with her hand resting on his arm—would be too much for even the most resilient individual to bear. But Mary also experienced hallucinations. In 1875 she told of being afflicted by the ghost of an Indian who scalped her, pulled the bones from her face, and drew wires out of her eyeballs. Mary's defenders argue that, given all she had suffered, the poor woman was understandably overwrought, but her behavior was merely unconventional, perhaps a bit eccentric. On the other side of the fence are scholars and students of the Lincolns who believe that Mary's behavior points to serious mental and/or emotional instability.

In 2006 independent historian Jason Emerson asked John M. Suarez, M.D., of the department of psychiatry, Neuropsychiatric Institute, University of California Medical Center in Los Angeles, and James S. Brust, M.D., chairman of the department of psychiatry and medical director of the psychiatric unit at San Pedro Peninsula Hospital, San Pedro, California, to review Mary Lincoln's symptoms. Although it is impossible to be absolutely certain about the diagnosis of an individual who has been dead for almost 130 years, Suarez and Brust stated that Mary's behavior suggested she suffered from bipolar disorder. Today she could be treated with medication, but in nineteenth-century United States the only treatment was confinement in a sanatorium where it was hoped rest and calm would restore the patient to good mental health. For this reason in 1875 Robert Todd Lincoln, Mary's sole surviving child, had her committed to a private sanatorium, Bellevue Place, in Batavia, Illinois, where the physician in residence, Richard J. Patterson, prescribed "rest, diet, baths, fresh air, occupation, diversion, change of scene, no more medicine than… absolutely necessary, and the least possible restraint."

Four months later, Mary was released from Bellevue after Patterson declared her sane. In fact, she continued to have unsettling episodes for the rest of her life. And it was years before she forgave her son Robert for sending her to Bellevue. She excoriated him as one "of the greatest scoundrels of the age," and took pleasure in the assurance that "God is just; retribution must follow those who act wickedly in this life."

Today, public opinion about Mary Todd Lincoln is deeply divided between those who regard her as emotional and perhaps a bit eccentric and those who believe that Mary suffered from some form of mental illness. The debate between proponents of these different points of view can be angry and even bitter, but one aspect of the debate has pretty much vanished from the scene—the condemnation of Mary Lincoln as a harpy who made Abraham Lincoln's life miserable. In the words of a music hall that was popular in Mary Lincoln's day, she is generally regarded as a woman "more to be pitied than censured."

———⋆———

CHAPTER 2

Ulysses S. Grant and the Whiskey Ring:

"LET NO GUILTY MAN ESCAPE"

———⋆———

s they climbed out of the hired carriage, Attorney General Edwards Pierrepont and Secretary of State Hamilton Fish held on tightly to their hats—a strong breeze blowing in off the Atlantic threatened to carry them away. They followed the gravel path to the front steps of a large, three-story, 28-room house that President Ulysses S. Grant and his family insisted upon calling a cottage. The exterior walls were covered with stucco, and embedded in the plaster were decorative timbers in an x pattern, giving the house a pseudo-Tudor appearance. As Pierrepont and Fish stepped into the shade of the long covered veranda that looked out on the ocean, a servant greeted them at the door and showed them inside where the president was waiting.

Since 1869 the Grant family had fled the heat and stifling humidity of Washington, D.C., for the sea breezes of Long Branch, New Jersey. It had been a sleepy beachfront village, but the arrival of the president transformed Long Branch into a summer boomtown. Soon prominent vacationers such as tycoon Diamond Jim Brady, newspaper magnate Horace Greeley, legendary actor Edwin Booth (brother of John Wilkes Booth), painter Winslow Homer, and author Robert Louis Stevenson took houses in Long Branch. Like the Grants, these celebrity "summer people" attended balls at the West End Hotel, went to the horse races at Monmouth Park, and took long carriage rides along the beach.

But it was government business that brought Pierrepont and Fish to President Grant's front door in July 1875. Another scandal had erupted, this time involving a wide-ranging conspiracy to embezzle funds from the federal government's tax on whiskey. Pierrepont and Fish had evidence that linked Orville Babcock, one of Grant's closest friends and most trusted aides, to the scandal, which meant the Grant Administration would be tainted in this whiskey scandal, too.

The president heard what Pierrepont and Fish had to say, then answered, "Let no guilty man escape if it can be avoided."

"LET US HAVE PEACE"

The assassination of Abraham Lincoln in 1865, just days after Confederate General Robert E. Lee had surrendered to Grant at Appomattox Court House in Virginia, followed by the troubled presidency of Andrew Johnson, led Grant to conclude that he must make the transition from the military to politics. The newly reunited nation needed him, so in the summer of 1867 he accepted the appointment as secretary of war. President Johnson made the move to oust Edwin Stanton, a fire-breathing Radical Republican who wanted to punish the South for the Civil War and the assassination of Lincoln. Grant was no Radical, and Johnson believed he would be loyal to the administration.

Yet within weeks after joining the Cabinet, Grant came to the conclusion that he ought to enforce the laws passed by Congress regarding Reconstruction rather than follow the orders of President Johnson. Although he had remained loyal to the Union during the Civil War, Johnson, a Tennessean, was a Southerner at heart, or at least understood Southern sensibilities, particularly regarding civil rights for the newly freed slaves. He clashed with Congress because he opposed civil rights legislation and advocated swift and painless methods to restore the civil rights of former Confederates. In general, Grant's sympathies lay with the newly freed slaves rather than with the newly defeated Confederates.

As Johnson's term in office was winding down, John W. Forney, editor of the *Washington Daily Chronicle*, began to use his newspaper to promote the nomination of General Grant for president on the Republican ticket. Forney's record as kingmaker was not good: He had been influential in bringing about the nomination of the dithering, do-nothing James Buchanan for president and the now nearly universally loathed Andrew Johnson as Lincoln's vice president. Yet he believed that in Grant he had found a guaranteed winner. Here was the commander who had saved the Union, who had been generous to the Confederates after the surrender. Grant had never held office so he brought no political baggage with him. And he had a reputation for honesty and loyalty.

John A. Rawlins, an old friend of Grant's from his days in Galena, Illinois, who had served as a member of his staff during the war, was now one of the general's closest confidants. Rawlins confided to Forney, "General Grant does not want to be president [but he] thinks the Republican party may need him, and he believes, as their candidate, he can be elected and reelected."

The presidency would also suit the candidate's family nicely. Grant had never been good at any occupation except warfare. In private life he had failed as a farmer and real estate broker; when the Civil War broke out he was barely making a living as a clerk in the family's leather business. The presidency came with an annual salary of $25,000—a fortune in 1867. Assuming that Grant served two terms he would leave the White House with a tidy sum to keep his family in comfort for the rest of his life. Following in the tradition of men such as Washington and Jefferson who lamented being dragged away from their homes and families to attend to affairs of state, Grant complained to his friend General William Tecumseh Sherman, "I have been forced into [the presidency] in spite of myself." In fact, he was not at all displeased to be nominated.

Grant, already a popular candidate with voters, especially veterans of the Union Army, ingratiated himself further by proclaiming modestly, "I shall have no policy of my own to interfere against the will of the people." He campaigned on the slogan, "Let us have peace." On Election Day 1868 Grant won by a margin of 300,000 votes, winning 214 votes in the Electoral College; the Democratic candidate, Horatio Seymour, won 80 Electoral College votes.

Although Grant entered the White House on a wave of popular enthusiasm, his administration was soon beset by scandal and controversial policies, including the president's attempt to annex the island of Santo Domingo in the Caribbean as a place where newly freed African Americans of the South would be relocated and live in peace, safe from the terrorism of the Ku Klux Klan and other white supremacist groups.

WHILE VACATIONING AT OAK BLUFFS ON MARTHA'S VINEYARD, PRESIDENT GRANT AND FIRST LADY
JULIA GRANT POSED WITH THEIR PARTY—INCLUDING TRUSTED AIDE ORVILLE BABCOCK, LEFT.
IN AN UNPRECEDENTED DECISION, GRANT OFFERED TO TESTIFY AT BABCOCK'S CRIMINAL TRIAL
ON HIS BEHALF. DESPITE THE EVIDENCE AGAINST HIM, GRANT REFUSED TO BELIEVE HIS AIDE
WAS GUILTY OF ANY KIND OF CRIMINAL BEHAVIOR.

———————★———————

Toward the end of Grant's first term, a group calling itself the Liberal Republicans was looking around for a new man who could run for president. One of the leaders of the Liberal faction was General Carl Schurz who, by 1871, was disgusted by the corruption rampant among Grant's cronies, as well as Grant's failure to deliver on civil service reform (a cause dear to political progressives in the last decades of the nineteenth century). In Missouri and other states of the Midwest Schurz was having great success raising funds for a Liberal Republican candidate to be named later. "The superstition that Grant is the necessary man," Schurz confided to a friend, "is rapidly giving way. The spell is broken, and we have only to push through the breach."

Like any incumbent, Grant did not want to leave office. He instructed John McDonald, his collector of internal revenue in the St. Louis district (which encompassed seven states in the Midwest), to begin raising funds for a "reelect Grant" campaign.

THE SLUSH FUND

John McDonald (sometimes spelled MacDonald) had fought for the Union during the Atlanta Campaign and won a promotion to the rank of general. McDonald was a friend of General Sherman and a close acquaintance of several members of the family of First Lady Julia Grant. McDonald was also known to Charles W. Ford, who managed the Grant family's farm outside St. Louis. In 1869, when Ford learned that McDonald had been given a government job, he wrote to the president, urging him to rescind the appointment. Ford described McDonald as "a bad egg…without sense, without truth and common honesty." But McDonald's friendship with Sherman and his links with Julia's family, several of whom recommended him to the president, carried more sway with Grant than Ford's blunt assessment of the man. McDonald kept his job.

As a campaign fund-raiser McDonald proved to be better than Grant had hoped. In a matter of months the reelection war chest was brimming with cash, and McDonald had raised enough additional funds to finance several pro-Grant newspapers that published articles and editorials in favor of the president and his administration. Unknown to the president, the money was not coming from his devoted and generous political base; McDonald was using funds that should have gone to the U. S. Treasury.

In the St. Louis district McDonald organized a vast conspiracy that involved government revenue agents and even clerks employed by the Treasury Department. By law, a tax of seventy cents was collected on every gallon of whiskey distilled in the United States. McDonald and his gang collected the tax but filed papers with the Treasury Department that reported a much lower level of whiskey production: McDonald's numbers were off by more than 1.7 million gallons, thereby defrauding the Treasury of $1.2 million in revenue. The $1.2 million was divvied up among the reelection campaign, the pro-Grant newspapers, and McDonald and his partners in crime. It is not certain exactly how much McDonald and his four chief colleagues who operated the scam received, but the amount is estimated to be between $45,000 and $60,000 each. Four distillers who participated in the swindle received about the same amount.

Chicanery in the whiskey industry was nothing new, but after the Lincoln Administration raised the tax on whiskey to seventy cents a gallon in order to defray the costs of the Civil War, efforts to circumvent the tax had boomed. By the early 1870s between 10 and 12 million gallons of whiskey went untaxed. For the first time whiskey money was being used as a slush fund to reelect a president.

PRINCIPLE AND AMBITION

The Whiskey Ring remained in business even after Grant's successful reelection bid in 1872—it was just too profitable to give up. And that is when McDonald and his colleagues made their mistake, because in June 1874 President Grant appointed a new secretary of the treasury, Benjamin H. Bristow. Although a Kentuckian, Bristow had remained loyal to the Union. He raised the 8th Kentucky Cavalry and enlisted himself. He was badly wounded at the Battle of Shiloh and was offered the brevet rank of major general, but out of modesty he declined it.

———★———

BY THE EARLY 1870S BETWEEN TEN AND TWELVE MILLION GALLONS OF WHISKEY WENT UNTAXED. FOR THE FIRST TIME WHISKEY MONEY WAS BEING USED AS A SLUSH FUND TO REELECT A PRESIDENT.

———★———

After the war Bristow was appointed U.S. attorney for the Kentucky district where he proved to be a tireless defender of law and order. In the late 1860s the state was being torn apart by racial violence, usually led by the Ku Klux Klan. Bristow hauled into court as many of the miscreants as he could capture. In three-and-a-half years he won thirty convictions, including the conviction of a Klansman for murder. During his tenure in Kentucky, Bristow also targeted whiskey distillers who were defrauding the government; ultimately, Bristow's agents discovered and seized 100 stockpiles of illegal whiskey.

Grant had a completely honest man in Benjamin Bristow, but in the end the president would not be entirely pleased with his choice. As Grant biographer William S. McFeely put it, "Benjamin Bristow possessed that sticky double commodity, principle and ambition,

RESURRECTIONISTS AT WORK.

U. S. G.—"*Ben, this fellow has been dead so long, I hardly think that we can use him.*"
B. F. B.—"*Oh, he'll do, if for nothing else, to divert attention from our live subject.*"

BENJAMIN BRISTOW TRIES TO DIG UP THE DEFUNCT WHISKEY RING IN ORDER TO GENERATE FUNDS FOR PRESIDENT GRANT'S RE-ELECTION CAMPAIGN IN AN 1872 POLITICAL CARTOON FROM *FRANK LESLIE'S ILLUSTRATED PAPER*. ALTHOUGH GRANT HAD NO KNOWLEDGE OF THE WHISKEY RING'S CONSPIRACY TO DEFRAUD THE U.S. TREASURY OF MILLIONS OF DOLLARS IN TAX REVENUE, HE DID TRY TO INTERFERE IN THE PROSECUTION OF CLOSE ASSOCIATES WHO HAD BEEN INVOLVED IN THE SCANDAL.

JOHN MCDONALD, A TRUSTED FRIEND OF PRESIDENT GRANT, WAS SUPERVISOR OF
INTERNAL REVENUE FOR THE CITY OF ST. LOUIS AND THE SURROUNDING AREA.
AS ONE OF THE LEADERS OF THE WHISKY RING, MCDONALD WAS TRIED FOR FRAUD.
IN COURT HE TRIED TO DEFLECT BLAME FROM HIMSELF BY CHARGING—FALSELY—THAT GRANT
HAD KNOWN OF THE FRAUD AND ACCEPTED EXTRAVAGANT GIFTS FROM MCDONALD.

———— ★ ————

and he was in the uncommon position of being able to rise to the first while advancing to the second. Ulysses Grant found the man and his cause cloying; he never fully owned up to how crooked things were that Bristow discovered."

A conspiracy as vast as the Whiskey Ring—it included more than 300 members—could not be kept secret. On the day Bristow took office he found waiting for him reports of fraud in the St. Louis district and evidence of collusion among government employees. Later he recalled, "Although I did receive further evidences of the existence of combination and conspiracies to defraud the Government, in which there was reason to believe that certain officers of the Government were participants, I still was unable through the medium of the Internal Revenue office to get hold of a thread by which we could be enabled to follow it to the end."

Bristow suspected that supervisors at the Internal Revenue were obstructing him, so in January 1875 he transferred all the supervisors. Those who were crooked would be cut off from their trusted subordinates and the fraud would collapse—that is what Bristow hoped. But a week after Bristow issued his transfer orders, Grant intervened, demanding that the orders be rescinded. Grant argued that transfers across the board punished unjustly faithful, hardworking supervisors such as John McDonald, who had been invaluable in the months leading up to the election of 1872. Furthermore, even a hint of scandal in the Grant Administration would be fodder for Carl Schurz and his allies. Finally, and this may be the lamest of Grant's arguments, because the transfers were not instantaneous, any scoundrels at the Internal Revenue would have time to correct their books or destroy evidence of wrongdoing.

THE RING INFILTRATED

Grant's interference was galling, but then Bristow received a letter that cheered him up. George W. Fishback, owner of the *St. Louis Democrat,* had heard of Bristow's efforts to break up the Whiskey Ring. He wrote to the secretary, "There has been much talk of late of the fraudulent whisky traffic in the west. If the Secretary wants to break up the powerful ring which exists here, I can give him the name of a man who, if he receives the necessary authority and is assured of absolute secrecy about the matter, will undertake to do it, and I will guarantee success."

The informant Fishback had in mind was a reporter named Myron Colony, a man McFeely characterizes as "nosy, shrewd, and not overly scrupulous." On Fishback's recommendation Bristow and the solicitor of the Treasury Department, Bluford Wilson, hired Colony to snoop around and see what he could learn. It wasn't a difficult assignment for Colony—his beat was the business news in St. Louis, and he served as secretary of the city's Cotton Exchange.

Colony recruited his own gang to infiltrate the Whiskey Ring in St. Louis. It kept detailed records of how much whiskey was actually distilled, compared to how much was reported, and how much tax revenue had been collected. In spring of 1875, Colony reported back to Bristow and Wilson that he had enough evidence to shut down the ring. And he had learned that the man at the heart of the Whiskey Ring in the St. Louis district was General John McDonald.

Bristow unleashed a wave of federal officers who swept through the St. Louis district, arresting 300 members of the ring. Also caught in the dragnet were two of General McDonald's closest collaborators—Internal Revenue Agent John A. Joyce and Collector Constantine Maguire.

As for McDonald, Bristow requested that he call upon him at his office in Washington. Some days later, when McDonald arrived at the Department of the Treasury, Bristow laid out before him the evidence that placed him at the heart of the Whiskey Ring. McDonald admitted his guilt, but as Bristow had no warrant for his arrest, the general was permitted to go—for the time being.

From Bristow's office McDonald went directly to see Bluford Wilson. He tried to make a deal—if the Treasury did not prefer charges against him he would collect and deliver the missing tax revenue. Then he had the audacity to ask Wilson to keep the scandal quiet. It would be bad for the Republican Party in Missouri and the St. Louis district, McDonald said, if the Whiskey Ring scandal was exposed. Wilson was outraged. He told McDonald bluntly that he wished he had the authority to fire such a scoundrel (at this point McDonald was still on the government payroll).

Next Bristow and Wilson went to the White House to inform Grant of the scandal. The president was grieved that McDonald, whom he had considered a friend, had betrayed him and the American people. Then Grant said that he wanted the prosecutions against the Whiskey Ring conspirators to proceed.

But Bristow had not revealed to the president everything he knew—one fact he shared only with Secretary of State Hamilton Fish. After meeting with Bristow, Fish confided to his diary, "Bristow tells me that [Orville E.] Babcock is as deep as any in the Whiskey Ring; that he has most positive evidence, he will not say of actual fraud, but of intimate relations and confidential correspondence with the very worst of them."

THE PRESIDENT'S MAN

Why did Bristow fail to tell Grant that Babcock had come under suspicion? Because Babcock was one of the president's most intimate confidants and most trusted aides. If Babcock was involved in the Whiskey Ring, then it was not beyond the realm of possibility that Grant might be implicated, too. So Bristow hung back, waiting to see what the evidence would reveal, before confronting his president.

JOHN RAWLINS, ONE OF GRANT'S MOST TRUSTED AIDES AND HIS CHIEF OF STAFF DURING THE CIVIL WAR,
BECAME THE PRESIDENT'S SECRETARY OF WAR. UNLIKE OTHER MEMBERS OF GRANT'S INNER CIRCLE,
RAWLINS NEVER BETRAYED HIS BOSS. EVEN WHEN HE CONTRACTED TUBERCULOSIS RAWLINS REFUSED
TO FOLLOW HIS DOCTOR'S ADVICE TO RETIRE TO ARIZONA. RAWLINS REMAINED IN OFFICE, WORKING
FAITHFULLY FOR GRANT UNTIL HIS DEATH IN 1869.

———★———

BENJAMIN BRISTOW SPEARHEADED THE PROSECUTION OF THE WHISKY RING CONSPIRATORS, WHICH LED TO MORE THAN 100 CONVICTIONS AND THE RECOVERY OF MORE THAN $2.5 MILLION IN TAX REVENUE. THE PROSECUTION OF ORVILLE BABCOCK, GRANT'S PRIVATE SECRETARY, CREATED A RIFT BETWEEN BRISTOW AND GRANT THAT WAS NEVER HEALED. BRISTOW RESIGNED FROM OFFICE IN 1876.

★

Babcock was born in Vermont and had graduated from West Point. During the Civil War he saw action at the Battle of Vicksburg, the Wilderness, and Cold Harbor. And in 1864 he joined General Grant's staff as an aide-de-camp. In April 1865, it was Babcock who delivered Grant's invitation to surrender to General Lee; Lee accepted, and Babcock escorted him to Wilmer McLean's farmhouse at Appomattox Court House, Virginia, for the formal ceremony of surrender.

Grant had great affection for Babcock and trusted him. After his election to president he made Babcock his assistant, giving him a desk outside his office. In fact Babcock was more than an assistant, he became the gatekeeper, the man who decided who would and who would not see the president. But the confidence of the president and the prestige of a White House post were not enough for Babcock. For that matter, neither was his salary: he had recently married and he and his bride yearned for a comfortable life, in a large house, tended by servants. So Orville Babcock kept an eye open for moneymaking opportunities that were more lucrative than working as an assistant to the president. When John McDonald—another man Grant trusted—invited Babcock into the Whiskey Ring, assuring him a healthy share in the profits, Babcock leaped at the chance.

On May 13, 1875, federal officers arrested approximately 350 men on suspicion of involvement in a plot to defraud the United States government of tax revenue. In June a grand jury in Missouri handed down several indictments, John McDonald among the men charged. Babcock was not named in the indictment, but a few weeks later, as the evidence against Grant's aide became more damning, Attorney General Pierrepont and Secretary of State Fish made the journey to the Grant family's summer retreat in Long Branch to lay the facts before the president personally. "Let no guilty man escape if it can be avoided," Grant said. But in August 1875 the president was having second thoughts.

A year later Bluford Wilson testified before a Congressional committee investigating the Whiskey Ring that initially President Grant had approved of the investigation into the swindle and wanted the swindlers brought to justice. One congressman asked Wilson whether at any point "there was a change in the demeanor of the President of the United States in reference to these prosecutions." Wilson replied, "It was not until we struck Babcock in what seemed to be strong suspicious evidence of his complicity that we began to grow apart." In fact, once he understood how close McDonald and Babcock had become, Grant even asserted McDonald's innocence. In a conversation with Bristow, Grant declared that in this scandal John McDonald was the "one honest man... as he was an intimate acquaintance and confidential friend of Babcock's." Bristow replied, "[McDonald] was the head center of the frauds; that he was at that time in New York with $160,000 fraudulently obtained."

In desperation Bristow appealed for help from James Harrison Wilson, a cavalry commander under Grant during the war and a member of his inner circle of officers. (He was also the brother of Bluford Wilson.) Bristow pleaded with Wilson to break the news of Babcock's guilt to Grant. "Well, that was one hell of a contract for me," James Wilson recalled later.

James Wilson sent the president a note requesting a private meeting, but Grant could not accommodate his old friend until evening. Describing the scene later, Wilson said, "I told him Babcock [was] concerned in the Whiskey Ring and that [he was] making use of the White House, and imperiling [the president's] good name." Grant refused to believe the charge, but Wilson told him it could be corroborated by Dr. Alexander Sharp, one of Julia Grant's brothers-in-law. So the president sent for Sharp, who confirmed the unhappy news that Wilson had brought the president. Sharp reported later that Grant was so distressed that he wept. And he blamed the Wilson brothers for his distress. "[They] disappointed me more than any persons I ever reposed confidence in," Grant said years later. It was out of friendship that James Harrison Wilson came to the White House to tell the president the truth about Orville Babcock, but Grant never forgave him for it. Their friendship ended that night.

THE "PERSECUTION" OF BABCOCK

Also caught up in the dragnet was another member of the president's staff, Horace Porter, who, like Babcock, had also been a member of Grant staff's during the war. Before any arrest had been made, before any indictments had been handed down, a series of telegrams passed between McDonald and Babcock in which they kept each other informed of the progress of the investigation. Some of these telegrams were signed, "Sylph." When Bluford Wilson confronted Porter with one of these "Sylph" telegrams, Porter came up with an especially vile alibi. "Sylph had been a lewd woman with whom the President of the United States had been in intimate association," he explained to Wilson. Grant tired of her, but the woman made a pest of herself, so much so that Babcock asked McDonald whether he could do anything to get rid of Sylph. By chance, McDonald was acquainted with her, too, and he persuaded her to leave the president in peace. Since then "Sylph" had become a private joke between McDonald and Babcock and they sometimes signed notes and telegrams to each other with that name when they were involved in a government task that called for discretion.

Wilson saw through Porter's elaborate and outrageous lie.

In August 1875, as Grant was backing away from his position of "Let no guilty man escape," Bristow confronted Babcock with a handful of "Sylph" telegrams, written in his hand, and bearing not-too-cryptic messages about how to escape the Whiskey Ring investigation. Babcock adopted a tone of moral indignation, declaring that the "Sylph" telegrams referred to instructions for having a series of bridges constructed. Grant chose

To deflect attention from his own acts of political chicanery, Horace Porter invented the story that President Grant had a mistress known to his staff as "Sylph." According to Porter, Grant had broken off the affair, but Sylph continued to pester him until John McDonald intervened and convinced the lady to leave the president alone.

Library of Congress

to believe Babcock's explanation, but when Bristow and Wilson expressed skepticism the president concluded that Bristow's and Wilson's persecution of Babcock was the first step in a scheme to bring down the president himself.

Between August and December, Bristow and Wilson continued to assemble more and more evidence against Babcock, which they showed to Grant. On several occasions, sometimes with President Grant present, Bristow and Wilson confronted Babcock with proof of his ties to McDonald and other top men in the Whiskey Ring, yet Babcock always countered their charges with some implausible excuse, and Grant always sided with his aide. Even when Attorney General Pierrepont caught Babcock in the act of composing a telegram to John Joyce, McDonald's associate in St. Louis, warning him that the government was becoming more aggressive in its investigation of the Whiskey Ring, Grant still refused to admit that Babcock was involved in the scheme.

Persuaded more by the evidence than by the president's unwavering support for his friend, on December 9, 1875, a grand jury handed down an indictment against Orville Babcock. The president's son, Fred Grant, called on a reporter for the *New York Herald*, a newspaper friendly to the Grant Administration, to give the man a scoop: Babcock was the innocent victim of a conspiracy hatched by Bluford Wilson and the president's political nemesis Senator Carl Schurz to make Grant guilty by association in the whiskey swindle.

Then, on January 27, 1876, Grant made things even more complex. He summoned Wilson to the White House and ordered him to stop offering immunity to members of the Whiskey Ring who agreed to testify against their former associates. It was and still is a standard procedure among prosecutors, but Grant feared that one of those men who turned state's evidence would give proof of wrongdoing against Babcock.

THE PRESIDENT'S DEPOSITION

In February 1876 Grant made an announcement to members of his Cabinet that sent them reeling: he would go to the Whiskey Ring trial in St. Louis and offer to testify on behalf of Orville Babcock.

It was unprecedented. No sitting president had ever testified in a criminal case, let alone been cross-examined in the dock. If Babcock were convicted—and virtually everyone involved in the case expected that he would be—Grant's testimony on behalf of a criminal would sully his name forever. After lengthy debate the president agreed not to go to St. Louis but to testify instead at the White House. One of the prosecutors, Lucien Eaton, traveled to Washington to question the president. William A. Cook, a member of Babcock's defense team, was invited to cross-examine the president. Bristow and Pierrepont attended as witnesses, as did the chief justice of the Supreme Court, Morrison Remick Waite, who

107   GEN. O. E. BABCOCK.

PRESIDENT ULYSSES GRANT FOUND IT HARD TO BELIEVE THAT HIS FRIEND, GENERAL ORVILLE E. BABCOCK, WOULD BE INVOLVED IN A SCHEME TO DEFRAUD THE U.S. GOVERNMENT OF TAX REVENUE. SINCE THE CIVIL WAR GRANT HAD REGARDED BABCOCK AS ONE OF HIS MOST TRUSTED AIDES. IN APRIL 1865 AT APPOMATTOX, VIRGINIA, IT WAS BABCOCK WHO DELIVERED TO GENERAL ROBERT E. LEE GRANT'S DEMAND FOR THE SURRENDER OF THE CONFEDERATE ARMY OF NORTHERN VIRGINIA.

———★———

AS THE INVESTIGATION INTO THE WHISKEY RING CLOSED IN ON HORACE PORTER, PORTER TRIED TO
DEFLECT ATTENTION FROM HIMSELF BY INVENTING THE STORY THAT THE PRESIDENT HAD HAD AN AFFAIR
WITH SYLPH, THE PET NAME FOR LOUISE HAWKINS OF ST. LOUIS. ONE OF SYLPH'S CONTEMPORARIES
PRAISED HER "TEMPTING LUSCIOUS DELICIOUSNESS." ALTHOUGH GRANT AND SYLPH WERE NEVER
ROMANTICALLY INVOLVED, SHE MAY HAVE HAD A FLING WITH GENERAL BABCOCK.

———★———

gave the president the traditional courtroom oath to tell "nothing but the truth." Grant turned over to the defense a deposition—signed and witnessed by Chief Justice Waite—attesting to Babcock's innocence.

Back in St. Louis, Cook and Babcock's other defense attorneys characterized their man as "warmhearted, confiding, generous;" they dismissed the incriminating telegrams as "wretched, purposeless, meaningless;" and they paraded before the court a series of character witnesses from Babcock's service during the Civil War, including General William Tecumseh Sherman, who said of Babcock, "His reputation has always been good. I never heard it questioned until these troubles."

———★———

"NO SITTING PRESIDENT HAD EVER TESTIFIED IN A CRIMINAL CASE, LET ALONE BEEN CROSS-EXAMINED IN THE DOCK. IF BABCOCK WERE CONVICTED— AND VIRTUALLY EVERYONE INVOLVED IN THE CASE EXPECTED THAT HE WOULD BE—GRANT'S TESTIMONY ON BEHALF OF A CRIMINAL WOULD SULLY HIS NAME FOREVER."

———★———

On February 17, President Grant's deposition was read aloud in the hushed courtroom. A newspaper reporter wrote, "The solemnity of the occasion was felt by all present, for all understood that on these depositions depended the conclusion as to whether the defendant was guilty of using his influence with the President . . . in any corrupt manner."

In his closing arguments one of Babcock's defense attorneys, Emory Storrs, shifted the jury's attention from Babcock's purported crimes to President Grant's selfless act of giving testimony in a court case like the humblest honest citizen in the land. "The President, who remained silent to the last moment, and who only spoke in obedience to the law whose majesty he recognizes," Storrs assured the jurors, "now stands fully vindicated." In his deposition, Storrs said, the president had spoken as plainly as Christ had in his Sermon on the Mount. It was a gamble to remind the jurors that Grant's reputation would be sullied if Babcock were convicted, but it paid off. After deliberating for two hours the jurors, described in one newspaper as "plain, honest, farmer-looking" men, returned to the courtroom to deliver a verdict of "not guilty."

Orville Babcock was the only Whiskey Ring defendant to be acquitted. One hundred and ten men were convicted of defrauding the federal government in the Whiskey Ring scandal; among them was John McDonald who served 18 months in prison. In 1880, after McDonald had served his sentence, President Grant gave him a full pardon. McDonald's response was to publish a book in which he stated that Babcock and the president had been deeply involved in the Whiskey Ring conspiracy. Fortunately for Grant, very few people believed McDonald's claim concerning the president.

Secretary of the Treasury Benjamin H. Bristow indulged in a little mythmaking himself. In 1876, as he lay on his deathbed, he told David Dyer, one of the prosecutors in the Whiskey Ring case, that President Grant had visited him, held his hand and said, "General Bristow, I have done you a great wrong and I cannot afford to die without acknowledging it to your face. In the prosecution at St. Louis you were right and I was wrong." It's a wonderful story, but there is no evidence that Grant called on Bristow as he lay dying.

Grant's Cabinet refused to let Babcock return to his old job at the White House. But the president found another job for his friend—chief inspector of lighthouses. When he left office Grant made a point of thanking Babcock, although he was no longer a member of his staff, "for faithful and efficient service." The president added, "He has my acknowledgments and thanks, and the assurance of my confidence in his integrity." In 1884 Babcock was in Florida supervising the construction of a new lighthouse at Mosquito Inlet (now known as Ponce de Leon Inlet). On June 2 the boat carrying him from the building site back to shore overturned and he drowned.

Once his second term was over, the president and Mrs. Grant went on a two-year journey around the world, hoping their experiences in foreign lands would help them forget eight scandal-plagued years in Washington. In 1880 the Grants were back in the United States and the former president let the Republican Party know that he was prepared to accept their nomination for a third term. The Republicans did not take Grant up on his offer.

Grant then became involved in a number of businesses, none of which were successful. Even in private life scandal haunted him: he became entangled in a stock swindle in which thousands of people lost their investments. Grant felt personally responsible and made a point of repaying the investors, but it left him destitute. To provide for his family he began writing his memoirs (with the help of his friend, Mark Twain). He completed the manuscript just days before dying on July 23, 1885.

Although scandal after scandal erupted during the eight years Ulysses S. Grant was president, he was never involved in any of them. Grant was an honest man, a good man, and when it came to his friends, Major General Greenville M. Dodge said Grant felt bound to them by "hooks of steel." Loyalty was a religious principle with Grant, but the question remains: Did he suspect

Orville Babcock was involved in the Whiskey Ring, but his concept of friendship demanded that he do everything in his power to shield his aide from the law? Or was Grant so devoted to his friends that he could not believe them capable of criminal behavior?

President Grant was not corrupt, but he was almost certainly naïve. He was a trusting soul whose personal sense of honesty and decency apparently made him incapable of recognizing chicanery in others. For example, in 1869, with the assistance of one of President Grant's brothers-in-law, two robber barons, Jay Gould and Jim Fisk, attempted to corner the gold market. (The full story of the scandal is told in chapter 3.)

And in 1867 Congressman Oakes Ames of Massachusetts formed the Credit Mobilier, a company that was advertised as having been hired to complete the last 600 miles (965.5 km) of the transcontinental railroad. Members of the U.S. public and even representatives of the U.S. government invested heavily in the company, but it was a scam: None of the funds went to complete the railway line. When Congress was about to investigate the company, Ames bribed some of his most influential fellow congressmen to block the inquiry, including Schuyler Colfax, Grant's vice president.

Nonetheless, naiveté is no excuse. Grant was president of the United States; if some of the men he placed in office were corrupt, the ultimate responsibility was Grant's. In a president a misguided sense of loyalty is not merely an eccentricity, it has real-world consequences. The Grant Administration scandals diminished the president's effectiveness, undermined the federal government, and reached deep into the pockets of the American taxpayer.

It was one of the tragedies of Grant's presidency that such an honorable man was surrounded by "friends" who proved to be scoundrels. Years later Grant's youngest son, Jesse Root Grant, published a life-with-father memoir entitled *In the Days of My Father, General Grant*. Writing of the scandals that plagued his father's years in the White House, Jesse said, "Father has been criticized for his loyalty to his subordinates. Perhaps this loyalty was, at times, imposed upon. It was part of the man. Where he believed he would not question, and he did not readily credit evil report. It required more than apparent facts to convince him, for behind the facts he sought to know and understand the equities."

---- ★ ----

CHAPTER 3

Ulysses S. Grant and the Gold Ring:

"A COMBINATION OF DAMNED THIEVES!"

---- ★ ----

The gentlemen began the evening with drinks at the 23rd Street apartment of Josie Mansfield, a Rubenesque showgirl who was the mistress of their host, New York stockbroker extraordinaire, Jim Fisk. From Josie's place the party headed south to lower Manhattan where Fisk had arranged a private dinner for his principal brokers in the offices of William Heath & Company, just steps away from Wall Street. The date was Thursday, September 23, 1869. For months Fisk and his colleague, Jay Gould, a financier reputed to be the ninth wealthiest man in the United States, had been manipulating the precious metals market to corner the U.S. gold supply. They wanted all of it. And on that festive Thursday evening it appeared that Fisk, Gould, and their friends had just about succeeded.

The men dining with Fisk that evening were all members of a clique or circle of select investors who called themselves the Gold Ring. Together they had purchased more than $100 million in gold coins and certificates. As Kenneth D. Ackerman, historian of the Gold Ring, put it, "For all practical purposes, the clique owned all the gold within reach. No one could buy gold except from the clique. No one could sell gold without borrowing it from the clique." Every time the price of gold rose by a $1, the Gold Ring made $1 million.

Of course, at any time the U. S. Treasury might undercut the Gold Ring by flooding the market with gold from the government reserve. Such action would cause the price of gold to drop, and the Gold Ring would not see the extraordinary profits it expected. Timing was everything, and for such delicate business, Gould, the thoughtful, methodical businessman, was a better judge than Fisk, the flamboyant playboy. Led by the jolly, overconfident Fisk, the members of the Gold Ring adopted a "the sky's the limit" faith in the future price of gold. But Gould did not share their confidence. He believed the price of gold would start to fall, probably soon. And that is why on that Thursday morning, September 23, 1869, without saying a word to his partners, he had started selling his gold. By the time he finished unloading the precious commodity, Gould would clear between $11 million and $12 million. Other speculators would not be so lucky.

DISTASTEFUL AND UNPATRIOTIC

In 1869 the United States had a national paper currency as well as gold coins, both of which were legal tender. Abraham Lincoln had authorized the national currency in 1862. Supplying the Union Army was a vastly expensive enterprise; there was not enough gold on hand in the U.S. Treasury or in the vaults of U.S. banks to pay the bills, so Congress, with Lincoln's blessing, issued $450 million of paper money. Because the paper money was not tied to the gold standard (Congress had suspended it for the duration of the war), the value of the currency and of gold fluctuated, sometimes on a daily basis.

Since the U.S government did not have $450 million in gold to back up the paper money, there was always the risk that the currency might prove to be worthless. Gold, on the other hand, would always have value, and investors found that the value of gold rose and fell according to the fortunes of the Union Army. A Confederate victory made Northern investors nervous; they would want gold in their strongboxes, not paper currency, and so the demand for gold (along with its price) rose, while the demand for greenbacks fell (along with their value). For example, when General Ulysses S. Grant and his army were bogged down besieging Petersburg, Virginia, in 1864, it cost $300 in paper money to buy $100 in gold. Once General Robert E. Lee surrendered to Grant at Appomattox Court House and the national crisis was over, Northern investors felt less edgy and the price of gold settled at approximately $144 in paper money.

But trade in gold ended with the war. It was, after all, an extremely valuable commodity, and if the price was not as volatile as it had been between 1861 and 1865, there was still money to be made speculating in gold. The trading took place at the Gold Room, in a building on William Street, around the corner from the New York Stock Exchange on Wall Street. During the war, stockbrokers at the Stock Exchange found gold speculation distasteful, even unpatriotic, as gold speculators profited every time the Union lost a battle. The stockbrokers barred the gold traders from the premises, so the gold traders moved to new quarters nearby.

Throughout the Civil War merchants in Europe, South America, and Asia who did business with the United States insisted upon payment in gold. Greenbacks were too unpredictable. After the war was over, greenbacks remained the primary domestic currency in the United States, but overseas traders still insisted upon being paid in gold. U.S. farmers and factory owners discovered that this arrangement could be advantageous. While overseas merchants were paid in gold, U.S. farmers and manufacturers were paid in greenbacks. If a ship full of U.S. manufactured goods and grain sailed from Boston on a day when the price of gold was $130 and the ship arrived in London on a day when the price of gold had risen to $135, then U.S. farmers and manufacturers would get more greenbacks for their goods.

FAMILY AND BUSINESS

Jay Gould was a quiet, thoughtful man from the little upstate New York town of Roxbury. In 1859, like other ambitious young men, he came to New York City to make his fortune. He began as a leather merchant, but was soon drawn to Wall Street, the place where serious money could be made. Gould observed that a stockbroker could do well, but a speculator could do even better. To help finance his speculations, he developed friendly business relationships with several New York bankers.

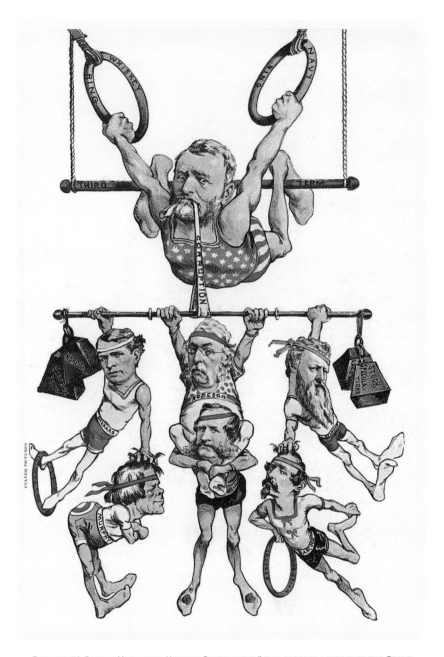

ENTITLED "A STRONG MAN AT THE HEAD OF GOVERNMENT," THIS CARTOON LAMPOONED THE GRANT
ADMINISTRATION AS A CIRCUS ACT, WITH THE PRESIDENT DOING HIS BEST TO SUPPORT HOPELESSLY
CORRUPT PARTY BOSSES AND PROFITEERS. THE CARTOON, WHICH APPEARED IN *PUCK* IN 1880, SHOWS
GRANT ON A TRAPEZE LABELED "THIRD TERM." NO U.S. PRESIDENT HAD EVER RUN FOR A THIRD TERM,
AND IF GRANT HAD TRIED IT IS VERY LIKELY THAT HE WOULD HAVE LOST. THE VOTERS WERE
FED UP WITH SCANDAL-PRONE GRANT ADMINISTRATION.

By 1863 Gould was building a considerable fortune, and he was ready to marry. He fell in love with Helen Day Miller, a shy, soft-spoken young woman. Her father, Daniel S. Miller, had made a tidy sum in the produce business, then retired in 1853 to manage his various investments. He and Gould met on Wall Street, and it is likely that he introduced Gould to his daughter. The couple married in 1863 and moved in with the Millers in the genteel Murray Hill section on the East Side of Manhattan.

Gould's quiet, reserved demeanor was misleading: He was driven by a nearly all-consuming ambition to be wealthy and successful. In his business transactions he was daring, even cunning, but he was also methodical: While Jim Fisk dashed about from one entertainment to the next, Gould spent his evenings studying ledgers and keeping up with the financial news. His grand passions were his wife, his children, and his business, and he divided his energy equally among them.

In 1868 Gould become president of the Erie Railroad, a line with connections across western New York, Ohio, Indiana, Illinois, and up into Wisconsin. In the 1860s these states comprised the Wheat Belt of the United States, and it was the Erie Railroad that carried the grain to New York so it could be shipped and sold overseas.

After the Civil War Gould began speculating in gold. He remarked, "A man with $100,000 of money and with credit can transact a business of $20 million." Gould certainly had $100,000, and thanks to his bankers he had access to credit. And $20 million was about all the gold there was in New York state. Gould bought up as much gold as he could, then loaned it to merchants and other businessmen who needed it for overseas transactions. With virtually all the state's gold in Gould's pocket, supply was short, demand was high, and the price of gold rose accordingly. During a speculation in gold Gould made in April 1869, he managed to drive up the price from $130 to $142, at which point he sold the gold for a tremendous profit.

Other investors in gold did not follow Gould's lead. In May the price of gold had risen to $145, and at that point the secretary of the treasury, George S. Boutwell, stepped in to correct the price. He announced that the federal government would sell twice as much gold from its reserve than usual. In other words, the Treasury was flooding the market with gold. And it had the effect Boutwell desired—the price of gold dropped. Investors, who had been much less cautious and much greedier than Jay Gould, lost large sums.

Gould's experience in spring 1869 convinced him that because no one knew when the Treasury would step in to reduce the price of gold, speculating in gold would always be risky. Now Gould began to consider how to eliminate that risk. The answer was inside information.

THE INFLUENCE PEDDLER

Gould found the insider he needed, not in Washington, but in New York. One of the speculators with whom he was acquainted was Abel Rathbone Corbin, a 61-year-old

TO THE U.S. PUBLIC, JAY GOULD RANKED HIGH AMONG THE MOST UNSCRUPULOUS ROBBER BARONS.
BUT HIS PRIVATE LIFE WAS UNIMPEACHABLE—HE SPENT ALMOST EVERY EVENING AT HOME,
WITH HIS WIFE AND CHILDREN.

★

widower. Tall, thin, round-shouldered, with gray hair and pale brown eyes that gave him a washed-out appearance, Corbin had just made a brilliant second marriage—to Virginia Grant, the younger and favorite sister of President Ulysses S. Grant.

Virginia, 37 years old and never married, had been living quietly with her father in Galena, Illinois. After her brother won the presidential election of 1868, Virginia Grant decided to join her family in Washington for the inaugural celebrations. At one of these fetes she met Corbin and within three months she married him and moved to New York City. Julia Grant, the new first lady, once praised Virginia for her "golden hair and dark, dove-like eyes. Her complexion was exquisitely fair with just a tinge of pink, and this sweet girl was as good as she was beautiful."

In spite of his age and physical shortcomings, Abel Corbin attracted lovely, vivacious women. A reporter for the *New York Times* described him as "a good talker, original, versatile, and well-informed." Corbin attended the Methodist church and was given to making edifying comments on almost any topic. Yet there were aspects of Corbin's character that he kept under wraps: Gould described him as "shrewd," others would come to regard Abel Corbin as a shameless hypocrite.

After a brief career as a newspaper editor in St. Louis in the 1830s, Corbin moved to Washington where he was hired as a clerk to the House of Representatives. Here Corbin found his niche. He had access to every senator and representative in Congress, and he began to peddle his connections, primarily to businessmen who came to the Capitol to lobby congressmen to introduce, support, or oppose various business-related pieces of legislation. Corbin convinced some of these visitors that he could shepherd their pet legislative initiatives through the House and Senate—for a fee. And the fees rolled in, enough for Corbin to buy a fine house in an exclusive part of I Street, next door to the renowned senator from Illinois, Stephen A. Douglas. In addition to soliciting bribes, Corbin also cultivated influential people, becoming friendly with Douglas, future Vice President Andrew Johnson, and the poet William Cullen Bryant.

In 1852 Corbin promised a Boston textile manufacturer that he could get a bill through Congress that would lower the tariff on wool and dyes. For his efforts he required a fee of $1,000. The measure failed, but during the Congressional session of 1855–56, Corbin wrote to the Boston firm saying he was ready to try again. He would need $50,000 to persuade key members of Congress to vote for the bill. For his services he wanted $25,000 up front and another $25,000 when the president signed the bill into law.

The Boston firm balked and appears to have passed along Corbin's letter to its representative in Washington. Humiliated at having been discovered, Corbin promptly resigned his office, but remained in Washington. Shortly after the Civil War, he sold his house on I Street to General Grant, then moved to New York City to pursue new interests.

Gould and Corbin met in 1866 or 1867 at Saratoga, New York, a summer resort favored by the well-to-do. At the time Corbin was investing in railroads and New Jersey real estate. He lived in a five-story brownstone mansion on West 27th Street in New York. Late in 1868 or early in 1869 Corbin showed an interest in the gold market. About that time the two men did their first piece of business together—the Erie Railroad wanted to lay track across land in New Jersey that belonged to Corbin, and rather than hand over the matter to subordinates, Corbin and Gould worked out the deal personally.

Then Gould had an inspiration: The great and dangerous variable in attempting to corner gold was the U.S. Treasury's ability at any time to flood the market with gold and drive down the price. But if Gould had an informant inside the Grant Administration, he would know when the Treasury was ready to act and sell his gold before disaster struck.

AN UNWILLING CANDIDATE

By manipulating the price of gold Gould saw an opportunity to enrich himself while increasing the profits of the Erie Railroad. If wheat farmers in the Midwest were making more money by selling their grain overseas, they would want to sell even more of their crops to Europe. This would translate into increased traffic on the Erie line, which would mean greater profits for the railroad. Gould could almost convince himself that by cornering gold he was performing a public service to hardworking U.S. farmers and increasing dividends for the Erie Railroad's shareholders.

Rather than act boldly and invite Corbin to participate in a grand swindle, Gould adopted a subtle approach. He told Corbin that he had stumbled upon a way to increase the prosperity of U.S. farmers and manufacturers, strengthen the U.S. economy, and boost the popularity of President Grant among voters. All the president had to do was restrain his secretary of the treasury and let the price of gold rise. And rise. And rise. The idea excited Corbin, but as the two men discussed their plan, they agreed that it might be best to have several sources within the administration who could supply them with inside information.

They discovered that the post of assistant U.S. treasurer in New York was open. Whoever held this job would know when the Treasury was preparing to buy or sell gold. Corbin suggested they win the appointment for Robert Catherwood, his stepdaughter's husband (by a previous marriage). Gould approved of the idea and the two men called upon Catherwood to make him a simple offer—Corbin would persuade President Grant to appoint Catherwood assistant treasurer; for his part, Catherwood would alert Corbin and Gould every time the government was about to make a gold- or currency-related transaction. But Catherwood refused to become Corbin's and Gould's informant. They would have to find someone else.

THE SILENT PRESIDENT

In June 1869 President Grant traveled to Boston to attend a peace conference. En route he stopped in New York City where his wife and children would stay with Abel and Virginia Corbin. The parlors, halls, and reception rooms of the Corbin mansion were crammed with politicians, businessmen, and the cream of New York society, all come to greet the president. In this throng Corbin introduced Gould to Grant, but amid such a crush of guests the two men could not make much conversation. It did not matter; shortly the president would leave for the wharves along the Hudson River where he would board the *Providence*, the finest of the steamships that followed the coast between New York and Boston. Jim Fisk, a business crony of Gould's, owned the line—they would both accompany Grant on his cruise up the Long Island Sound.

———★———

THE PRESIDENT KNEW HE WAS IN THE COMPANY OF TWO ROBBER BARONS, BUT HE HAD SUPPRESSED HIS MISGIVINGS BECAUSE ABEL CORBIN, THE HUSBAND OF HIS BELOVED SISTER VIRGINIA, HAD VOUCHED FOR THEIR CHARACTER. AND GRANT TRUSTED ANYONE WHO WAS A MEMBER OF HIS FAMILY.

———★———

Fisk was a year older than Gould, a Vermont peddler's son who made his fortune securing textile contracts from the U.S. government during the Civil War and running the Union blockade of Southern ports to bring cotton to the Northern textile mills. He was as flamboyant as Gould was subdued; while Gould spent his evenings with his family, Fisk craved the limelight. But there was more to Fisk than his being the self-indulgent playboy; he was a shrewd speculator, although more willing to take risks than Gould. They became close associates after Fisk joined the board of directors of the Erie Railroad. When Gould first broached the subject of cornering the gold market, Fisk expressed interest.

Late in the afternoon of June 15, 1869, Gould and Fisk boarded the *Providence* as part of President Grant's entourage. The president knew he was in the company of two robber barons, but he had suppressed his misgivings because Abel Corbin, the husband of his beloved sister Virginia, had vouched for their character. And Grant trusted anyone who was a member of his family.

Gould and Fisk had agreed to broach the subject of gold after dinner; they expected that with a few drinks in him, the president would be in a receptive mood. But Grant had declined whiskey before the meal and wine during dinner. Many of the dinner guests were businessmen, and their conversation turned naturally to the economy—that made it easy for Gould to urge that the Treasury should permit gold to rise so that farmers and manufacturers could sell their grain and goods overseas at a better price.

Grant did not volunteer a response to Gould's proposition, so Fisk asked the president what his thoughts were on the subject. Grant said, "There is a certain fictitiousness about the prosperity of the country." He believed paper money already was too cheap, and he would never permit the power of the federal government to be used by speculators who wanted to see the price of gold rise.

But Gould was not yet prepared to give up. If the government permitted the price of gold to collapse, he said, "It would produce strikes among the workmen, and their workshops, to a great extent, would have to be closed, the manufactories would have to stop." The government's action "would produce great distress," Gould said, "and almost lead to civil war." That was a daring thing to say to the former commander of the Union Army, only four years after the Civil War had ended, but Grant still held his peace. For three hours the gentlemen discussed the gold question, but the president never wavered from his refusal to use the Treasury to keep the price of gold high. Gould and Fisk could expect no help from Grant.

The next morning when the *Providence* docked at Fall River, Massachusetts, Gould went ashore to find a telegraph office—he wanted to send a message to his office to sell his gold. When he reached the Western Union branch he met William Marston, one of his fellow guests from the presidential dinner—Marston was ordering his office to sell his gold, too.

GOULD'S INVESTMENT

Gould and Fisk wrote off the conversation with Grant as a momentary setback. In New York they met with Abel Corbin and once again reviewed possible candidates for the post of assistant U.S. treasurer in New York. Corbin recommended General Daniel Butterfield, a hero of the Civil War who had fought at Fredericksburg, Chancellorsville, and Gettysburg. President Grant considered Butterfield a trusted friend, a man who had gone out of his way to be of assistance to the Grants and their friends. After the war, when the New York department store magnate Alexander T. Stewart floated the idea that the wealthy families of New York should present General Grant with a cash honorarium in appreciation for his services to the Union, it was Butterfield who made the rounds among well-to-do New Yorkers soliciting contributions; then he presented Grant with a check for $105,000. When two of Grant's closest associates, General

JAY GOULD GAVE DANIEL BUTTERFIELD, ASSISTANT TREASURY SECRETARY, A "LOAN" OF $10,000.
IN RETURN, BUTTERFIELD PROVIDED GOULD WITH ADVANCE INFORMATION REGARDING ANY
GOVERNMENT TRANSACTION THAT WOULD IMPACT THE PRICE OF GOLD.
LIBRARY OF CONGRESS

————★————

Horace Porter and General Orville Babcock, wanted to invest in New York real estate, Butterfield found properties for them, arranged the mortgages, and even advanced the gentlemen the necessary down payments. As a result, when Abel Corbin approached Grant and recommended Butterfield for the assistant U.S. treasurer post, the president appointed him at once.

On June 29 Butterfield moved into his office on Wall Street, and two days later Jay Gould called upon him. Before he left, Gould presented Butterfield with a "gift" of $10,000 (Butterfield's salary as assistant U.S. treasurer was $8,000 per year). Butterfield would later explain that the $10,000 was a loan. It is probably best characterized as an "investment," and the return Gould expected was advance information regarding any pending government transaction involving gold.

In August Gould enjoyed an even greater coup than installing Butterfield in the Treasury Department—the president himself assured him that he was now a believer in permitting the price of gold to rise. While in New York to attend a funeral, Grant met with Gould. The harvest of 1869 had been especially bountiful, and Grant now was of the opinion that the federal government should not take any action that would prevent U.S. farmers from making a tidy profit selling their grain overseas. Gould was euphoric, and he would have been even more so if he knew that on September 4 Grant sent written instructions to Secretary of the Treasury Boutwell that it was "undesirable to force down the price of gold."

GRANT'S SUSPICIONS

Only days after he received the president's instructions, Secretary of the Treasury Boutwell traveled to New York where he was to be honored with a dinner at the Union League. Gould, Fisk, and Corbin were not on the guest list, but many of Wall Street's bearish investors were, and this put Fisk in a state of agitation. Suppose the bears of Wall Street persuaded Boutwell to dump government gold on the market—would Butterfield be able to warn them in time? Then Corbin began to panic, too. He had called upon the Treasury secretary at his hotel and Boutwell had treated Corbin coldly. Corbin feared that the Gold Ring's $100 million was in jeopardy.

Gould tried to reassure Fisk and Corbin, but eventually their anxieties infected him, too. He declared that Corbin must write a letter to Grant, who was vacationing in Washington, Pennsylvania, outside of Pittsburgh. The purpose of the letter would be to urge the president to stand firm in his commitment to let the price of gold rise without any interference from the government. Fearful that Boutwell might reach the president first and persuade him to suspend the ever-rising price of gold, Gould decided to send Corbin's letter to Grant by confidential messenger. Gould selected the Erie Railroad's most trusted courier, a young New Yorker named William Chapin.

Chapin performed his task perfectly, but the arrival of a courier from New York bearing a lengthy letter from Corbin about the vital importance of barring the Treasury secretary from interfering in the price of gold made Grant suspicious. Given Corbin's friendship with Gould and Fisk, Grant concluded that his brother-in-law was also involved in gold speculation. "It is very sad," Grant said to his wife Julia and General Porter. "I fear [Corbin] may be ruined—and my poor sister." Then he instructed Julia to write to Virginia to warn her of rumors that Corbin was involved in gold speculation. "If you have any influence with your husband," Julia wrote, "tell him to have nothing to do with [New York gold speculators]. If he does, he will be ruined, for come what may [President Grant] will do his duty to the country and the trusts in his keeping."

———— ★ ————

GRANT CONCLUDED THAT HIS BROTHER-IN-LAW WAS INVOLVED IN GOLD SPECULATION. "IT IS VERY SAD," GRANT SAID TO HIS WIFE JULIA. "I FEAR [CORBIN] MAY BE RUINED—AND MY POOR SISTER."

———— ★ ————

With this warning Grant hoped to save his sister and brother-in-law from the shame of bankruptcy, and his family and administration from being linked to scandal. It did not occur to the president that Corbin would pass the warning along to Gould and Fisk.

Julia Grant sent her note by regular mail; the soonest her warning would reach Virginia Corbin was September 22.

"I MUST GET OUT INSTANTLY!"

In New York Gould and Fisk had no idea that President Grant had seen through them at last. In fact, they had no reason to believe that he would change his gold policy: William Chapin sent Fisk a telegram with the message, "Letter delivered all right." But the telegraph operator sent the message this way: "Letter delivered. All right." Fisk and Gould read it as meaning Grant still favored rising gold prices.

Fisk, overdressed and overperfumed as usual, all but charged onto the trading floor of the Gold Room shouting orders for gold and offering to wager any man present $50,000 that gold, languishing at the moment at $137 ⅝ would soar to $145. Incredibly, he also declared for all to hear that he had President Grant's personal assurance that no Treasury gold would be sold.

Fisk's flamboyance paid off: on Wednesday, September 22, the trading closed with gold at $141 ½. According to Gould's biographer Maury Klein, "To accomplish this required enormous purchases later estimated at between $50 and $60 million."

That evening Gould dropped in on the Corbins. Julia Grant's note had arrived, and Corbin was on the verge of panic. "I must get out instantly—Instantly!" he cried. It was a moment of revelation for Gould, too. He understood now that Corbin had misled him, that he did not exercise great influence over the president.

Corbin wanted to sell his gold as soon as the market opened the next day, but Gould wanted to protect the Gold Ring's profits if he could, and a sudden sale of Corbin's millions in gold might set off a panic among other investors. Instead Gould offered to advance Corbin $100,000—the profit he could expect if he sold his gold the next morning. In return Corbin would not tell anyone about the Julia Grant note. Corbin accepted Gould's offer.

The next morning, Thursday, September 23, Fisk discovered that Corbin was losing his nerve. Fisk, still boisterous and overconfident, responded by ordering his brokers to buy more gold and drive the price up to $144. It was at that point that Gould, without Fisk's knowledge, gave his brokers orders to sell. To mask the sales, he instructed them to buy small amounts of gold so it would appear to other investors that he still had confidence that the price would continue to rise. That day gold climbed to $145 before settling at $143 ¼.

That evening, as Fisk and his brokers celebrated at their gala dinner, Secretary of the Treasury Boutwell met with President Grant, newly returned from his vacation in Pennsylvania. Gold investors had driven the price up to $145, Boutwell reported. What did the president want to do? Grant authorized Boutwell to sell government gold.

MEN OF FORESIGHT

The Gold Room did not open for business until 10 in the morning, but hours earlier crowds began to throng William Street and neighboring Broad and New streets, eager or anxious to see what would happen to the price of gold that day, Friday, September 24. Gould and Fisk rode to lower Manhattan in a carriage; to stay out of the public eye they went to the offices of William Heath & Company, site of the previous night's dinner party. En route Gould had his driver stop at Daniel Butterfield's office. Dependable informant that he was, Butterfield reported that so far he had received no communication from Washington.

The tension was so great in the Gold Room that men began to trade before business opened at 10 a.m. In fact, by the time the president struck his gavel, gold already stood at $150. Before 11 a.m. it would inch beyond the $150 mark. Meanwhile, as Gould's brokers continued quietly to sell off his gold, Gould made no mention of this fact to Fisk or any

ON SEPTEMBER 24, 1869, ON ORDERS FROM PRESIDENT GRANT, THE SECRETARY
OF THE TREASURY DUMPED $4 MILLION OF TREASURY GOLD ON THE MARKET.
WITHIN MINUTES THE PRICE OF GOLD PLUMMETED FROM $162 TO $135 AND HUNDREDS,
PERHAPS THOUSANDS, OF INVESTORS WERE RUINED. THE WOOD ENGRAVING,
WHICH APPEARED IN FRANK LESLIE'S *ILLUSTRATED NEWSPAPER* ON OCTOBER 9, 1869,
DEPICTS THE CHAOS OF THE EVENT.

HULTON ARCHIVE/GETTY IMAGES

———★———

other member of the Gold Ring. People who had been at the Heath offices with Gould and Fisk would recall later that they did not hear Gould say a word; he sat, calm and silent, methodically tearing up bits of paper and rolling them into tiny balls.

Gold had risen to $162 when news arrived in the Gold Room that Secretary of the Treasury Boutwell had dumped $4 million of Treasury gold on the market. Cries of despair rose from the 300 brokers crammed onto the trading floor, and from the hundreds of investors packed into the galleries above. Within minutes gold fell to $135. Investors who had purchased gold for any price higher than $135 were ruined. But Gould was not among the bankrupted. And neither was Butterfield who, like Gould, had the foresight to sell his gold before the price collapsed.

JIM FISK'S BLOODY NOSE

The crowd of investors and brokers surged out of the Gold Room into the streets of lower Manhattan where, within minutes, they became an angry mob. They gathered in front of the offices of members of the Gold Ring, including Gould's office and Heath & Company, where Gould and Fisk were hiding in a back office, protected by three muscle-bound bodyguards who stood in front of the door.

Squads of New York policemen and New York State Militia rushed to the scene to keep order. One part of the mob chanted, "Jay Gould! Jay Gould!" while another part answered "Lynch! Lynch! Lynch!"

Gould and Fisk slipped out of the Heath building through a back entrance, then scurried down an alley to Gould's office, half a block away. But they were observed, and now the bloodthirsty crowd gathered in front of Gould's building on Broad Street. No police or militia had arrived at the building yet; Gould wondered aloud if there were any guns in the offices so they could defend themselves when the mob broke in. But Fisk insisted he could disperse the crowd. He considered himself a first-rate speechifier, an orator who could charm even hundreds of irate bankrupt investors and brokers.

So he went downstairs, unlocked the lobby doors, and stepped out to face the crowd. They closed in on him, shrieking threats and curses. As Fisk raised his arms and called for the crowd's attention, someone hauled off and punched Fisk in the face. At that moment, a few policemen arrived, and as they made for the attacker, Fisk staggered back inside the building, holding his handkerchief to his bloody nose.

Not until nightfall were Gould and Fisk able to escape in a closed carriage that took them swiftly to their uptown offices in the Grand Opera House on West 23rd Street and Eighth Avenue. They called in hired guards and posted them at every entrance. Then the two men sat down to plot their next move.

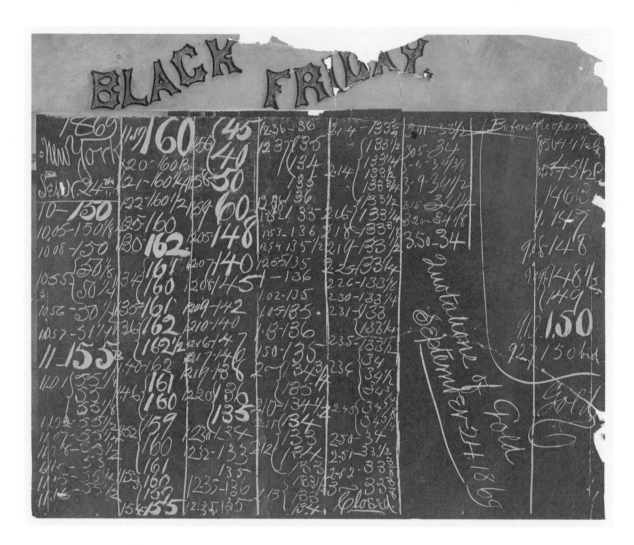

THIS BULLETIN BOARD FROM THE GOLD ROOM ILLUSTRATES THE COLLAPSE OF THE PRICE OF GOLD

ON "BLACK FRIDAY," SEPTEMBER 24, 1869. THIS PHOTOGRAPH OF THE BULLETIN BOARD WAS PRODUCED

AS EVIDENCE BEFORE THE COMMITTEE ON BANKING AND CURRENCY HEARINGS IN 1870.

THE HOUSE OF REPRESENTATIVES HAD CHARGED THE COMMITTEE "TO INVESTIGATE THE CAUSES

THAT LED TO THE UNUSUAL AND EXTRAORDINARY FLUCTUATIONS OF GOLD IN THE CITY OF NEW YORK,

FROM THE 21ST TO THE 27TH OF SEPTEMBER, 1869."

———————★———————

They had some breathing space. The trades of Thursday and what became known as Black Friday were so numerous and so tangled that no one was entirely sure yet how much money had been lost. The investors and brokers howling for Gould's and Fisk's blood knew they had been badly hurt, possibly ruined, but they didn't have a dollar amount. Over the weekend Gould and Fisk devised a plan.

———★———

SQUADS OF NEW YORK POLICEMEN AND NEW YORK STATE MILITIA RUSHED TO THE SCENE TO KEEP ORDER. ONE PART OF THE MOB CHANTED, "JAY GOULD! JAY GOULD!" WHILE ANOTHER PART ANSWERED "LYNCH! LYNCH! LYNCH!"

———★———

First thing Monday morning, Gould's and Fisk's attorneys hurried to court to obtain a series of injunctions. The Gold Exchange Bank, which handled most gold transactions in New York, was put into receivership with a court-appointed administrator to take control of its assets; furthermore, the bank was barred from selling any of its gold until the snarl of more than $800 million in transactions had been sorted out. Meanwhile, the ripple effect of Black Friday was beginning to become apparent: Foreign traders stopped buying U.S. goods, and U.S. banks were driving up interest rates for loans—since Black Friday the interest rates had risen three percentage points. And stock prices tumbled. One especially dramatic example was Commodore Cornelius Vanderbilt's New York Central Railroad—its shares fell from $177 to $150. When a reporter asked the commodore who was responsible for the wreck of the gold and stock markets, Vanderbilt replied, "A combination of damned thieves!"

GRANT'S VIRTUES

Between Black Friday, September 24, and October 1, the value of gold and stocks dropped by approximately $100 million. Investors remained skittish for the next year—between January and September 1870, only four million shares were traded on Wall Street, half of what had been traded in 1869. For months after the collapse, the price of gold languished beneath $130. Dozens of brokerage houses went out of business. The number of personal fortunes ruined by the Gold Ring will never be known—hundreds certainly, very likely thousands.

Gould had won President Grant to his side by arguing that high gold prices would be good for U.S. farmers. After the collapse, the farmers were badly hurt. Overseas traders were still wary of doing business with the United States, and so U.S. grain found no market. The price of wheat dropped from $1.40 per bushel to 77 cents, corn from 95 cents to 68 cents.

Eager to deflect attention from himself, Fisk invited the *New York Herald*'s financial reporter, George Crouch, to the Grand Opera House for an exclusive interview about the Gold Ring. Crouch was suspicious, but he accepted the invitation. During the interview Fisk dropped a bombshell: "Members of the president's family were in with us," he said. "The president himself was interested with us in the corner." Then Fisk went on to tell of meetings with Grant and payoffs. When Crouch asked why Fisk was revealing these secrets, he replied, "Because they went back on us and came near ruining us. Grant got scared."

The *Herald* ran the story, but newspapers across the country leaped to the president's defense. Editorial writers reminded their readers that the president's relatives may be corrupt, but that did not mean that he was tainted. Furthermore, it was Grant who destroyed the Gold Ring by putting Treasury gold on the market. Fisk's ploy failed. He remained the villain of Black Friday, and Grant, the hero of the nation who had defeated the Confederacy was a hero once again, this time saving the United States from unprincipled swindlers.

But it was a near-miss. If Corbin hadn't panicked and written to the vacationing president to let the price of gold rise, it is likely that Grant would not have suspected that he was being manipulated by Gould, Corbin, and the Gold Ring. The speculators, aided by Daniel Butterfield, might have enjoyed an indefinite field day. By playing upon one of Grant's most prominent traits—personal loyalty—they almost got away with the swindle. The speculators were undone by another of the president's virtues—unimpeachable honesty.

Unlike the Whiskey Ring scandal, Grant kept the Gold Ring schemers at arm's length. True, he placed his trust—for a time—in Abel Corbin, for the sake of his sister Virginia. But when it became clear to Grant that Corbin was corrupt, the president took action to destroy the Gold Ring. He knew that Gould and Fisk were unscrupulous, but he was persuaded by their argument that high gold prices would be good for the U.S. public. He listened to their arguments, but he did not consider them friends, and so the demands of loyalty did not apply to Gould and Fisk. Tragically, it was U.S. investors, farmers, and manufacturers who bore the brunt of the collapse of the price of gold. It was such crashes that would lead, in time, to government regulation of the financial markets.

In the 1880s Jay Gould gained controlling interests in the Western Union telegraph company and four railroads, including the Union Pacific. He purchased a Gothic mansion, Lyndhurst, overlooking the Hudson River in Tarrytown, New York. He gave generously to various charities, yet he never managed to shake off his reputation as one

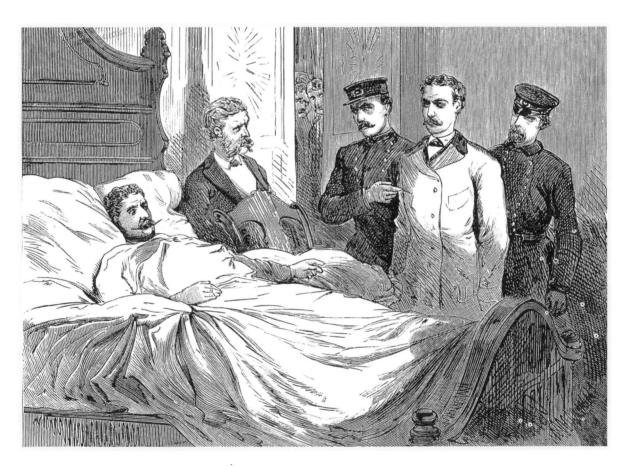

IN 1872 JOSIE MANSFIELD AND HER NEW LOVER, EDWARD STOKES, ATTEMPTED TO EXTORT MONEY
FROM HER FORMER LOVER, FINANCIER, AND GOLD RING SCHEMER, JIM FISK. WHEN FISK REFUSED,
STOKES SHOT HIM. ON HIS DEATH BED, FISK IDENTIFIED STOKES AS HIS MURDERER.

———— ★ ————

of the most unprincipled businessmen in the United States. He died in 1892 and lies buried in a grand mausoleum in Woodlawn Cemetery. The tomb does not bear the family name—apparently Gould feared it would be desecrated by vandals if the public knew whose body was inside.

After the Gold Ring debacle Josie Mansfield left Fisk for the much more handsome Edward S. Stokes. The couple were blissfully happy, but short on cash. Mansfield and Stokes threatened to publish Fisk's letters to Mansfield if he did not hand over a large pile of cash (the exact amount is unknown), Fisk refused. In January 1872 Stokes and Mansfield were on the brink of bankruptcy; in frustration, Stokes shot Fisk, then ran off. On his deathbed Fisk identified Stokes as his killer. Stokes served four years in prison for manslaughter.

Josie Mansfield married three times, although between her second and third husbands she declared her intention to enter a convent. In 1931, while shopping in a department store in Paris she fell. Her injuries proved fatal; she was 84 years old.

In 1870, within months of the Gold Ring scandal, Abel Corbin and his wife Virginia had a child, a daughter, who died about four weeks later. They had no other children. The couple left New York City and bought a house in Jersey City, New Jersey, where Corbin died in 1880. Virginia Grant Corbin survived her husband by thirty-three years, dying in 1913.

In the wake of the Gold Ring scandal the federal government did not impose any regulations on commodities trading—decades would pass before the government would try to control commercial and investment transactions. As for Grant, historians have tended to exonerate him. C. Vann Woodward summed up the historians' perspective in an article he published in *American Heritage* magazine in April 1957: "It must be admitted that the President was grossly careless about his associates…he seemed incapable of spotting a rogue. His heavy responsibility for some of the scandals of his time was indirect and grew out of his blind loyalty to friends and his weakness for men of wealth."

———★———

CHAPTER 4

Warren Harding and the Teapot Dome Scandal:

AMERICA'S OIL BARONS STRIKE A GUSHER DURING THE ROARING TWENTIES

———★———

n the morning of July 27, 1923, the naval transport ship USS *Henderson* steamed into Puget Sound on its way to Seattle. Heavy fog had settled on the water, forcing the ship to a cautious pace. Suddenly another vessel loomed out of the murk. Henderson's helm struggled to veer off, but to no avail, and the racket of colliding steel cut through the gray stillness.

The other vessel, USS *Zeilin*, was a destroyer. She had been sent to escort *Henderson* and her precious cargo, only to find herself the unwitting victim of the transport's considerable momentum in the confusion of a typically foggy Pacific Northwest morning. Crippled from the impact into her side, *Zeilin* took on water before beaching herself to avoid sinking.

Henderson, though barely scratched, shuddered from the impact. Safe in his cabin and unaware of the accident unfolding outside, the ship's most important passenger murmured, "I hope the boat sinks."

He was Warren Harding, president of the United States—the very cargo that *Zeilin*, along with other naval vessels, had been assigned to escort on this executive tour of the American West. The president's acid remark was entirely in character, the result of a recent skepticism that his abilities were not up to the crushing burdens of his office. He had acquired, at moments of unguarded cynicism, a defeatist attitude. Literally and figuratively, Harding's ship of state was in troubled waters.

Nothing convinced him of this more surely than the scandals that seemed to fester within his administration. Like tumors, he had uncovered a few of them almost by accident, which served only to make him wonder how many others remained to be found. Men in his own clique, on whose support he had relied to become president, were cashing in on their closeness to the commander in chief. "I have no trouble with my enemies," Harding once complained to newspaperman William Allen White. "But my friends…my goddamn friends, White, they're the ones [who] keep me walking the floor nights!"

Harding didn't have many more sleepless nights to worry about. On August 2, in the finest suite of San Francisco's Palace Hotel, he suffered convulsions and died, either from some respiratory infection or as a result of deeper pulmonary issues that had gone undiagnosed (and that remain a mystery to this day). He was fifty-seven years old.

The extent to which Harding's "goddamn friends" bilked the U.S. taxpayer would come out in dribs and drabs over the course of the ensuing years; ironically, Warren Harding died a popular leader whose nation mourned his untimely death in complete ignorance of the malfeasance that ultimately defined him as president. In the end, none of these scandals made as big an impact on history as the one whose name has come to symbolize government corruption of the first order: Teapot Dome.

EVERYMAN FROM OHIO

"Well, Warren Harding, I have got you the presidency," said his wife Florence famously after his 1920 electoral victory. "What are you going to do with it?" Known as "the Duchess" to everyone in the Harding circle, Florence Kling Harding had rebuilt her husband's failing newspaper business in Marion, Ohio, and helped hammer his Senate career into shape. Despite misgivings about the prospect of her husband's presidential nomination, she ended up playing a leading role in his campaign, regularly holding court with reporters and uttering nary an offbeat remark. She was ambitious, domineering, adventurous, and a natural administrator. But she could not have done it on her own.

That's because her husband was not necessarily presidential material. To be sure, Warren Harding had certain assets: He had experience in the scrum of newspaper culture and its attendant political fights; he embraced, in an intelligently articulated manner, the Republican Party's most progressive ideas on business; and he was handsome in an old Hollywood sort of way, with piercing eyes and a rangy, athletic frame. But Harding wasn't even sure he *wanted* to be the chief executive. He found the U.S. Senate congenial enough, with its gentleman's club atmosphere and manageable schedule. A small-town businessman by nature, he treasured his leisure time, whether it was spent golfing, playing poker, or sleeping with his twenty-three-year-old mistress, Nan Britton. The notion of winning the White House had always been tempting and terrifying by turns, and on several occasions during the campaign he threatened to quit.

Of those in his entourage who refused to let him, none was as determined as Harry Daugherty, Harding's campaign manager. Daugherty was a veteran operator in the Republican organization who had known Harding for years and had groomed him for great things, hoping to ride the newspaperman's coattails to the White House itself. But like the Duchess, Daugherty knew that gregariousness and good looks weren't enough to get Harding the presidency.

From the beginning, he took no chances. Going into the Republican National Convention in Chicago, Harding ran near the bottom of a list of candidates led by General Leonard Wood. The *Wall Street Journal* reckoned Harding's odds at eight to one. Fortunately for Daugherty, an extremely wealthy segment of the population had decided to bet everything on a Republican victory in 1920. For the last eight years, U.S. oil barons had had a very unsympathetic president to cope with. Woodrow Wilson, a Democrat, had consistently refused to intervene on the oil companies' behalf both at home, where government-owned oil reserves remained unexploited, and in Mexico, where U.S.-owned wells were being nationalized by the Mexican government. As GOP delegates from around the nation converged on Chicago in 1920, two of the oil industry's richest players—Jake Hamon, "the Oil King of Oklahoma," and Harry Ford Sinclair, president of the Sinclair Consolidated Oil Corporation—joined them. Soon their money was lining the pockets of every delegate and party boss who promised to vote their way.

IN THIS CONTEMPORARY CARTOON FROM THE *WASHINGTON STAR*, THE OUTBREAK OF THE TEAPOT DOME

SCANDAL THREATENS TO FLATTEN THE WHITE HOUSE.

LIBRARY OF CONGRESS

But which candidate would they throw their weight behind? Leonard Wood, a bona fide, riding-crop-wielding war hero and former sparring partner of Theodore Roosevelt, proved morally unimpeachable. By contrast, Warren Harding was open for business—the debonair, whiskey-drinking poker player from Ohio with the firm handshake was clearly a man Hamon and Sinclair could reason with. Daugherty's deft and relentless schmoozing brought them all together, and soon the eight-to-one dark horse was leading the pack.

Harding secured the nomination. Six months later, in the first presidential election in which women could vote, he handily defeated Democrat James Cox with the help of contributions from the petroleum lobby. The oilmen had their president.

"OPENING UP EVERY RESOURCE"

The Harding presidency was in many ways an accurate reflection of the times. Prohibition had been in effect since 1920, but seemingly nobody in the nation took it seriously. The new administration was no exception. Harding held regular poker soirees in the White House study in which whiskey, much of it confiscated from bootleggers by the U.S. Treasury Department, was as common as cigar smoke. The Roaring Twenties were getting under way, a period defined by loosening morals and reckless entrepreneurialism, and the Harding White House was right in the thick of it all.

Harry Daugherty's prize for masterminding his boss's elevation to the presidency was the attorney generalship, a post he now used to enrich himself and his friends through a loosely organized network of corruption. Known as the "Ohio Gang," this throng of delegates, Harding associates, and party faithful from the president's home state now reaped the rewards of their service. But there were other bigger players in need of payment as well.

Jake Hamon had always intended his enormous campaign contributions to pave the way for his appointment as secretary of the interior, which he had been promised by Harding himself in the event of victory. By assuming the Cabinet post, Hamon would be in an ideal situation to open domestic oil reserves to exploitation. These reserves on state land—at Elk Hills and Buena Vista, California, and Teapot Dome, Wyoming—had been set aside by the previous two administrations for emergency use by the Navy in wartime, an arrangement that also suited conservationists who opposed their immediate exploitation. Hamon, as point man for the oil barons, would, with the legal assistance of Attorney General Daugherty, transfer control of these untapped petroleum assets from the Navy to the Department of the Interior. Once in control of them, Hamon could release them for drilling to the oil industry the support of which had put Harding in office, opening up a mind-boggling bonanza worth hundreds of millions of (1920) dollars.

But as historian Laton McCartney makes clear in *The Teapot Dome Scandal*, there was a snag in Hamon's plan. Harding assured him after being elected that the post to the Department of the Interior was his. But Hamon had to give something up in exchange:

PRESIDENT WARREN HARDING RECEIVES A FLOWER FOR HIS LAPEL FROM THE WOMAN WITH WHOM HE
SHARED A STRAINED AND COMPLEX RELATIONSHIP: HIS WIFE, FLORENCE KLING HARDING,
A.K.A. "THE DUCHESS." THOUGH ORIGINALLY HESITANT TO LET HER HUSBAND RUN FOR THE WHITE
HOUSE, FLORENCE GRADUALLY CAME AROUND IN 1920, PARTLY AS A RESULT OF HEARING FROM
"MADAME MARCIA," A WASHINGTON, D.C., FORTUNE-TELLER, WHO PREDICTED THAT HARDING WOULD WIN.

LIBRARY OF COMGRESS

————★————

namely, his mistress. Since 1910 Hamon had been living and traveling with Clara Smith, eighteen years his junior, making a mockery of his marriage. To the Duchess, no stranger to mistresses, Hamon's behavior was more than merely inexcusable—it was an insult to the Duchess's family. By the purest of coincidences, Florence Harding and Hamon's wife, Ruth, were second cousins. Upon learning of this, the Duchess insisted that Warren make Hamon's acceptance of the Department of the Interior post contingent on ending his affair with Clara. They called Florence "the Duchess" for a reason, and Warren agreed.

Hamon had to choose between the opportunity of a lifetime and the great love of his life. He seems to have chosen poorly. Several weeks after the election, Hamon turned up in an Oklahoma sanatorium with a bullet in his liver. The wound proved fatal. Though she would ultimately be acquitted of the charge of attempted murder years later, Clara Smith Hamon (she had been using his last name since marrying Hamon's nephew in a farcical ceremony) doubtless shot her paramour. Self-defense was the plea; only Clara knew the truth.

In any event, President-elect Harding was now without a secretary of the interior. An obvious replacement was Albert Fall, Republican senator from New Mexico who had become a member of the Harding circle during the campaign. Fall was something of a legend in the Senate—a tough-talking product of the New Mexico frontier who bullied his opponents, both on and off the chamber floor. He was uncompromising. "He has no acquaintances," claimed a 1911 article in the *Saturday Evening Post*. "Every New Mexican is either his steadfast friend or his bitter enemy; and they are all his admirers."

Harding was certainly an admirer, especially as Fall was already up to speed on the idea of leasing the oil reserves and was more than willing to do so. A wealthy rancher and mine owner, the colorful New Mexican looked on the scheme as a means of underwriting big plans throughout the West. "I stand for opening up every resource," said Fall, upon becoming head of the Department of the Interior.

On May 31, 1921, President Harding authorized the transfer of the Navy's petroleum reserves to the Department of the Interior. Fall was now responsible for making sure they didn't go to waste.

ANTE UP

There were several reasons why Fall's scheme was likely to go forward without a hitch. First, there was nothing illegal about it, at least not on the face of things. Though conservationists were against the plan, exploiting the reserves was arguably a matter for executive policy. Second, both the president and the new secretary of the Navy, Edwin Denby, were on board—there would be no trouble from them. And lastly, the scheme had a practical and believable raison d´être: the widely held assumption that the government's reserves were likely either to "seep" or drain into neighboring privately owned lands, or to be surreptitiously

FOR HARRY MICAJAH DAUGHERTY, SHOWN HERE IN 1924, THE ATTORNEY GENERAL'S SEAT
WAS A REWARD FOR GETTING WARREN HARDING THE PRESIDENCY IN 1920. A VETERAN
REPUBLICAN OPERATOR, HE REFUSED TO LET HARDING QUIT, WHICH HE THREATENED TO DO
SEVERAL TIMES DURING THE PRESIDENTIAL CAMPAIGN.

LIBRARY OF COMGRESS

————————★————————

tapped by those neighbors through transverse drilling techniques that went in at an angle, or both. By drilling sooner rather than later, the government would make the most of its petroleum assets.

In fact, this "assumption" was a debatable one. In February 1922, Secretary Fall met with a gentleman named Arthur Ambrose, a government geologist who had examined the ground at Teapot Dome (so named for the rock formation that dominates it, which vaguely resembles the profile of a teapot). To Fall's disappointment, Ambrose had found no evidence that the area's reserves were at risk of drainage. A blow to Fall's plan, the secretary resolved to keep the information to himself and focus on the other findings that Ambrose brought him: specifically, the fact that Teapot Dome and the neighboring Salt Creek oil reserves, which were already controlled by the Department of the Interior, were together worth nearly half a billion dollars.

———————★———————

"THE NEWLY CREATED U.S. VETERANS' BUREAU WAS MAKING A KILLING AT THE TAXPAYERS' EXPENSE. ACCORDING TO ONE ESTIMATE, THE VETERANS' BUREAU SCAMS COST TAXPAYERS IN THE AREA OF $200 MILLION AT THE TIME."

———————★———————

The following April, Secretaries Fall and Denby gave their signatures to a contract assigning Sinclair's Mammoth Oil Company (newly created by the oil giant specifically for Teapot Dome) the rights to drill petroleum at the Wyoming site for twenty years. Later that same month, the Elk Hills reserve in California was leased to Edward Doheny, the so-called "Rockefeller of the West"—a longtime friend of Fall's, president of the Pan American Oil Company, and one of the richest oil barons in the world.

Even before the signing of the Elk Hills contract, Teapot Dome's lease to Mammoth Oil caused a stir in Washington. On April 15, the Senate passed a resolution demanding more information from the administration about a transaction that had been announced as a fait accompli and that seemed, without any deliberation or proper bidding, to place a vast portion of state-owned resources in Wyoming at the disposal of a wealthy developer unshackled by obligations to the public trust. As Wisconsin Senator Robert La Follette fumed, "Who were the real organizers of the Mammoth Oil Company who were to be favored by the government with a special privilege in the value beyond the dreams of Croesus?" An investigation was soon under way.

Forced by the Senate to produce all the paperwork on the leases, Secretary Fall issued a detailed, illustrated report that made much of the dubious "drainage" issue and that often descended into a verbose quagmire of geological terminology. It is entirely possible that it was intended to buy time or convince the investigators to desist. At any rate, the president passed it along with his own signature, staking his reputation on the report's veracity and legality.

What Harding didn't know was that the most scandalous facts regarding Teapot Dome and Elk Hills would never be found in either Fall's report or any of the other reams of paperwork handed over to the Senate. Simply put, they were this: The previous year Doheny had offered Fall $100,000, ostensibly as a loan, to cover the cost of buying an extensive ranch in New Mexico. Then, in May 1922, Fall received $233,000 in interest-paying Liberty Bonds from none other than Harry Sinclair, who wished to buy an interest in the very same ranch. Together these payments amounted to around $3.5 million (in today's dollars).

"AN HONEST, ABLE, AND HARDWORKING MAN"

As he had planned to do since accepting the post, Albert Fall resigned from the Harding Cabinet in March 1923 to pursue private matters. Ironically, the president's statement regarding the event praised Fall for having served at great financial loss to himself.

By that time the Harding Administration was up to its eyeballs in corruption. In addition to Fall's shenanigans, which had yet to be discovered, the newly created U.S. Veterans' Bureau was making a killing at the taxpayers' expense. Charles Forbes, an army colonel and friend of Harding's since the two first met in 1915, had been appointed to direct the bureau no doubt because of his upstanding reputation. In fact, once in charge, he and his general counsel, Charles Cramer, began accepting bids for new hospital sites, buying them at radically inflated prices, and pocketing the overpayment themselves. They also had a side business selling surplus government medical equipment. Warned by friends of the activity, President Harding was witnessed confronting Forbes and calling him a "double-crossing bastard." The colonel eventually served two years in prison, by which time Cramer had committed suicide. According to one estimate, the Veterans' Bureau scams cost taxpayers in the area of $200 million at the time.

Then there was Jess Smith, the longtime friend and housemate of Attorney General Daugherty, who became the go-to man for bootleggers interested in purchasing immunity from prosecution. Smith also dispensed permits for the withdrawal of government-bonded liquor for up to $20,000 a pop, and was involved on at least one occasion in the illegal transfer of a foreign firm to a U.S.-based one, making a profit for the fix of nearly a quarter of a million dollars. Smith, sensing imminent exposure, committed suicide in Daugherty's apartment on May 30, 1923.

DEMOCRATIC SENATOR THOMAS WALSH, SHOWN HERE CIRCA 1928,
BECAME THE HERO OF TEAPOT DOME FOR RELENTLESSLY PURSUING THE FACTS.
AN ESTEEMED CONSTITUTIONAL LAWYER, HE HAD A REPUTATION FOR RIGID MORALITY,
SUPPORTED PROHIBITION, AND DETESTED UNSCRUPULOUS BEHAVIOR IN PUBLIC OFFICIALS.

———★———

Such goings-on plagued the president, whose habit of losing himself in poker and golf did little to rein things in. Naïve and insecure, Harding put a premium on loyalty only to gradually discover that the circle of people he had come to rely on in good times and bad were using him. It is uncertain how much he knew before his death in July 1923; the nation, however, had yet to discover how deeply the administration was immersed in corruption. "No one can hurt you now, Warren," said the Duchess to the corpse that lay in state at the White House. Thirty-five thousand mourners filed past the casket on August 8, the day of the service.

The following October, in Room 210 of the Senate Office Building, the formal inquiry into Teapot Dome, that Senator La Follette and his allies had pushed for eighteen months earlier, finally got under way. Their choice, of all the men on the Senate Committee on Public Lands and Surveys who were responsible for the investigation, to spearhead the inquiry was an unusual one. Thomas J. Walsh, senator from Wisconsin since 1913, was a Democrat who had backed virtually all of Woodrow Wilson's provocative agendas. But he was also a Westerner who shared many of Fall's opinions on public land. Indeed, he was a friend of Edward Doheny's who had also advocated the transfer of domestic oil reserves to private exploitation, having once been dismissed by conservationists as "an unscrupulous spoilsman and enemy" of U.S. public parks.

But if all this made Walsh an unlikely candidate to take on the Teapot Dome affair, other qualities made him a natural. To begin with, he was an old foe of Fall's with whom he had locked horns over Wilson's Versailles Treaty during long and often acrimonious debates. Moreover, Walsh had a reputation for rigid morality. He was stern, terse, intense, an esteemed constitutional lawyer who supported Prohibition and detested unscrupulous behavior in public officials. As one of Fall's own subordinates would later note, Walsh was "an honest, able, and hardworking man."

He needed to be. With few leads and a wagonload of documents to wrestle with, Walsh was heading into an investigation that virtually no one believed would go anywhere. Rumors, however, abounded of malfeasance in the old Department of the Interior. What's more, it was no secret that Fall's spread at Three Rivers Ranch, New Mexico, had undergone considerable renovations and development, a curious fact given the former secretary's alleged financial difficulties upon retiring from public office.

Fall was the first to testify. The Republican-dominated committee refused to subpoena Fall outright, offering him the opportunity to appear without compulsion. Curiously, the committee also decided to forego the ritual of swearing him in.

For two days the soft-spoken, businesslike Walsh sparred with Fall, who dominated events like a monarch whose appearance was a magnanimous, albeit irritating, gesture on his subjects' behalf. Fall was at the time offering unofficial counsel on Mexican and other affairs to President Calvin Coolidge, the former vice president who had assumed the presidency upon Harding's demise. He clearly felt a palpable impatience with the proceedings, and often responded to Walsh's inquiries with condescension. Nevertheless, his testimony was solid and convincing, clearly setting forth as it did the assertion that leasing the fields had been good business as well as good for national security; after all, it readily made hundreds of thousands of barrels of oil available to the Navy. Why had there not been any bids? Because he could get a better deal without them, Fall insisted. Why all the secrecy? "National security" came the reply, invoking the sanctity of the Navy's need for silence on matters of such import. After all, the deal had opened up a new source of fuel for the growing Pacific Fleet stationed at Pearl Harbor, whose new storage installations were part of the contract Fall had signed with Doheny.

———★———

FOR TWO DAYS THE SOFT-SPOKEN, BUSINESSLIKE WALSH SPARRED WITH FALL, WHO DOMINATED EVENTS LIKE A MONARCH WHOSE APPEARANCE WAS A MAGNANIMOUS, ALBEIT IRRITATING, GESTURE ON HIS SUBJECTS' BEHALF.

———★———

Over the ensuing days other witnesses appeared, including Navy Secretary Denby, Sinclair, and Doheny. But bereft of anything to hang a case on and faced with open cynicism from Republican committee members looking to avert a party scandal, Walsh floundered. The hearings commenced a monthlong recess on October 30, and the press, interpreting the affair as a Democratic gambit to slander the GOP, predicted an anticlimactic denouement. As events would ultimately prove, they—and everyone else—were sorely mistaken.

FALL GUY

When the hearings resumed in December, Walsh could rely on a new set of witnesses. Mostly from New Mexico, they offered a new perspective on Albert Fall. Chief among them was a *Denver Post* investigative reporter named D. F. Stackelback who had tracked down evidence that Fall had rather suddenly come into money the previous year, including records of paid overdue taxes. Though he never testified, Stackelback volunteered the fruits of his labor to the Senate committee, setting Walsh on a course that ultimately took him to his quarry.

A picture began to emerge from the New Mexico witnesses that didn't add up. On the one hand, Fall was a respected, almost legendary figure of the West who had brought himself up from nothing to become a national figure. On the other, he was a man whose

OIL BARON HARRY FORD SINCLAIR (1876–1956, RIGHT) STANDS WITH FORMER
SECRETARY OF THE INTERIOR ALBERT BACON FALL (1861–1944), CIRCA 1924.
A VETERAN OF THE SPANISH-AMERICAN WAR AND A FAMOUS ATTORNEY WHOSE CLIENTS
INCLUDED THE ACCUSED KILLER OF PAT GARRETT, FALL BECAME THE FIRST FORMER CABINET
OFFICER IN U.S. HISTORY TO DO TIME FOR MISCONDUCT IN OFFICE.
HULTON ARCHIVE/GETTY IMAGES

———★———

sudden turn of fortune came about under mysterious circumstances. Even the die-hard Republicans on the committee stopped nodding off during testimony, and the papers began treating the Teapot Dome hearings as something more than a back page dead end. But the questions remained: Where had the money come from? And was it tied to the oil leases?

Walsh, through sheer doggedness, stirred things up. Nevertheless, he was working on circumstantial evidence in a case involving a powerful public figure. Though impressive enough, how far could this really go?

Fall made the next move, and it was a fateful one. Feeling the heat (apparently he had drastically underestimated Walsh), the former secretary of the interior decided to take matters into his own hands. Making his way east by train, he succumbed to sickness, probably exacerbated by nerves, eventually settling in Washington's Wardman Park Hotel shortly before Christmas 1923 to be near the hearings. There, visited around the clock by advisors, friends, and fellow Republicans eager to stanch the Teapot Dome wound, he gave in to pressure to head off Walsh before the tenacious Wisconsin senator had the GOP over a barrel. If the money had come from someone other than the benefactors of the oil leases, urged his colleagues, why won't Fall simply divulge the name of the benefactor who had allowed him to buy Three Rivers and turn it around?

In the final days of 1923, Albert Fall dictated a letter to the Senate Committee on Public Lands and Surveys that the money required to buy his New Mexico ranch—some $100,000, worth just over a million dollars today—came not from Sinclair or Doheny but from longtime friend and newspaper owner Edward McLean. McLean soon confirmed the testimony himself from his home in Palm Beach, Florida. Fall, a veteran poker player, had made his bluff. Would Walsh call him on it?

Yes, he would. Walsh had long since exhibited an uncanny willingness to wade into the hardest challenges of a case that would otherwise have assuredly gone away. Truly he had the scent of his prey, and something about the notion that Ned (Edward) McLean had lent so large a sum to his friend smelled fishy. For one thing, McLean, though a successful publisher, was unlikely to have so much cash on hand; in fact, rumor had it that he had been in dire financial straits himself.

Fall, considering the matter closed, accepted an invitation to join McLean in Florida for a bit of much needed R and R. As far as the New Mexican was concerned, he had dodged a bullet. Much of the nation concurred. Newspapers began bemoaning the hearings' fruitlessness, at taxpayers' expense no less. Fall had been the victim of partisan brinkmanship.

Walsh went after McLean nonetheless, insisting in the first week of January 1924 that the newspaperman appear in person before the committee in Washington. At this point Walsh looked like an obsessive who'd gone off the rails, making it easier for McLean to say no on account of illness. Walsh insisted, eventually agreeing with the committee's insistence to go to McLean and get his testimony in Florida.

While Fall and his wife hid in another part of the Palm Beach hotel under assumed names, McLean testified to Walsh. To the senator's astonishment, a somewhat nervous McLean—with very little provocation on Walsh's part—denied having lent his friend the money, reversing his previous statement to the committee. Walsh was stunned.

Albert Fall was ruined.

STRIKING THE MOTHER LODE

On the afternoon of January 24, 1924, Room 210 of the Senate Office Building was packed. Even the halls outside burst with people trying to hear or see the drama that was unfolding inside the chamber. Most of the Senate had joined the throng of reporters and curious spectators, their business for the day having taken a backseat to what had developed into the trial of the century.

The man everyone was there to see was Edward Doheny, who had come to testify before the committee to help shed light on recent spectacular events that had gripped Washington and much of the country.

Since returning from Palm Beach with McLean's electrifying testimony, Walsh had found himself leading an entirely new investigation. McLean's words, read before the committee, exposed Albert Fall as a liar and stunned the nation. Things began moving quickly. On January 21, Archie Roosevelt, a son of Theodore Roosevelt and a war hero, took the stand. A former employee of Harry Sinclair, the 29-year-old Roosevelt had recently tendered his resignation after discovering that his boss was acting, to say the least, suspiciously. Indeed, Sinclair had asked Roosevelt to buy him a ticket on a steamship bound for Europe with the stipulation that it be reserved under an alias. Roosevelt was followed by G. D. Wahlberg, Sinclair's private secretary, who claimed that he, too, had quit in light of evidence that Sinclair was acting like a fugitive. Sinclair insisted, for instance, that all his papers and financial documents be removed from his office pronto before departing for his transatlantic trip.

In Walsh's mind, all of this pointed to one scenario: Harry Sinclair had bribed Fall for the oil leases. And what of Fall? The former secretary had absconded to New Orleans to regroup and plan a counterattack with friends and advisors. He was a broken man. Once the hale and hearty personification of Western ruggedness, a man who used to brag about gunfights in his youth, he now quavered on the brink of a nervous collapse, frail and sickly. In Palm Beach Edward McLean's wife, Evalyn, had been struck by the transformation: "For the first time in my life, I saw a man crumble right before my eyes."

In Washington, the committee arranged a twenty-four-hour watch on Fall in New Orleans to ensure that he didn't leave the country. He was also called to make another appearance, and this time he didn't have a choice: A subpoena was issued. For his part, the embattled New Mexican attempted a bit of damage control by asking Doheny to come clean before the committee about the loan he had made to buy the ranch back in 1921. With luck, they would be able to make it look like a transaction between old friends with no ties to the oil fields. In any event, Fall was running out of options.

Now surrounded by a crowd of captive onlookers (Senator La Follette sat right behind him like a vulture eyeing its meal), Doheny confronted Walsh and the other committee members with a prepared statement. "I wish to inform the committee," went part of the speech, "that on the 30th of November, 1921, I loaned Albert B. Fall $100,000 upon his promissory note to enable him to purchase a ranch in New Mexico." When asked by Walsh in the cross-examination that followed how the loan was made, Doheny responded, "In cash." How was it transported? "In a satchel," came the reply. Was this not an extraordinary way of transmitting money? Doheny's response to this was that the sum, though large by the standards of most, was "a mere bagatelle" to him, like $25 or $50 to most men.

———★———

TEAPOT DOME SERVED AS THE GOLD STANDARD OF POLITICAL CORRUPTION UNTIL WATERGATE SURPASSED IT IN THE 1970S.

———★———

In the end the oil baron came off like a folksy millionaire with nothing to hide or, for that matter, no reason to hide in the first place. The loan was an affair between two old friends, and nothing more. If it put him in favor with the secretary when the issue of the leases came up, so be it, but that was not his intention.

Few of those in the murmuring crowd in the Senate Office Building believed him. Walsh, who had been working under the hypothesis that Fall had received a bribe from Sinclair, now realized that the secretary had likely taken money from *two* sources. It was a bombshell.

SILENT CAL

Senator Walsh was no longer the most important person in Washington who believed the oil leases were a scandal. In fact, virtually no one in the capital—Democrat or Republican— believed that Albert Fall was clear of wrongdoing. And few of them had as much to lose from that revelation as President Calvin Coolidge.

A laconic New Englander whose gift for concision earned him the sobriquet "Silent Cal," Coolidge was a devotee of the "less is more" school of government. For weeks the new president had been pressed by colleagues and reporters alike about Teapot Dome, only to receive such famously curt replies as, "There is no action that could be taken by the President relative to it." But after Doheny's testimony, the president could no longer afford *not* to do something. After all, he had inherited the presidency from the man whose incompetence had allowed the Teapot Dome scandal, and many others, to fester. He had been the vice president, for goodness sake, leading many to wonder just how much he knew about this den of thieves and their cons. He was the face of the GOP, whose fortunes had definitely suffered of late. And by seizing the initiative from Walsh, a Democrat, he could be seen as having taken control of a national tragedy in a nonpartisan quest for the truth.

It was with these calculations in mind that, immediately following the Doheny testimony, President Coolidge appointed a pair of federal prosecutors to pursue the matter in a court of law. By the time a weakened, tottering Fall had answered his subpoena and appeared again before the committee, he was able to plead Fifth Amendment rights to silence on the perfectly legal grounds that, as of the president's announcement of official judicial proceedings, he did not wish to incriminate himself before appearing in court.

On the committee's advice, Navy Secretary Denby was fired. This was the first time that Coolidge, who had made it a point of maintaining Harding's Cabinet, was compelled to fire a Cabinet officer. Attorney General Daugherty, who had gotten the ball rolling in 1920 by helping to entwine the Harding Administration in oil and in whom the nation at large had lost all trust, was also forced to resign.

Walsh's hard work had paid off—sort of. In the ensuing trials, Fall was convicted of taking bribes while in office. He served nine months of a one-year sentence, but never paid his $100,000 fine. As for Doheny and Sinclair, they both escaped convictions for bribing an official. Only Doheny did time, serving a brief sentence for jury tampering. Congress simply abrogated the oil contracts.

All of which served to advance the president's agenda. No party in power is ever likely to survive a corruption scandal like Teapot Dome. Yet Calvin Coolidge quietly ensured that all parties involved were prosecuted, cleaning up—or at least appearing to clean up—the mess that his late boss had bequeathed to him. The result was that the Republicans never suffered the sort of punishment in the polls their Democratic opponents assumed they would. Despite this, Teapot Dome served as the gold standard of political corruption until Watergate surpassed it in the 1970s.

———★———

CHAPTER 5

John F. Kennedy and Vote-Buying in West Virginia:

"I WON'T PAY FOR A LANDSLIDE"

———★———

During a visit to Boston in 1966, Senator Hubert Humphrey of Minnesota paid a call on Cardinal Richard Cushing, archbishop of Boston and an intimate friend of the Kennedy family. The 71-year-old cardinal met the senator at the door. In his memoirs, Humphrey would recall Cushing's appearance: "tall, already gaunt from illness and heavy-featured in his old age, but bantering in a cheerful mood."

Cushing led his visitor to the library where very quickly the conversation turned to politics, in particular the 1960 campaign when John F. Kennedy defeated Humphrey in the Democratic primaries. Since the late president's assassination three years before, there had been a blizzard of books written by JFK's friends and advisors, and Cardinal Cushing had read them all. "I keep reading these books by the young men around Jack Kennedy and how they claim credit for electing him," the cardinal told Humphrey. "I'll tell you who elected Jack Kennedy. It was his father, Joe, and me, *right here in this room*."

As Humphrey sat "in stunned silence," the cardinal went on. "I believe you should know that the decisions on West Virginia were made here, in this library. Joe Kennedy and I sat and discussed the strategy of that campaign in this room. We decided which of the Protestant ministers would receive a contribution to their church." In the history of the United States no Catholic had ever been elected to the presidency.

When the last Catholic nominee, Alfred E. Smith, ran for president in 1928, he was vilified in Protestant pulpits and Protestant newspapers and magazines as the advance guard of a Catholic conspiracy to take over the United States and install the pope in the White House. Kennedy rarely experienced such blatant animosity, but anti-Catholic sentiments still simmered beneath the surface in America in 1960, and in West Virginia, where Catholics were a tiny minority, the Kennedy campaign feared he would suffer a severe defeat. On the other hand, if he won the primary in such a heavily Protestant state, the victory would send a message to other parts of the country that a Catholic was electable.

In an effort to reduce the chances of anti-Catholic or anti-Kennedy sermons being preached in West Virginia's Protestant churches, the candidate's father and Cardinal Cushing decided to make financial contributions, which would come from the campaign's war chest, directly to Protestant ministers, particularly pastors of small black congregations who tended to be more favorable to the Kennedy candidacy. Joe Kennedy and Cardinal Cushing worked up a list of names and dollar amounts: some pastors got $100, others received $200, and still others $500.

Humphrey recalled that Cushing concluded his stunning revelation "with a whimsical, if not beatific smile, asking rhetorically, 'What better way is there to spend campaign money than to help a preacher and his flock? It's good for the Lord. It's good for the church. It's good for the preacher, and it's good for the candidate.'"

A FATHER'S PLAN

For all his adult life Joseph Patrick Kennedy had laid the groundwork so his eldest son, Joseph, Jr., could become the first Catholic to be elected president of the United States. It was an ambitious dream for a man whose father had been a Boston saloonkeeper and ward boss, and whose grandparents had arrived in the United States as penniless refugees fleeing from Ireland's potato famine. But from childhood Joe Kennedy had a motto: "If you can't be captain, don't play."

Joseph Kennedy was born in Boston in 1888. By that time many Irish families had escaped the slums and joined the United States' comfortable middle class. Irish-Americans dominated the Catholic Church in the United States and in the cities they dominated the Democratic Party. Nonetheless, the fine, old families of Boston—the Cabots, the Lodges— still looked down on the Irish as rowdy Papist thugs. In politics the Boston Brahmins may have had a point: Joe Kennedy remembered one Election Day during his childhood when his father was serving as election commissioner. Two cronies, both Irish, came by to report proudly, "Pat, we voted 128 times today!"

As a teenager and young man, Joseph Kennedy asked himself two questions—how could he make money and how could he make connections? He came to the conclusion that the answer was to learn to be as much at ease among Protestant Yankees as among his fellow Irish-Catholics. Although most of the children in his neighborhood went to parochial school, Joe Kennedy went to Boston Latin School. When the young men of the parish enrolled at Boston College or Holy Cross, Joe Kennedy was admitted to Harvard. As an Irish-Catholic he was barred from all of the socially prominent undergraduate clubs at Harvard, yet by the time he graduated in 1912 Joe Kennedy managed to ingratiate himself with members of the Protestant upper crust.

He came out of Harvard eager to make a name for himself. As he told a reporter, "I want to be a millionaire by the age of 35." Of course, he would need a wife, and he courted Irish-Catholic Boston's most admired debutante—Rose Fitzgerald, the polished, accomplished, convent-educated daughter of Boston's popular mayor, John "Honey Fitz" Fitzgerald.

Joe Kennedy did become a millionaire, thanks to his work in banking, in Hollywood, and on Wall Street. He and Rose had nine children who would become a political dynasty. But the golden boy of the Kennedy clan was the eldest son, Joseph Jr. He was handsome, athletic, daring, a born leader, and his father intended to see him become president of the United States. That dream ended during World War II. In August 1944, Joe Jr. took off for a bombing mission over Nazi Germany. His aircraft, loaded with explosives, accidentally exploded in midair. Joe Jr.'s body was never recovered; he was 29 years old.

Joseph Sr. shifted his hopes to his next eldest son, John. Like his elder brother, Jack was good-looking, athletic, charismatic, but physically he was frail, underweight, and often sick with a host of ailments and chronic conditions. Because he was often confined

IN 1960, AS JFK'S CAMPAIGN FOR THE DEMOCRATIC NOMINATION GAINED MOMENTUM, CARTOONIST
BILL MAUDLIN DREW AN ATTIC PACKED WITH OUTDATED OBJECTS—A BUTTER CHURN, A VICTROLA,
AND A SAMPLER THAT READS, "A CATHOLIC CAN'T WIN." MANY FEARED JFK'S CATHOLICISM WOULD
PREVENT HIM FROM OBTAINING THE NATION'S HIGHEST OFFICE.

LIBRARY OF CONGRESS

———★———

to his bed, Jack was more bookish than his big brother Joe. In spite of his physical shortcomings he was a combative boy who, as his mother once said, "could fight like fury when he had to."

Jack Kennedy may have been his father's second choice but he was not second best. A year before Joe's death, Jack's PT boat had been rammed and sunk in the Pacific by a Japanese destroyer. Kennedy saved the life of a badly injured crewman, and worked tirelessly to find food, water, and eventually rescue for his men. At age 26 he came out of the war a hero decorated with the Navy and Marine Corps Medal.

After the war Joseph Kennedy got his son into politics quickly. He was elected to the House of Representatives in 1946 and in 1952 defeated the Boston blue blood, Henry Cabot Lodge Jr. in a race for the Senate.

In 1953 the wedding of John F. Kennedy and Jacqueline Bouvier was the social event of the year. In 1956, while convalescing from back surgery, Kennedy wrote *Profiles in Courage*, a book that won him the Pulitzer Prize. (There are persistent rumors that the work was coauthored, perhaps even ghostwritten, by Kennedy's friend, advisor, and speechwriter Ted Sorensen.)

On January 2, 1960, John Kennedy stood amid the marble columns of the grand Senate Caucus Room, before a packed house of 300 cheering supporters, and announced his candidacy for the office of president of the United States.

ALL THE MARBLES

John Kennedy had been running for president since 1956 when his political allies, urged on by Kennedy's father, tried to convince the Democrats' nominee, Adlai Stevenson, to put JFK on the ticket as vice president. Even if Stevenson lost the election (and he did), Kennedy would become a nationally recognized political figure, which would make his bid for the presidency in 1960 easier.

It was Sargent Shriver, Kennedy's brother-in-law, who put the question to Stevenson. The candidate hedged. In spite of a recent Gallup Poll that found that three out of four respondents said they would have no trouble voting for a Catholic candidate for the presidency, Stevenson feared that a Catholic running mate would prove to be a disadvantage. And one poll was not about to change his mind. Rather than respond with a simple "yes" or "no," Stevenson threw the nomination for vice president to the convention delegates. They chose Senator Estes Kefauver of Tennessee, but that did not mean that John F. Kennedy became the wallflower of the convention. He narrated the film shown at the beginning of the convention and delivered the main speech nominating Stevenson for president. He got attention. He garnered press coverage. And seen from the perspective of 1960, by not being Stevenson's running mate he did not have to address awkward questions about why he and Stevenson had failed to win over voters in 1956. Shortly after the 1956 election, JFK told David Powers, one of his aides, "If I work hard for four years I can pick up all the marbles."

And he did work hard. After the 1956 election Kennedy's staff put out the word that he was available for speaking engagements. He addressed college graduating classes, ecumenical groups, and political and fraternal organizations. Between January 1958 and May 1958, he delivered ninety-six speeches across the country, from Eugene, Oregon, to Casper, Wyoming, to Morgantown, West Virginia. Kennedy also made himself available to journalists, who more often than not wrote in praise of the young senator from Massachusetts. *Newsweek* described him as "candid, informal, and disarmingly relaxed." A profile in the *New York Times Magazine* said, "Jack Kennedy is a singularly gifted young man in looks, bearing, intelligence, and personality. There is about him a subtle blending of deference and self-confidence, of engaging shyness and mature forthrightness."

But not everyone was charmed by Kennedy. In a 1958 television interview, Eleanor Roosevelt declared that among the current crop of Democratic hopefuls for the White House, only Senator Hubert Humphrey had "the spark of greatness." Then Mrs. Roosevelt stated that Joseph Kennedy was spending "oodles of money all over the country" to advance JFK's presidential candidacy and "probably has paid representatives in every state by now." Kennedy denied the allegations, but such an accusation coming from a Democrat as revered and respected as Eleanor Roosevelt stung. Worse, it might put his nomination in jeopardy.

DEPLOYING THE FAMILY

In 1960 the leaders of the Democratic Party picked their nominee for president. They were not obligated to nominate the candidate who had won the greatest number of primaries. Nonetheless, a good showing in the primaries did carry weight, and Kennedy intended to win the majority of primaries to prove that he was the most viable choice.

Primary season began in New Hampshire on March 8, 1960. The Kennedys sent Rose across the border where she displayed the political skills she had learned as a child from her father. JFK swept the state, taking 85 percent of the vote. Wisconsin was next, and here Humphrey had the advantage. He was well-known, popular, viewed as such a staunch friend and ally of Wisconsin that he was often referred to as the state's third senator. To counteract Humphrey's lead, JFK's campaign deployed virtually the entire family. Rose and Jackie Kennedy hosted countless teas and receptions where their combination of warmth and elegance charmed women voters. When Bobby Kennedy learned that pro-Kennedy Democrats in Wisconsin were throwing house parties to gather support for JFK, he demanded that each of his three sisters attend nine such parties a day. Kennedy won Wisconsin, taking 56 percent of the vote to Humphrey's 43 percent.

ARCHBISHOP OF BOSTON, CARDINAL RICHARD J. CUSHING, SHOWN HERE IN 1961 WITH JFK, WAS
DETERMINED TO SEE KENNEDY BECOME THE FIRST CATHOLIC PRESIDENT OF THE UNITED STATES. IN THE
WEEKS LEADING UP TO THE WEST VIRGINIA PRIMARY, CUSHING AND JOSEPH KENNEDY SR. SENT GIFTS
OF CASH TO PROTESTANT CLERGY IN WEST VIRGINIA. THE CARDINAL AND THE CANDIDATE'S FATHER
BELIEVED THAT IF THE PASTORS ACCEPTED THE MONEY, THEY WOULD NOT DISCOURAGE THEIR
CONGREGATIONS FROM VOTING FOR JFK.

ASSOCIATED PRESS

———— ★ ————

IN A 1931 PHOTOGRAPH JOSEPH KENNEDY SR. STANDS BETWEEN HIS TWO ELDEST SONS: JOSEPH JR.,
LEFT, AND JOHN, RIGHT. KENNEDY HAD PLANNED TO MAKE JOSEPH THE FIRST CATHOLIC PRESIDENT.
AFTER JOSEPH WAS KILLED IN ACTION DURING WORLD WAR II, HE SHIFTED HIS HOPES TO JFK.

JOHN F. KENNEDY LIBRARY

————— ★ —————

Kennedy went on to win Illinois, Massachusetts, Pennsylvania, Indiana, and Nebraska. During this period Humphrey took only a single primary—in the District of Columbia.

In spite of these victories, JFK could not get over Wisconsin. Yes, he had won, but he had not enjoyed the stunning victory he expected, a win so decisive that Humphrey would withdraw from the race. For that reason the Kennedy team identified West Virginia as the place where they would crush Hubert Humphrey.

CAMPAIGNING IN WEST VIRGINIA

The Kennedy advance team arrived in West Virginia confident of another victory. A poll taken before Christmas 1959 found that 70 percent of likely Democratic voters favored Kennedy. But then the advance team discovered that no one had told the voters that John Kennedy was Catholic. And in West Virginia, 95 percent of the population was Protestant.

In a less-than-subtle effort to distinguish their candidate from Kennedy, Humphrey's staff wrote a campaign song set to the tune of the traditional gospel hymn, "Give Me that Old-Time Religion." They played it endlessly across West Virginia.

And there were examples of anti-Catholic hostility. Anonymous individuals or organizations printed flyers and left them in mailboxes and on front doorsteps in the night. The pamphlets warned of what would happen if a Catholic moved into the White House: Catholics would arm themselves with guns stored inside their churches. Then they would unleash a bloody war against American Protestants, led by the Knights of Columbus and directed by the pope himself.

Religion, however, was not the only issue. West Virginia had the highest unemployment rate in the nation, and Humphrey had a reputation as a champion of the common man, a senator who worked hard to support labor unions and create jobs. Kennedy had no reputation as a hard-fighting liberal.

And the Kennedy campaign faced another serious challenge: West Virginia's Senator Robert Byrd opposed JFK—he wanted to see Lyndon B. Johnson of Texas win the Democratic Party's nomination. The combination of anti-Catholicism, high unemployment, and the active opposition of some leading Democratic politicians in the state seemed enough to sink the Kennedy campaign.

To counteract the Humphrey offensive and anti-Catholic hysteria, the Kennedys brought in Franklin D. Roosevelt Jr., son of the late president who was still beloved in West Virginia for his New Deal initiatives to end the Great Depression. During his standard stump speech Roosevelt usually raised his hand and showed two fingers pressed tightly together. Then he'd assure the crowd, "My daddy and Jack Kennedy's daddy were just like that." It was a bald-faced lie. FDR loathed Joseph Kennedy who, at the outset of World War II, had declared that the Nazi war machine could not be beaten and called upon the Allies to find a way to appease Hitler.

Meanwhile, Jack Kennedy addressed the religion issue directly when he reminded audiences of his war service and that of his brother Joe. "Nobody asked me if I was Catholic when I joined the United States Navy," he said. "Nobody asked my brother if he was Catholic or Protestant before he climbed into an American bomber to fly his last mission."

The Kennedy campaign produced a documentary about Jack that was shown on statewide television. It featured clips of PT boats, of Jack receiving the Pulitzer Prize, of Jack reading to his two-year-old daughter Caroline. The journalist and historian Theodore H. White wrote, "Over and over again there was the handsome, open-faced candidate on the TV screen, showing himself, proving that a Catholic wears no horns."

But the Kennedy campaign staff believed these strategies were not enough.

A billboard appeared in West Virginia that showed ballots cast for Humphrey falling into a garbage can, while ballots cast for Kennedy drifted down upon the White House. In New York state was a coterie of influential Democrats who wanted to see Adlai Stevenson appointed secretary of state in the next Democratic Cabinet. Kennedy staffers traveled to New York and told the Stevenson people bluntly that if they did not stop supporting Humphrey, Jack Kennedy would not appoint Stevenson his secretary of state.

During their junket the Kennedy people also met with well-to-do New York Democrats who were contributing to Humphrey's campaign. After that meeting, Humphrey saw contributions from his New York friends dry up. One donor, named Bill Benton, explained to Humphrey that the JFK staffers had assured him that if he continued to support the senator from Minnesota, JFK would never forgive him. And if Kennedy won the election, the White House and access to all high levels of the federal government would be closed to him permanently.

Hardball tactics came into play in West Virginia, too. Urged on by Bobby Kennedy, Franklin D. Roosevelt Jr. issued a press release in which he accused Humphrey of dodging the draft during World War II. In fact, a physical disability disqualified Humphrey for military service, and JFK publicly repudiated the accusation. Not that JFK's repudiation mattered—the charge was already circulating among voters.

TEN DOLLARS PER VOTE

Kennedy's staff was not leaving anything to chance. In addition to the gifts Joseph Kennedy and Cardinal Cushing had sent to Protestant pastors in West Virginia, Larry O'Brien, director of the campaign, presented West Virginia politicians with gifts of cash—reimbursements, it was said, for the expenses they incurred assisting the Kennedy campaign.

Most of the money came from the Kennedy family, but according to Seymour Hersh there was also an infusion of cash from the Mafia. In February 1960, while JFK was in Las Vegas, Frank Sinatra had introduced him to an actress named Judith Campbell; within a few weeks

A PROFILE OF JOHN F. KENNEDY PUBLISHED IN THE *NEW YORK TIMES MAGAZINE*
DESCRIBED HIM AS "A SINGULARLY GIFTED YOUNG MAN IN LOOKS, BEARING, INTELLIGENCE,
AND PERSONALITY." JFK USED THOSE QUALITIES WHENEVER HE INTRODUCED HIMSELF
TO VOTERS IN WEST VIRGINIA, AS IN THIS 1960 PHOTOGRAPH.
TIME & LIFE IMAGES / GETTY IMAGES

———— ★ ————

SAM GIANCANA, SHOWN HERE IN 1965 IN NEW YORK CITY, WAS ONE OF THE LEADING FIGURES IN THE
CHICAGO MAFIA AND IS BELIEVED TO HAVE DONATED HEAVILY TO KENNEDY'S CAMPAIGN IN WEST VIRGINIA.
IN RETURN, JFK'S FATHER, JOSEPH KENNEDY, PROMISED TO USE HIS INFLUENCE TO DERAIL ANY FUTURE
FEDERAL INVESTIGATION INTO GIANCANA'S ACTIVITIES.

GETTY IMAGES

———— ★ ————

Kennedy and Campbell were having an affair. Through Sinatra, Campbell had also met a man who called himself "Sam Flood." In fact, he was Chicago mob boss Sam Giancana. In April, with the West Virginia primary just a few weeks away, Kennedy asked Campbell to arrange for him to meet Sam. "I think I may need his help in the campaign," Kennedy told her.

In an interview Tina Sinatra gave to author Seymour Hersh, the singer's daughter recalled that Joseph Kennedy invited Frank Sinatra to Hyannis Port. During lunch the senior Kennedy said, "I think that you can help me in West Virginia and Illinois with our friends. You understand, Frank, I can't go. They're my friends, too, but I can't approach them. But you can." Not long after his visit to Hyannis Port Sinatra played a round of golf with Giancana. The golf course was one of the few places where the mobster was free from FBI surveillance, and Sinatra took the opportunity to raise the subject of John Kennedy's candidacy. "I believe in this man," Sinatra told Giancana. "I think he's going to make us a good president. With your help, I think we can work this out."

According to Kennedy biographer Thomas C. Reeves, "FBI wiretaps later revealed large Mafia donations to the Kennedy campaign in West Virginia that were apparently distributed by Frank Sinatra....Paul "Skinny" D'Amato, an Atlantic City casino owner and Giancana henchman, distributed more than $50,000 to local sheriffs to get out the vote—for Kennedy—by any means possible." Reeves goes on to say that an examination of FBI documents reveals that Joseph Kennedy promised Giancana that he would use his influence to derail any future federal investigations into the mobster's activities.

There was a tradition in West Virginia of political candidates paying the county bosses $2 or $3 for every vote they delivered. The bosses justified the payment as a fee for their time and also for their expenses, as many of their constituents in these districts had no cars and had to be picked up, driven to the polls, then taken home again.

The Humphrey campaign, which was woefully short of cash by the time it arrived in West Virginia, scraped together enough to "buy" one such county. Days before the election a Humphrey staffer received a call to meet a local representative of the Democratic Party in a public men's room. There the West Virginian handed over a bag of cash and told the staffer the deal with Humphrey was off. Kennedy's people were paying much more—as much as $10 per vote.

PAYING THE RIGHT PEOPLE

Humphrey's campaign spent no more than $30,000 in West Virginia. At one point his war chest was completely empty; in order make a television appearance he was obliged to write a personal check for $750 before the station manager would agree to let him go on the air.

Historian W. J. Rorabaugh estimates that Humphrey spent $2,000 on television appearances in West Virginia to the Kennedy campaign's $34,000. Cash was never a problem for Kennedy staffers. When asked how much he would need to buy votes for

Kennedy, Logan County political boss Raymond Chafin told a Kennedy staffer, "about thirty-five." He meant $3,500, but a courier brought him $35,000 in cash. When Chafin called James McCahey Jr., his contact at Kennedy's campaign headquarters, to report the error, McCahey told Chafin to keep the money and put it to good use. "I spent every dime of it," Chafin wrote in his memoirs. "And we won."

Another Logan County boss, Claude "Big Daddy" Ellis, received $50,000 from Kennedy's people. Ellis said Kennedy didn't "buy West Virginia, he just rented it for the day."

Jerry Bruno, one of Kennedy's advance men in West Virginia, recalled how the Kennedy campaign's reputation for paying top dollar made an impression, especially on county pols who had already been paid by Humphrey's advance men. "The Hubert people," Bruno said, "they'd take [Humphrey's] money and then come to see us."

———★———

ANOTHER LOGAN COUNTY BOSS, CLAUDE "BIG DADDY" ELLIS, RECEIVED $50,000 FROM KENNEDY'S PEOPLE. ELLIS SAID KENNEDY DIDN'T "BUY WEST VIRGINIA, HE JUST RENTED IT FOR THE DAY."

———★———

But the money had to go to the right people in the county. James McCahey recalled how Teddy Kennedy had gone to West Virginia in the fall of 1959 to lay the groundwork for his brother's primary campaign, but he made the mistake of handing out cash to the county committeemen. "It didn't work at all," McCahey told Seymour Hersh. "You don't go into a primary [in West Virginia] and spread money around to the committeemen. The local committeemen will take your money and do nothing. The sheriff is the important guy. You give it to the sheriff."

Victor Gabriel, a supervisor of the West Virginia Alcoholic Beverage Control Commission, was responsible for the Kennedy campaign in Harrison County. He told Bobby Kennedy he could deliver his county for JFK for only $5,000. Some of the Kennedy people scoffed, but Gabriel insisted he knew exactly who to pay and how much they would demand. On Election Day Harrison County went for JFK. Bonn Brown, the attorney for West Virginia Governor W.W. Barron, told Hersh that some sheriffs had demanded $50,000 from the Kennedys, which made Gabriel's accomplishment appear to be even more of a bargain.

FRANK SINATRA, SHOWN IN THIS UNDATED PHOTO, WAS A CLOSE FRIEND OF JFK.
IT IS BELIEVED THAT SINATRA SOLICITED MORE THAN $50,000 FROM HIS MAFIA CONNECTIONS,
WHICH HE HAD DISTRIBUTED AMONG LOCAL OFFICIALS IN WEST VIRGINIA
TO CONVINCE THEM TO GET THEIR CONSTITUENTS TO VOTE FOR KENNEDY.

AFP/GETTY IMAGES

———————★———————

Rorabaugh writes of Kennedy's people passing out $150,000 to politicians in Charleston County, $100,000 in Logan County, and $100,000 in Huntington County. "The campaign thus spent $350,000 for just three counties," Rorabaugh writes, "and the state had fifty-five counties."

No one knows how much the Kennedys spent in West Virginia—estimates run as high as $4 million or $5 million. Rorabaugh believes "a more realistic estimate" would be between $1.5 million and $2.5 million. There is a story that after his victory in West Virginia Kennedy told friends and staffers about a telegram he received from his father a day or two before the primary. It read, "Don't buy another vote. I won't pay for a landslide."

FIXING THE POLLS IN CHICAGO

The Kennedy campaign's voting interference wasn't limited to West Virginia. Mayor Richard Daley of Chicago had promised Joseph Kennedy he'd deliver his city for JFK. Because Chicago represented almost half the votes cast in Illinois, to win the city was pretty much a guarantee of winning the state.

Vote fraud was not new in Chicago. Historian W. J. Rorabaugh quoted one Chicago precinct captain as saying, "We don't know how many [votes] we got until we find out how many we need."

As Election Day 1960 approached, Daley gave each precinct captain and ward boss a number that represented how many votes he had to deliver for Kennedy. Any member of the city's Democratic machine who failed to produce could be assured of losing his job. With such motivation the precinct captains and ward bosses outdid themselves: An impressive 89.3 percent of registered voters turned out on Election Day.

Daley's operatives did everything in their power to elect John F. Kennedy. They removed the names of registered Republicans from the voter rolls; when these individuals appeared at their neighborhood polling place to cast their ballots, they were turned away. Long-dead Democrats voted for JFK. Vans full of Kennedy enthusiasts traveled from precinct to precinct, voting for Jack at each one.

One precinct captain cast his vote for Kennedy—twice. Then went outside where he passed out cash to persuade his constituents to vote for Kennedy, too.

Kennedy won Illinois by a margin of 8,858 votes. But he won Chicago's Cook County by 318,736 votes.

THE POWER OF THE PRESS

Back in West Virginia, it was difficult to keep quiet so much money passing through so many hands, so Joseph Kennedy's operatives put pressure on newspaper owners to pull any story about vote-buying. In some cases they were successful: A reporter for the *Baltimore Sun* who wrote an investigative piece on vote-buying during the primary found his story eviscerated and buried inside the paper.

The editors of *Life* magazine did not cave in to Kennedy pressure. Staff reporter Donald Wilson traveled to Logan County where he met an attorney named Dan Dahill who was extremely forthcoming on the topic of vote-buying on the county level. "With $5,000 you can elect a man to any office except sheriff in this county," Dahill said. "[Sheriff] costs $40,000. Why, heck, all you need is the right boys pulling the levers and you can't miss."

Alan L. Otten, the correspondent for the *Wall Street Journal* covering the primary in West Virginia, was stunned when Kennedy won. During the weeks he had spent traveling through the state, especially in coal country, his impression had been that Kennedy's Catholicism was a serious obstacle and Humphrey would be a shoo-in. Otten suspected that Kennedy's people had bought votes on a massive scale. Several other *Journal* reporters shared Otten's suspicion and worked together on an investigative piece, but the newspaper never published it. According to Robert D. Novak, a reporter for the *Journal* in 1960, the newspaper's management believed that an exposé of corruption in the West Virginia primary could influence which candidate the Democrats nominated at their national convention in Los Angles, and they did not want to bear responsibility for anything so momentous.

A SURE THING

On Election Day JFK left his brother Bobby in West Virginia to monitor the results while he returned home to Washington, D.C. (Jack and Jackie had purchased a three-story brick house in Georgetown.) After dinner Jack and several friends went to downtown Washington to see a pornographic movie. Ben Bradlee of *The Washington Post* was in the party. He recalled that every twenty minutes or so JFK went out to the lobby to call Bobby for the latest on the returns.

Kennedy won West Virginia, 219,246 votes to Humphrey's 141,941. Of West Virginia's fifty-five counties, Kennedy won forty-eight. That night Hubert Humphrey withdrew from the Democratic primary.

About midnight Humphrey received a call in his hotel room from Bobby Kennedy—he wanted to stop by for a moment. Upon entering the room Bobby went directly to Muriel Humphrey and kissed her on the cheek. Humphrey wrote in his memoirs, "Muriel stiffened, stared, and turned away in silent hostility, walking away from him, fighting back tears and angry words."

Back in Congress Humphrey explained his loss this way: "You can't beat a billion dollars." Then he made a bitter joke, "The way Jack Kennedy and his old man threw the money around, the people of West Virginia won't need any public relief for the next fifteen years."

It was money well spent. The Kennedy victory in overwhelmingly Protestant West Virginia struck many Democrats as a watershed moment. Perhaps the people of the United States were ready for a Catholic president. Both Lyndon Johnson and Adlai Stevenson were angling with party leaders to be nominated at the Democrats' national convention, but as Kennedy moved from victory to victory in state primaries, his nomination appeared more and more to be a sure thing.

PAYING THE PRICE

John F. Kennedy presented himself to the U.S. public and the world as a witty, thoughtful, idealistic young man. He was the handsome husband of a stunningly beautiful wife; the father of an enchanting little girl, and another baby was on the way. He belonged to a large, loving, devout Irish-Catholic family. He was a war hero. He was extremely wealthy, but he had dedicated his life to public service. All of that was JFK's public image, and his father had begun crafting it for him, and for every other member of the Kennedy clan, years earlier. Joseph Kennedy was a public relations genius who taught his sons and daughters how to do what he did: keep their private lives as secret as possible while presenting an attractive mask to the world.

The great masses of the voting public in West Virginia and elsewhere in the United States had no idea that Kennedy the idealist was buying votes in every county of West Virginia.

In the decades since Kennedy's assassination, revelations of his sordid private life, his links to organized crime, and his political hijinks have all been revealed. Some people, perhaps still influenced by the notion of the Kennedy years as a kind of American Camelot, tend to excuse JFK's peccadilloes, saying he was a complex man. Others consider him a brazen hypocrite.

However one sees JFK, the vote-buying and dirty tricks of the West Virginia primary were pure Kennedy: Joseph Kennedy had taught all nine of his children that winning was the most important thing, and when the prize was the White House, John F. Kennedy was prepared to pay a high price for victory.

————⋆————

CHAPTER 6

Richard Nixon:

"VESCO IS A CROOK"

————⋆————

23. Bribery, Fraud. Solicited and obtained for the reelection campaign of President Nixon, from Robert Vesco, on April 10, 1972, a contribution of $200,000, which was not reported to the General Accounting Office as required by law, in exchange for conferring upon Vesco governmental benefits, to wit, arranging a meeting between his attorney, Harry Sears, and federal law enforcement officials, to wit the Chairman of the Securities and Exchange Commission, and promises of other benefits, to wit, that John Mitchell and Maurice Stans would use their influence to prevent law enforcement action from being taken against Vesco; in violation of article II, section 4 of the Constitution and sections 201, 371, 872, 1503, and 1505 of the Criminal Code.

Beginning on July 24, 1974, and continuing for six days of nationally televised hearings, the U.S. House of Representatives Judiciary Committee debated the impeachment evidence against President Richard Nixon. In the end, the committee voted to charge Nixon with three articles of impeachment—obstruction of justice in the cover-up of the Watergate break-in, general abuse of presidential powers, and contempt of Congress for refusal to comply with subpoenas for evidence. The Bill of Particulars supporting all three impeachment charges included the above charge of bribery and fraud having to do with a certain briefcase filled with $200,000 in $100 bills. It was delivered by Robert Vesco's lawyer directly to Maurice Stans, who was the finance director of Nixon's Committee to Reelect the President, known by its notorious acronym CREEP.

However, by the time the committee's 528-page report was released on August 20, Richard Nixon had already resigned his office, becoming the first president of the United States to do so. The charge that Robert Vesco—the pencil-mustached, indelibly sleazy tycoon—had influenced a Security and Exchange Commission (SEC) investigation against him by contributing a sum worth about $1 million today to the President's reelection campaign was never proven. Nixon himself is heard saying on the White House audiotapes, which would be responsible for bringing about the downfall of his presidency, "Vesco is a crook. I never met the man."

But in fact the president had met Robert Vesco on at least two different occasions. Vesco was a friend of Nixon's brother Donald, and Nixon's nephew Donald Jr., or "Don-Don," who worked for Vesco as a personal aide. All of these interwoven connections led to what one writer has described as "an episode that, had even its bare outline become known at the time, might have been as great a scandal as Watergate itself."

THE QUAKER

Richard Nixon was born in 1913 in Yorba Linda, California, the second of five sons of Francis and Hannah Nixon. He grew up in a strict Quaker family where hardship was the order of the day—Francis Nixon ran a corner grocery store after failing as a lemon farmer—and where two of his admired brothers died young of disease. Although Nixon liked to place a certain popular magazine gloss on his childhood ("We were poor, but the glory of it was, we didn't know it"), he was an unpopular child and, as one biographer has written, "a collector of resentments," something he would remain all his life.

However, he was also one of the most dogged and persistent workers anyone who knew him had ever seen. After graduating from Whittier College in Whittier, California, as senior class president, and having excelled in debating and student politics, he went to Duke University on a full scholarship, earning the name "Iron Butt" for his marathon studying stints in the college library. During World War II, Nixon joined the Navy as a supply officer, eventually being stationed in the South Pacific. He did not see combat, but became renowned for his poker-playing ability, managing to amass about $10,000 in winnings before returning to the United States in 1945. He used the money to bankroll a career in politics, running for and winning a seat in Congress as a California Republican in 1946 and then leaping to a Senate seat in 1950.

In both instances, Nixon became known as a superb practitioner of the art of dirty politics, attacking his opponents as soft on Communism. His 1950 Senate race against Democratic Senator Helen Gahagan Douglas is still thought of as one of the dirtiest races ever run in California—Nixon accused her of being a Soviet sympathizer, a "Pink Lady," who was "pink right down to her underwear." After only two years as senator, Nixon was tagged by Dwight Eisenhower to become vice president and served in that office for Eisenhower's two terms. Ironically, when Nixon ran for president against his old friend and fellow freshman Congressman John F. Kennedy, he lost in a close race whose outcome was probably decided by dirty tricks the Democrats played against him in Chicago and Texas. After this, a supremely resentful Nixon told a press conference: "You won't have Nixon to kick around anymore because, gentlemen, this is my last press conference."

But Nixon couldn't stay away. After garnering the Republican nomination for president in 1968, he beat Hubert Humphrey in one of the most extraordinary comebacks in U.S. political history. By 1972, faced with an easy Democratic opponent in George McGovern, Nixon was ready to win by a landslide for what he hoped would be a historic second term in office.

But then his resentments got in the way.

THE CROOK

It's strange how Robert Vesco's life parallels that of the man with whom he would later be inextricably linked. Vesco was born on Detroit's near east side in 1935 to parents who were the children of immigrants. His father was a Chrysler assembly line worker and Vesco and his older sister were raised amid humble surroundings. Vesco dropped

ROBERT VESCO IS HUSTLED THROUGH THE CROWD BY PRIVATE SECURITY GUARDS AT AN EXTRADITION
HEARING IN THE BAHAMAS ON NOVEMBER 13, 1973. HE WAS NEVER RETURNED TO THE UNITED STATES
TO FACE CHARGES, DESPITE NUMEROUS ATTEMPTS BY THE DEPARTMENT OF JUSTICE TO BRING HIM BACK.

ASSOCIATED PRESS

———★———

out of high school at the age of seventeen to marry another teenager, Patricia, who had become pregnant with the first of what would be their five children (a sixth was to die shortly after birth).

While working at a body shop and moonlighting as a gypsy cabdriver, Vesco took correspondence courses to try to finish his high school degree—courses, according to Vesco's biographer Arthur Herzog, in which the young man did quite well. Yet he never finished them or the courses he claimed he was taking in engineering at nearby Wayne State University—Herzog says Wayne State has no record of Vesco's enrollment. Despite all of this, Vesco was hardworking and extraordinarily ambitious and it was his goal, as he later said, "to get the hell out of Detroit." After a series of jobs in auto parts companies, he got himself hired as an administrative assistant in the engineering division of the Olin Mathieson Chemical Corporation and was able to get transferred to New York City. He brought a modest house in Connecticut and lived the 1950s suburban dream with Patricia and the kids—commuting to work, having weekend barbecues, playing poker with the neighbors.

———— ★ ————

SHOWING UP IN A LEASED LINCOLN CONTINENTAL WITH AIR-CONDITIONING AND A TELEPHONE, WITH A STAFF ASSISTANT POSING AS A CHAUFFEUR, VESCO MANAGED TO CONVINCE HH INDUSTRIES TO INVEST $100,000 IN HIS BUSINESS.

———— ★ ————

But Vesco was different. Unlike the other men in their gray flannel suits, he quit his job, announced that he was going to be a millionaire "within five years" and went off to do business on his own. Moving his wife and children to New Jersey, he borrowed money from a bank and started a business that turned out aluminum garage doors, siding, and awnings. He then took over a nearly moribund company called Captive Seal that owned the rights to a valve and a pressure switch that were used in the aerospace and defense industries. Then he went looking for investors on Wall Street, and found a venture capital company, HH Industries, owned in part by Baron Edmond de Rothschild. Vesco, the high school dropout from Detroit, managed to finagle a meeting with Rothschild and other partners in the firm. Showing up in a leased Lincoln Continental with air-conditioning and a telephone, with a staff assistant posing as a chauffeur, Vesco managed to convince HH Industries to

FROM LEFT, G. GORDON LIDDY, WHITE HOUSE COUNSEL JOHN DEAN III, FORMER U.S. ATTORNEY
GENERAL JOHN MITCHELL, AND JEB MAGRUDER, DEPUTY CAMPAIGN MANAGER FOR RICHARD NIXON'S
CAMPAIGN TO RE-ELECT THE PRESIDENT. EACH MAN WAS TAINTED IN SOME WAY BY ROBERT VESCO'S CASH
CAMPAIGN CONTRIBUTION TO THE NIXON CAMPAIGN.

ASSOCIATED PRESS

———★———

invest $100,000 in his business. Within 18 months, Rothschild received a return on his investment of $1 million and he and his partners were impressed with Vesco, who struck them as intelligent, if grandiose.

At home in Denville, New Jersey, Vesco was considered something of a character. His nickname was Rapid Robert because he wanted everything now, now, *now*. He borrowed a high-priced oil painting from a gallery, pretending to be considering it for purchase, then had it copied and returned it. He hired limousines to chauffeur himself and his wife around. He gambled wildly, took numerous trips to Las Vegas, womanized, drank heavily, but still came home to coach his son's Little League baseball team. Moving from Denville to nearby Boonton, he built himself a palatial home on 80 acres, replete with an indoor riding ring for his daughter, her own stables, and a landing pad for helicopters.

Around this time—the mid-1960s—Vesco created a company called International Controls Corporation (ICC) that took over other businesses, including an airline and several manufacturing firms. Vesco purchased a small company called Cryogenics, which manufactured ultracold devices, simply because it was a publicly traded company. This meant that Vesco could now list ICC without having to go through the SEC filing and registration procedures—"we became a public company through the back door," he was to say.

By 1968, worth, at least on paper, in the neighborhood of $50 million, Vesco contributed $25,000 to Richard Nixon's election campaign and was invited to the annual Alfred E. Smith Memorial Dinner in New York, a prestigious political event attended both by outgoing President Lyndon Johnson and President-elect Richard Nixon. It was here that Vesco was introduced to Nixon for the first time.

"A THIRD-RATE BURGLARY"

By the time the presidential campaign of 1972 rolled around, Richard Nixon was a troubled man. His first-term triumphs had been largely on the foreign affairs front, with historic summit trips to China and Russia. At home, however, he faced growing opposition to his policies, especially in Vietnam, and an economy shored up by wage and price controls. Intense opposition made Nixon paranoid and, increasingly, he walled himself off inside his presidency, sticking close to the White House and relying on the same group of advisors and rich friends.

Wanting to have a record of everything said in the Oval Office, both in case he was misquoted and so that he could better write his memoirs when he left the presidency, Nixon had in 1971 installed a tape recording system, with seven microphones planted in his presidential desk alone. This was nothing new; presidents had taped themselves ever since FDR. (These tapes are collected at http://millercenter.org/academic/presidentialrecordings

and it is a pleasure to listen to John F. Kennedy calling up his doctor to ask for "one of those little blue pills" or Lyndon Johnson browbeating the president of the Haggar Clothing Co. into giving him some free slacks.) However, Richard Nixon insisted that the tapes be voice-operated, so they would turn on at the sound of someone talking, unlike those used by Kennedy or Johnson, which had to be switched on manually and only caught accidental conversations if the president forgot to switch them off.

But Nixon's tapes caught everything and when 1972 rolled around, they found a president increasingly profane and divorced from reality. When FBI Director J. Edgar Hoover died in his sleep in May 1972, aides brought Nixon the news while he sat at his desk in the Oval Office. There was a long pause, and then he exclaimed, "Jesus Christ! That old cocksucker!" Then he ordered a national day of mourning. As Hoover's body lay in state in the Capital Rotunda, an antiwar rally was in progress on the National Mall. Hearing that some protestors had a Vietcong flag, Nixon ordered CREEP operative G. Gordon Liddy to take a group to attack the protestors and seize the flag. This Liddy did, using some old Cuban Bay of Pigs operatives, although it turned out there was no Vietcong flag to seize—its existence had just been a rumor.

And on May 15, when conservative third-party candidate Governor George Wallace—whose run for presidency threatened to siphon votes away from Nixon—was shot and paralyzed by a gun-wielding assassin, Nixon became privately "agitated" and wondered whether a member of CREEP had actually done the shooting. However, when it was realized that the assassin, Arthur Bremer, was acting alone, Nixon speculated, "Wouldn't it be great if they had some left-wing propaganda in [Bremer's] apartment?...Too bad we couldn't get somebody in there to plant it...."

In early 1970, Nixon had told top advisor John Ehrlichman to "set up a little group right here in the White House" to fix leaks, and so Ehrlichman assembled a task force that included ex-CIA agents E. Howard Hunt and Liddy. This Special Investigations Unit, a group more informally known as the "Plumbers," performed any number of "dirty tricks" against Nixon's political opponents, and also broke into the office of Daniel Ellsberg's psychiatrist, looking for damaging information on the former Defense Department analyst, who had leaked the Pentagon Papers to the *New York Times*.

On June 17, 1972, police discovered these same Plumbers inside the offices of the Democratic National Committee (DNC) in the Watergate apartment and office complex in Washington, D.C. They carried with them surgical gloves, bugging equipment (tiny microphones hidden in phony Chapstick tubes), cameras, forty rolls of unexposed film, and $3,500 in brand-new, consecutively numbered hundred dollar bills. They had apparently bugged the office of DNC chairman Larry O'Brien, and were coming back to replace bugs that didn't work.

AN IRONIC, AND ICONIC, FINAL IMAGE: ON AUGUST 9, 1974, RICHARD NIXON GIVES HIS "V FOR VICTORY"
SIGNS AS HE IS ABOUT TO BOARD HIS HELICOPTER AFTER THE ULTIMATE DEFEAT OF HIS LIFE:
RESIGNING AS PRESIDENT OF THE UNITED STATES.

ASSOCIATED PRESS

——— ★ ———

When reporters queried White House Press Secretary Ron Ziegler about the break-in, he dismissed it as "a third-rate burglary." If so, it was one that would bring down the president of the United States. And many now think those consecutively numbered hundred dollar bills came directly from Robert Vesco.

"THE TYPE THAT BRINGS OUT ANIMOSITY"

By 1970, Robert Vesco had wheeled-and-dealed his way into becoming one of the richest men in the world. International Controls Corporation (ICC) now owned thirteen subsidiaries in the United States and Vesco was looking to branch out overseas. At the time, beleaguered billionaire Bernie Cornfeld owned the massive, Geneva-based mutual fund company, Investors Overseas Services (IOS), and Vesco wanted a part of it, because offshore mutual funds were a source of mainly unregulated and untaxed capital investment possibilities. Cornfeld, born in Istanbul under the name Benno Cornfeld was a diminutive, profane, violent-tempered womanizer (he believed in what he called "sexual anarchy" and at one point lived with twelve women at the same time) whose poor business decisions meant that by 1970 IOS was running out of money.

———★———

IN 1972, VESCO HAD HIRED NIXON NEPHEW DON-DON NIXON TO BE HIS PERSONAL ASSISTANT, FLYING WITH HIM ON HIS 707, THE *SILVER PHYLLIS*—WHICH HAD A BEDROOM, A COMPLETELY EQUIPPED KITCHEN AND DINING ROOM, A DISCOTHEQUE WITH A HARDWOOD DANCE FLOOR AND STROBE LIGHTS, AND A MINI-GYM WITH THE WORLD'S ONLY AIRBORNE SAUNA—ALL OVER THE WORLD.

———★———

Vesco, whom Cornfeld considered a "hoodlum," decided to "rescue" IOS via a series of complicated maneuvers that gave him 6.6 million shares in the company; by February 1971, he had ousted Cornfeld and become chairman of the company, placing his men in key positions throughout IOS. However, within a month, the Securities and Exchange Commission had begun to investigate Vesco, in part because his involvement violated a consent order previously agreed upon with IOS, which kept it from operating in the United States. Vesco protested that this investigation was a "witch hunt," and there is the sense that it might have been to some extent. The white-collar types who ran the SEC, including

PRESIDENT RICHARD NIXON WAS WIDELY RIDICULED FOR TAKING TO THE AIRWAVES AND
TELLING THE AMERICAN PEOPLE, "I AM NOT A CROOK." THIS HERBERT BLOCK CARTOON OF 1974
CAPTURES THE PREVAILING SENTIMENT THAT HE WAS.

LIBRARY OF CONGRESS

———— ★ ————

Stanley Sporkin, director of the enforcement division, and SEC General Counsel G. Bradford Cook, didn't like Vesco at all. Sporkin said of Vesco and his men: "I knew these were not good people." Cook went further. Vesco, he said, "was crude, very sleek-looking…a slimer…the type that brings out animosity."

For his part, Vesco claimed that SEC stood for See Everything Crooked. He raged against Sporkin as a "rat bastard" and a "sheeny prick," especially as the SEC investigation continued and it became clear that the feds thought that Vesco was intent on transferring IOS funds to ICC ventures in Costa Rica and Bermuda, in effect milking the company. By the early spring of 1972, it was evident to Vesco, ICC president Laurence Richardson, and Vesco lawyer Harry Sears that they needed to "go over the heads" of the SEC people they were dealing with, to William Casey, head of the SEC (who would later go on to become director of the CIA under Ronald Reagan).

As far as Vesco was concerned, this was quite possible because of what he considered to be his relationship with the Nixons. He had contributed $25,000 to Nixon's 1968 presidential campaign through his business relationship with Nixon's brother, Donald. This had not only gotten Vesco a seat at the Alfred E. Smith Memorial Dinner, but, according to the longtime pilot of Vesco's private 707 jet, a tête-à-tête with the president-elect a few weeks later at the Rose Bowl. In 1972, Vesco had hired Nixon nephew Don-Don Nixon, twenty-four years old, to be his personal assistant, flying with him on his 707, the *Silver Phyllis*—which had a bedroom, a completely equipped kitchen and dining room, a discotheque with a hardwood dance floor and strobe lights, and a mini-gym with the world's only airborne sauna—all over the world.

Vesco also had reason to hope that he would be cleared of any wrongdoing by the SEC investigation because Attorney General John Mitchell had helped him late in 1971, when Vesco had been briefly imprisoned in a Swiss jail after an irate IOS stockholder brought charges against him. Harry Sears had gone to see Mitchell, who then made several phone calls to the U.S. Embassy in Switzerland, with the result that Vesco was soon released. Mitchell had recently resigned as attorney general to become Richard Nixon's campaign manager.

"HOW MUCH YOU GOT IN MIND?"

In the summer of 1971, Richard Nixon asked his aide H. R. Haldeman how much money CREEP had put away for "special operations" of the kind that the Plumbers performed.

"About $1 million," Haldeman said.

"Jesus Christ!" Nixon exclaimed. "We need $2 million…at least $2 million…."

With the president seriously concerned about the outcome of the 1972 election, Maurice Stans—6'5", white-haired, patrician looking—was trying to find money in his job as financial director of CREEP. Eventually, he would raise $62 million (worth about $304

ROBERT VESCO FOUND REFUGE FOR HIMSELF AND HIS FAMILY AT THIS LUXURIOUS PRIVATE COMPOUND IN
COSTA RICA, WHOSE PRESIDENT WAS A GENUINE ADMIRER OF THE FUGITIVE FINANCIER'S AND
REFUSED TO TURN HIM OVER TO U.S. AUTHORITIES.

TIME & LIFE IMAGES/ GETTY IMAGES

———★———

million today), a record amount at the time. It was apparent to most corporate contributors in 1971 and early 1972 that their arms were being twisted for large amounts of cash to be given to CREEP before April 7, 1972, when a new law would come into effect that stipulated that all large contributions be registered with the government's General Accounting Office. In his book *The Arrogance of Power: The Secret World of Richard Nixon*, Anthony Summers recounts numerous stories of corporate chiefs urged to give sums into the hundreds of thousands of dollars in return for "a friendly climate in Washington." In one case, writes Summers, "an order to McDonald's, canceling an unauthorized price increase levied on its quarter-pounder with cheese, was reversed—after the company's chairman had donated $255,000" to CREEP.

It was in this climate of quid pro quo, tit for tat, that Harry Sears met with John Mitchell on February 11, 1972, and told him that "Vesco was talking about giving very substantial amounts" to the Nixon campaign, that he wanted to be "among the top contributors" to CREEP. Mitchell then asked Sears how much Vesco had contributed in 1968 and Sears told him he couldn't remember, at which point Mitchell referred Sears to Maurice Stans.

On March 8, Vesco and Laurence Richardson arrived at CREEP headquarters (directly across the street from the White House) for a meeting with Stans that had been set up by Sears. Vesco told Stans that he wanted to contribute even more generously than he had in '68, but, as he said, "I have a problem. My company and I are under investigation by the SEC....It is completely without merit and amounts to a personal vendetta and harassment. I want to find a way to bring the case to a conference and a settlement."

Stans then replied, according to later testimony by Richardson, "Well, I can't help you with this, but let me see if we can get you an appointment with John Mitchell today while you're here."

Stans then picked up the phone but was unable to reach Mitchell. He then asked Vesco: "How much you got in mind?"

Vesco replied: "I want to be in the front row."

He then told Stans he wanted to contribute $500,000, in two installments. Stans told him that he would need to contribute it before April 7 because otherwise the new law would have to identify him and the size of the contribution, and Vesco replied that he would make the first half of the payment by then. How would Stans like the money?

"In currency," Stans replied.

"In cash?" Vesco said.

"That would be fine," said Stans.

Arthur Herzog was later to write in his biography of Vesco that Stans "knew exactly where to draw the line while giving Vesco the come-on...Vesco did in fact think he was buying influence."

A GUANT, NOTICEABLY OLDER ROBERT VESCO IS ESCORTED BY CUBAN STATE SECURITY OFFICERS TO HIS TRIAL IN HAVANA IN 1996, WHERE HE WAS CHARGED WITH ALLEGED ECONOMIC CRIMES AGAINST THE CUBAN STATE. SOME THOUGHT HE HAD RUN AFOUL OF FIDEL CASTRO BECAUSE OF A FAILED BUSINESS VENTURE WITH CASTRO'S BROTHER, RAUL.

ASSOCIATED PRESS

———★———

On April 10, 1972—missing the deadline by three days—Richardson and Sears met with Maurice Stans in his office. They were carrying a briefcase filled with $200,000 in $100 bills. Vesco had had trouble laying his hands on the money, had eventually had it wired to Barclays Bank on Wall Street, where the money was picked up by a Vesco aide and an armed guard, stashed in ICC's New Jersey offices overnight, and then transported to Washington.

"Here is your currency," Richardson told Stans. "Do you want to count it?"

Stans told him that would not be necessary. Then Richardson set out to deliver a message. Vesco was not present with him to deliver the cash, but he had told Richardson to tell Stans, "Get that fuckin' SEC off my back!"

In Stans's presence, Richardson translated more politely: "Mr. Vesco wants me to deliver you a message. He'd like to get some help."

"Tell him that's not my bailiwick," Stans said. "That's John Mitchell's department."

Stans then put the money in his safe. Later that same afternoon, Sears finally secured an appointment with John Mitchell. He told Mitchell about the cash contribution Stans had just received (Mitchell would later deny hearing about this from Sears) and pressed Mitchell for an appointment with William Casey, head of the SEC. Somewhat to Sears's surprise, Mitchell made a telephone call and set one up for him that very afternoon at 4 p.m. Sears met with Casey and Bradford Cook, who admitted that feelings had run high in the agency against Vesco and hinted to him that an injunction—and possibly a criminal charge—would be forthcoming against Vesco.

"I'LL BLOW THE LID OFF THE WHOLE THING"

In the meantime, what of the Vesco cash that disappeared into Stans's safe? Numerous people believe that it was used to finance the Watergate break-ins and also in part to pay hush money to the burglars once they had been caught. Vesco's chief biographer Arthur Herzog writes that "the money was used, of course, to finance the 'plumbers,' and led to the Watergate scandal."

Investigators later attempted to follow the trail. The hundred dollar bills found on the burglars were traced by their sequential serial numbers to the bank account of one of the burglars, Bernard Barker; this money was subsequently traced to CREEP via money that Maurice Stans deposited into the account of Kenneth Dahlberg, CREEP's finance chairman for the Midwest. Dahlberg then turned some of the money into a $25,000 cashier's check, which was deposited in Barker's Miami bank account.

There is no absolute proof that Vesco's money specifically was the money used, but it appears highly likely because the cash came in a month before the first of the burglaries, and because Stans did not report the contribution to the General Accounting Office.

Richard Nixon continued to wage a successful campaign for the presidency, ignoring a series of articles on the Watergate break-in that were beginning to appear in the summer of 1972, from two young *Washington Post* reporters, Carl Bernstein and Bob Woodward. Nixon beat George McGovern by a massive plurality in the popular vote and took the Electoral College 520 to 17. It was a debacle for the Democrats, but there were numerous reports from people who knew him that Nixon looked glum on Election Night. Instead of celebrating at his victory party, he closeted himself with a few close aides and drank Scotch. It may be that he was starting to understand that everything was going to unravel around him.

In the meantime, things started to unravel around Robert Vesco. From Cook's comments both to Sears and Vesco, it became apparent that the SEC planned to charge Vesco with looting the accounts of IOS of a sizable amount of money, as well as with perjury for lying to SEC investigators. At the end of September 1972, the SEC summoned Vesco to an October hearing in New York. Vesco went ballistic, threatening to Sears to bring the president of the United States down with him if questioned about his cash contribution to the Nixon campaign. "Those bastards would like nothing more than to nail me and the president to the wall together," he said. "Nixon may survive some of the other things, but this would be the crusher." Vesco told Sears to tell John Mitchell to have the SEC investigation closed down "or I'll blow the lid off the whole thing," the whole thing being Watergate and the part Vesco suspected that his cash had played in it.

The presidential campaign was still going on, and Sears went to Mitchell and told him that if Vesco testified it would have a "devastating effect" on Nixon's fortunes. He asked that the SEC deposition be postponed. "Do you think that is possible?" Sears later recalled asking Mitchell. To which Mitchell replied: "Well, I certainly would hope so, if they have any concern for the president of the United States."

Eventually, Vesco decided to plead the Fifth Amendment at his SEC deposition on October 18. When Mitchell heard about it, he told Sears to tell Vesco that he was "grateful" for Vesco's silence. The SEC also deposed several other Vesco employees, and they pleaded the Fifth as well. It didn't matter. At the end of November, Robert Vesco was charged with "diverting" more than $224 million from IOS shareholders into Bahamas and Luxembourg banks that were controlled by Vesco. This was an enormous amount of money, the equivalent in purchasing power of about $9 billion today, and Arthur Herzog casts some doubt as to whether the SEC estimation was accurate. But it is probably fair to say that Vesco was involved in some type of double-dealing with the IOS money that put him in personal control of millions.

By this time, however, Vesco was not prepared to wait around to see whether he might find himself in a U.S. jail. He had been making preparations since early in the summer to flee to Costa Rica whose president, Jose Figueres Ferrer, or Don Pepe, was a strong supporter of the

MAURICE STANS, FINANCE DIRECTOR OF RICHARD NIXON'S COMMITTEE TO RE-ELECT THE PRESIDENT,
MAKES A PREPARED STATEMENT BEFORE TESTIFYING IN FRONT OF THE SENATE WATERGATE COMMITTEE
IN JUNE 1973. IT WAS STANS, FORMER U.S. COMMERCE SECRETARY, WHO RECEIVED A BRIEFCASE FILLED
WITH $200,000 IN ONE-HUNDRED DOLLAR BILLS DELIVERED DIRECTLY BY ROBERT VESCO'S LAWYER.

ASSOCIATED PRESS

———— ★ ————

financier, as Vesco's company made investments in Ferrer's family businesses. But Ferrer was also a genuine admirer of Vesco's, who felt that he had been persecuted by the U.S. government because of his freewheeling ways and his refusal to kowtow to the SEC.

In November 1972, having been transferring his family and possessions to Costa Rica on numerous trips of the *Silver Phyllis*, Robert Vesco officially became a fugitive.

THE FAILED PRESIDENT AND THE FUGITIVE FINANCIER

After Robert Vesco was indicted, Domestic Affairs Assistant John Erhlichman predicted to Richard Nixon, in one of their taped conversations in the Oval Office, that Vesco "will probably go to Costa Rica, where he has bought the president."

"The son of a bitch," Nixon replied. And in one of the numerous anti-Semitic outbursts that would shock the American people, he called Vesco, who was not Jewish, "a cheap kike." He became increasingly upset thinking about Vesco. "Vesco is a crook," he told Erhlichman. "ICC didn't get anything. We indicted them…Vesco got indicted, too! Shit! It's stupidity, insanity!"

———★———

WHEN THE SENATE SELECT COMMITTEE BEGAN TELEVISED HEARINGS ON WATERGATE, DEAN TESTIFIED THAT THERE HAD BEEN A WHITE HOUSE COVER-UP AND THAT RICHARD NIXON WAS PERSONALLY INVOLVED IN PAYING HUSH MONEY TO THE FIVE BURGLARS.

———★———

It is interesting to speculate on why Nixon was so upset about the fate of one crooked financier. Obviously, at the time he was having this conversation with Ehrlichman (in the late winter of 1973, after his inauguration) the Watergate scandal was beginning to blow up into a problem of epic proportions. John Mitchell and Maurice Stans had been indicted on charges that they had taken cash from Vesco in return for attempting to influence the outcome of the SEC investigation against him (a New York jury would eventually acquit both men because of lack of concrete evidence). In February 1973, the U.S. Senate established a Select Committee on Presidential Campaign activities to investigate all activities surrounding the Watergate break-in and other possibly illegal activities of CREEP. On March 23, shortly after Erhlichman and Nixon discussed Vesco in the White House, James W. McCord, one of the five burglars caught in the Watergate office complex, told U.S. District Judge John J. Sirica that he was being pressured to remain silent.

A month later, acting FBI Director L. Patrick Gray resigned admitting he had destroyed Watergate evidence after being pressured by Richard Nixon's aides. With the scandal getting closer and closer, Nixon forced the resignation, two weeks later, of four of his aides—Ehrlichman, Chief of Staff H. R. Haldeman, Attorney General Richard Kleindienst, and Presidential Counsel John Dean. Dean refused to go quietly. When the Senate Select Committee began televised hearings on Watergate, Dean testified that there had been a White House cover-up and that Richard Nixon was personally involved in paying hush money to the five burglars.

And in mid-July, Alexander Butterfield, a former White House appointments secretary, informed the Senate Committee of the existence of a White House taping system, one that had been in place since Nixon's first term. Shortly thereafter, Nixon ordered the White House taping system disconnected, but it was too late. The Senate Committee and Special Prosecutor Archibald Cox demanded that Nixon turn over the tapes and he refused. A seesaw battle now began, with Nixon fighting court orders to turn over the tapes and eventually losing, even though he fired Archibald Cox in his attempts to keep the American people from hearing them.

By early in the spring of 1974, Nixon had released 1,254 pages of edited transcripts of the tapes, to avoid handing over 42 subpoenaed tapes themselves. Even in this censored form, the transcripts shocked the public. They heard Nixon's profanity and bigotry. They heard Nixon, shortly after the Watergate break-in, tell H. R. Haldeman to essentially obstruct justice—"to call the FBI and say that we wish, for the country, don't go any further into this case, period." They heard Nixon discussing hush money for the Watergate burglars, as in a conversation he had early in 1973 with John Dean: "We could get that. On the money, if you need the money you could get that. You could get a million dollars. You could get it in cash. I know where it could be gotten. It is not easy, but it could be done. But the question is, Who would handle it? Any ideas on that?"

Despite the fact that Nixon went on television and famously told the American people "I am not a crook!" they began to consider him one. It all came to a head in the summer of 1974. Leon Jaworsky, the new special prosecutor, pursued the Nixon tapes all the way to the Supreme Court, which ruled, on July 24, that Nixon had to surrender the tapes. Within a week, the House Judiciary Committee had approved three articles of impeachment against the president. With the handwriting on the wall, a distraught Nixon became the first U.S. president ever to resign, on August 9, 1974. His Vice President, Gerald Ford, took over and announced that the United States' "long national nightmare" was over, but a month later pardoned Richard Nixon for all crimes he may have committed while in office, therefore making sure that the full truth would never be known about his involvement in Watergate.

Nixon would eventually attempt to rehabilitate himself, without ever admitting wrongdoing in the Watergate scandal. He later told an interviewer: "I could never muster much moral outrage over a political bugging," and he had a point—Democrats and Republicans had been bugging each other with some regularity in the twenty years leading up to Watergate. But on what was CREEP's evident attempt to coerce corporations into giving money to his campaign and on leading Robert Vesco to believe that a $200,000 donation would solve his legal problems, Nixon was silent. Although his involvement cannot be proven with 100 percent certitude, it seems reasonable to believe that he knew about the Vesco situation and knew where the $200,000 in cash came from. This and the money CREEP extorted in the name of the 1972 Republican presidential campaign makes Nixon the king of presidential payola.

Richard Nixon wrote his memoirs (along with nine other books), founded his library, became a respected elder statesman, and died of a stroke in April 1994. Robert Vesco met a different fate. He lived in Costa Rica until 1978, when a change in the political climate made him an unwelcome visitor and then he made his way to the Bahamas and then Antigua. In 1982, he moved to Cuba, a country that would not extradite him to the United States. He formed a fairly close relationship with Cuban President Fidel Castro, advising him on financial matters, although it is also believed that Vesco paid a large sum, possibly as much as $50,000 a month, for Castro's protection.

In 1990, Vesco worked once again with his old aide Don-Don Nixon on the development of a new wonder drug called trixolan, which was supposedly a cure for cancer, AIDS, arthritis, and even the common cold. Vesco introduced Nixon to Castro and his brother Raul and became involved in trixolan's development in Cuba, but in 1995 Castro arrested Vesco, charging him with double-crossing him, and threw both him and his Cuban girlfriend into prison. He was released after about ten years and lived quietly in humble surroundings before dying of lung cancer in late 2007, at the age of 72. Despite photos taken of the dying Vesco, as well as pictures of his funeral, there were those who were skeptical that the man had actually passed away. An Italian passport was found in his belongings, and many people who knew him thought that he had orchestrated his death, to slip away from justice one more time.

CHAPTER 7

———★———

Ronald Reagan and the HUD Scandal:

"HOW ARE THINGS IN YOUR CITY?"

———★———

s the oldest president in U.S. history, Ronald Reagan became known for his gaffes. On one memorable occasion, he called Liberian leader Samuel K. Doe "Chairman Moe." He loved ethnic jokes, which did not necessarily go over so well with certain groups, such as the time reporters overheard him telling one that began: "How do you tell the Polish fellow at a cockfight?" The answer was: "He's the one with the duck."

Sometimes his remarks didn't make any sense at all. For instance, there was the occasion when he told a group of high school ambassadors, off on a youth goodwill mission to Europe, "And, yes, it's all right to have an affinity for what was the mother country for all of us, because if a man takes a wife until himself he doesn't stop loving his mother because of that. But at the same time, we're all Americans."

But one of his biggest faux pas was also quite a telling one. On June 12, 1981, Ronald Reagan stood at the head of a receiving line during a visit to the White House by a dozen big city mayors. Many of them were black and wished to talk about the plight of mainly black neighborhoods in deteriorating urban areas. Reagan greeted them politely one by one, finally reaching the last person in line.

"Hello, Mr. Mayor!" Reagan boomed, patting the man on the back and shaking his hand. "How are you? How are things in your city?"

But the man was not a mayor. He was, in fact, Samuel R. Pierce, secretary of Housing and Urban Development (HUD) and a member of Reagan's own cabinet. He had been picked by Reagan for the job and had spent six months attending Cabinet meetings at which the President was present. Pierce would go on to become the only Reagan Cabinet member to serve eight years for both of Reagan's terms in office. And yet Reagan, and not just on this occasion, had continual trouble recognizing Pierce, much to Pierce's lasting chagrin and mortification.

Some people suggested this was because Pierce was black and all black people looked alike to Reagan, and there may have been an element of truth to this—after all, Pierce was picked for the Cabinet spot almost solely because he was an African American. But the more likely explanation for not recognizing Samuel Pierce was that the Department of Housing and Urban Development was hardly on President Reagan's radar. He simply didn't care. And Reagan's disinterest allowed one of the most blatant and heartbreaking scandals in U.S. history to grow right under the nose of the White House.

A REVOLUTION IN HOME OWNING

The Department of Housing and Urban Development began in 1934 as the Federal Housing Administration (FHA), which was created by the National Housing Act, one of the New Deal bills signed into law by President Franklin Roosevelt. In the depths of the Great Depression, unemployment and bank failures had left the housing market in disarray and millions of homeless to wander the streets of the United States. Home building—or "starts" of housing construction—was way down and foreclosures were at an all-time high. One of the major purposes of the FHA was to insure mortgages against the risk of default, making banks more willing to extend credit, thus allowing more and more people to buy housing, which in turn increased the size of the market for houses.

For much of U.S. history, home owning was something that came late in life, after a person might have saved up enough money to make a hefty down payment on a house—at least one-third or more of the value of the house, in pre-New Deal days, at which point mortgages might extend for only five to seven years. This left home ownership mainly to those with a fairly hefty income and savings. The FHA changed all that. Millions of people purchased homes via FHA-approved loans and in its own way the FHA created a revolution in home owning, establishing the current home-buying model of relatively low down payments followed by long-term mortgages. Under the FHA, home ownership jumped from about 44 percent of Americans in 1940 to 63 percent in 1970.

---★---

THE DEPARTMENT OF HOUSING AND URBAN DEVELOPMENT WAS HARDLY ON PRESIDENT REAGAN'S RADAR. HE SIMPLY DIDN'T CARE.

---★---

Home ownership among whites, that is. Among African Americans, although the rate doubled, home ownership lagged 20 percent behind in the same period. This was because, whether it intended to or not, the FHA discriminated against blacks by failing to approve loans for houses in low-income neighborhoods. And once the FHA refused to insure a loan, a black would-be home owner would be unable to find a mortgage loan anywhere.

A second goal of the FHA was to assist low-income renters to find safe and affordable housing by providing rent subsidies to poor people who qualified for them. Most people today would be shocked to learn that, according to one study, 50 percent of housing in America in 1940 lacked even basic plumbing. The U.S. Housing Act of 1937 was designed to construct public housing, which, during the war, became mainly housing for defense workers. After 1946, Public Housing, as the department became known, worked to find homes for the population of newly returned veterans and their burgeoning families during a period when Washington, D.C., reported 25,000 homeless veterans and Chicago 100,000.

Finally, the Housing Act of 1949, signed into law by President Harry Truman, added a third goal of rejuvenating United States' cities by clearing slum areas—"urban renewal" as it became euphemistically known—and providing housing redevelopment in these areas.

IN JANUARY 1989, THE OUTGOING RONALD REAGAN SAYS GOOD-BYE TO CABINET MEMBERS
WHO INCLUDED SAMUEL R. PIERCE, HUD SECRETARY, LEFT. TRAGICALLY, PIERCE'S PROMISING CAREER
WAS RUINED BY HIS TENURE AT HUD, AND YET HE WAS ONE OF THE FEW CABINET MEMBERS WHO CAME
TO THE AIRPORT TO SEE REAGAN OFF AS THE FORMER PRESIDENT RETURNED TO CIVILIAN LIFE.
ASKED WHY, PIERCE SAID SIMPLY: "HE'S A FRIEND OF MINE."

TIME & LIFE IMAGES/GETTY IMAGES

★

PREY OF VANDALS

In 1965, President Lyndon Johnson combined these similar programs into one Cabinet-level department as part of his Great Society program. Known as the Department of Housing and Urban Development, HUD was a crucial initiative in the 1960s, with so many of America's urban centers suffering from the blights of crime and decay. With the Civil Rights Act of 1968, HUD was also tasked with fighting discrimination in housing markets on the basis of race, religion, or ethnic origin.

Judging by all its missions—to guarantee mortgage loans, provide subsidies to allow people to buy or rent good housing, clear decayed housing and provide safe, low-income alternatives, and make sure poor African Americans and other minorities weren't discriminated against—it would seem like HUD might be considered the saintliest of government agencies. But historically speaking, this has simply not been the case. One of the reasons for this is because HUD is the fulcrum where government subsidy money meets private capitalism, allowing for a wide array of fraudulent practices. For instance, because the FHA's previous policies toward black home owners had amounted to a kind of redlining—refusing to guarantee home mortgage loans in ghetto areas, even if the would-be home buyer had a secure job, simply because property values were so low—bureaucrats in the 1960s and 1970s set out to remedy this by providing overgenerous subsidies in urban areas.

A typical scam, as the late housing expert and sociologist Louis Winnick wrote in his 1990 book *New People in Old Neighborhoods*, took advantage of the fact that now HUD "provided more money to the poor than the poor could beneficially absorb."

Typically [Winnick says] speculators contrived the purchase of a house [in a decayed urban area] from a distressed owner for $5,000 or less. After cosmetic touch-ups, the property was sold for $20,000 to be provided by an FHA-approved mortgage of nearly equivalent amount. The buyers of these overpriced and overmortgaged houses were usually the Puerto Ricans, unwary families who lacked the means to meet monthly finance charges plus the cost of keeping oft-defective homes in good repair. Substantial numbers of homes went into default, turned back to the mortgagees and eventually to FHA…to become prey of vandals, drug dealers, and weather.

In other words, this type of fraud completely subverted the mission of HUD creating more homelessness and urban blight. Because of this, and because (as many home owners in the first decade of the twenty-first century were to discover) it makes sense to walk away from a decaying home whose mortgage outweighs its actual value, President Richard Nixon suspended subsidy programs to HUD in 1973. This led directly to the termination of subsidized housing programs, but only for about a year or so, before HUD was reorganized and practices began again. But it wasn't long before other HUD scandals arose and the agency got a reputation for corruption, waste, and neglect. The combination of Samuel Pierce and Ronald Reagan would bring that reputation to a new low.

"IN EVERY RESPECT, A SINGULAR MAN"

Samuel R. Pierce Jr. was born in 1922 in Glen Cove, New York, and received a football scholarship to Cornell, from which he graduated Phi Beta Kappa in 1947. After graduating a few years later from Cornell Law School, he launched what would become a distinguished career. He went to work as an assistant district attorney and assistant U.S. attorney in New York in the 1950s and later became an undersecretary for the Department of Labor in the second Eisenhower administration. After returning to New York to serve as a judge, he went into private practice and eventually founded the first New York commercial bank with mainly African American officers. From 1970 to 1973 he served as counsel for the Treasury Department under Richard Nixon.

Pierce had an unusual resume, a black man who had held positions of power in a mainly white Republican world, although as a lawyer in private practice he had also defended Martin Luther King Jr. in a court case and had taught at Yale. He was a tall, courtly, bespectacled, and soft-spoken man who actually did not want the job he had been nominated for when Reagan became president in 1981—he made it loud and clear that his preference was for secretary of labor. But Pierce was recommended for the job of HUD secretary by Alfred Bloomingdale, the powerful New York department store owner who was a member of Reagan's "kitchen cabinet" of wealthy old friends who advised the new president. Reagan wanted a black man in his Cabinet. Pierce was black and had a great resume and, just possibly, might be able to replace Justice Thurgood Marshall when the latter retired from the Supreme Court (Marshall, as it turned out, was not to retire until 1991, and would be succeeded by Clarence Thomas).

Pierce had not had any particular experience with HUD, but was a decent enough candidate, well-liked not only by Republicans, but also by Democrats. At his confirmation hearings, Senator Daniel P. Moynihan praised him as "a master of legal issues [who] is also cognizant of the fiscal and monetary consequences....He is in every respect a singular man."

Interestingly, this was higher praise than he received from Reagan himself, partially because Reagan, as his biographer Lou Cannon states, "was uninterested in many of the Cabinet positions" that he saw as minor. Thus he knew almost nothing about the secretary of commerce, Malcolm Baldrige, or his secretary of agriculture, John Block, an Illinois corn and pig farmer. His secretary of the interior, James G. Watt, was an obscure conservative attorney whose Christianity often appeared in his public utterances ("I don't know how many future generations we can count on before the Lord returns," he said, in talking about conserving resources) and who was forced to resign in 1983 after mocking affirmative action by saying publicly about his staff: "I have a black, I have a woman, two Jews, and a cripple."

Ronald Reagan set the tone for what would happen in the Department of Housing and Urban Development by never visiting its offices in the eight years that he was president.

HOMELESS BY CHOICE

Part of the reason for Reagan's lack of interest in HUD was philosophical—he felt the department was an example of big liberal government spending that did not need to exist. Soon after taking office, Reagan appointed a housing task force that was to call for "free and deregulated" housing markets, in keeping with Reagan's economic policies of reduced government intervention. During Reagan's eight years as president, the amount spent on subsidized housing programs was reduced drastically, from $26 billion annually to $8 billion annually. Subsidies for new low-income housing starts were drastically cut—from 175,000 to 20,000 a year—with a focus on repairing and rehabilitating current housing. When the numbers of homeless swelled dramatically, Reagan told an interviewer in 1984 on the *Good Morning America* show that these people "were homeless, you might say, by choice."

This lack of interest in the housing of poor Americans was made abundantly clear to Samuel R. Pierce, whose previous enterprise was sorely lacking as soon as he began the job as HUD secretary. Although he had sat on the boards of companies like General Electric and Prudential Insurance, writes Irving Welfeld, author of *HUD Scandals: Howling Headlines and Silent Fiascoes*, Pierce "had never run any large organization, let alone a federal agency. He came to HUD with but the scantiest knowledge of HUD programs and never mastered the details."

Pierce was notorious for spending part of the afternoon watching soap operas with the younger staff members in his office. He was quite the junketeer, taking five taxpayer-funded trips to the Soviet Union on trade missions (more visits than were made by the secretary of state). He had one staffer devoted full-time to working on a book entitled *The Pierce Years*, which became an 87-page, four-color pamphlet published at taxpayer expense. He became known as "Silent Sam," for his low profile and lack of any seemingly coherent public utterances.

Pierce's inattention at HUD imitated Ronald Reagan's own inattention and was in fact fostered by Reagan's belief that HUD was an unnecessary federal agency. Because of Reagan's attitude toward Pierce, the man he literally couldn't see, and HUD, the agency he didn't believe in, HUD was to become the most scandal-ridden federal agency of the 1980s. Pierce spent a good deal of time making sure that friends of his or friends of powerful Republicans received favorable HUD treatment. He backed a $4.5 million HUD grant to convert an aircraft carrier into a museum—a project pushed forward by a former law firm client, Larry Fisher, a wealthy real estate developer and Republican campaign contributor. He helped his friend and fellow Republican, jazz musician Lionel Hampton, receive a 20-year, $21 million subsidy on a housing project in Newark, New Jersey. And he overrode the recommendations of HUD's own civil servants in order to champion a Durham, North Carolina, project by Charles Markham, who was Durham's mayor but also a former law associate of Pierce's.

THIS 1989 PAUL CONRAD CARTOON SHOWS THE ENORMITY OF THE S&L AND HUD SCANDALS
OF THE REAGAN YEARS COMPARED TO THE TEAPOT DOME SCANDAL OF THE ERA OF WARREN G. HARDING.
INDEED, AS FAR AS HUD WAS CONCERNED, THE SCANDAL AS WIDESPREAD AND PERVASIVE
AS ANY THAT HAD HIT WASHINGTON.

LIBRARY OF CONGRESS

But these scandals were minor compared to the some of the major problems caused by Pierce and his lieutenants while the president of the United States was failing to mind the store.

"THE LIST OF LEMONS"

One of the biggest scandals of Pierce's years at the helm of HUD had to do with HUD's section 223(f) coinsurance program, which began in 1983, the goal of which was to rehabilitate multifamily housing units. Coinsurance was the FHA's policy of fully insuring any loan it approved, thus relieving the lender of any financial burden if the loan was defaulted on. In the past, it had insured all but 10 percent of mortgages—that last 10 percent was enough to make sure that banks lending money would be prudent in their loans, lest they be liable for that amount. But up through the 1960s, it was apparent that many banks simply would not make any mortgage loans to families in inner city or central city areas unless the FHA fully approved them. Legislation authorizing coinsurance was passed in 1974.

Once again the impetus behind coinsurance is understandable—trying to make sure that poor families had housing. But unfortunately, a lax HUD administration and a corrupt private market conspired to turn this into a lucrative cash cow.

In 1983, because of the Reagan Administration's lack of funding for new housing starts, HUD cut back staff for mortgage processing—the appraisers, underwriters, and inspectors it had needed to oversee bank loans to consumers, in both single-family and multifamily housing. However, the Reagan Administration allowed the refinancing, repair, and sale of existing multifamily housing stock, a process HUD also wanted to continue. Because it now did not have the staff to process these mortgages, Pierce's agency allowed private mortgage lenders to administer the entire process without oversight—from underwriting to foreclosure. The lenders were also allowed to charge consumers fees as high as 4.15 percent of the entire amount of the loan.

By 1988, participating lenders had coinsured 846 loans for the government, totaling $4.8 billion, according to Irving Welfeld. At the same time, 106 of these loans were in default, with the government now guaranteeing the mortgage lender $700 million in losses. (By 1990, when the program was hastily shut down, the defaults had reached $1.6 billion.)

The biggest winner in tearing money out of the hands of the U.S. taxpayer was the Washington, D.C.,-based mortgage firm of DRG, run by Donald De Franceaux, known to friends and associates as Donnie De. Welfeld likens the coinsurance business given by HUD to the politically well-connected Donnie De to giving "a hunting license in a game preserve." A typical case occurred in 1984, when the owner of Colonial House, an 1,800-unit public housing unit in Houston, wanted to renovate and refinance it. DRG appraised Colonial House's worth at $60 million, when HUD's number-two man in the Texas region,

A PENSIVE REPRESENTATIVE TOM LANTOS (D-CA) CHAIRED THE HOUSE GOVERNMENT OPERATIONS
COMMITTEE HEARINGS INTO THE HUD SCANDALS IN 1990. IT WAS LANTOS WHO PUT OUT THE REPORT
THAT READ "AT BEST, SECRETARY PIERCE WAS LESS THAN HONEST AND MISLED THE SUBCOMMITTEE
ABOUT HIS INVOLVEMENT IN ABUSES AND FAVORITISM IN THE HUD FUNDING DECISIONS.
AT WORSE, SECRETARY PIERCE KNOWINGLY LIED AND COMMITTED PERJURY DURING HIS TESTIMONY."

TIME & LIFE IMAGES/GETTY IMAGES

———————★———————

DEBORAH GORE DEAN, TOP AIDE TO SAMUEL R. PIERCE, TESTIFIES BEFORE A 1989 HOUSE GOVERNMENT OPERATIONS COMMITTEE HEARING IN WHICH SHE TOOK THE FIFTH AMENDMENT. ALTHOUGH GORE WAS ONLY 29 WHEN SHE TOOK THE JOB WORKING FOR PIERCE, SHE SOON BECAME THE POWER BEHIND THE THRONE, DISPENSING MILLIONS OF HUD DOLLARS TO REAL ESTATE DEVELOPERS IN WHAT *PEOPLE* MAGAZINE HAS CALLED "A BACCHANAL OF INFLUENCE PEDDLING." AMONG HER STAFF, THE STRONG-WILLED DEAN WAS KNOWN AS "THE DUCHESS OF DARKNESS" FOR HER IMPERIOUS WAYS.

TIME & LIFE IMAGES/GETTY IMAGES

★

Walter Sevier, thought it was worth only around $13 million. Sevier refused to approve a coinsured $47 million loan, but higher-ups in Washington did. Colonial House went into default 13 months later, sticking the taxpayer with millions in debt but making Donnie De a cool $1 million in fees with no liability.

When word of this got out in 1985, Samuel Pierce restricted DRG's access to the coinsurance program. But of course Donnie De just happened to be a big contributor to the Samuel Pierce scholarship fund at Georgetown Preparatory School. He hired a powerful lobbyist, Carla Hills, former HUD secretary under President Gerald Ford, to plead his case with Pierce. And his attorney, Lynda Murphy, was a good friend of Deborah Gore Dean, a young Washingtonian from a well-connected political family who was Pierce's executive assistant. Within a few weeks of restricting DRG access, Pierce completely lifted it. DRG went on to make $1 billion worth of loans before it was ousted from the program in 1989. Eventually, two-thirds of these loans would be in default, for a total of $709 billion.

This kind of interference by Pierce and his top staffers caused enormous angst among those honest civil servants at lower levels of the HUD administration. One mid-level HUD officer wrote in a memo, "This is the most fraud-prone system ever spawned by HUD, but we have been overruled so many times in matters of compliance that I have given up registering protests." Another regional HUD administrator wrote, "I am convinced that financial problems of national proportions are inevitable unless something is done."

He was right. The coinsurance program, as administered by Samuel Pierce, was an invitation for unscrupulous lenders to enrich themselves by overvaluing properties, as there was little risk to themselves. As Tom Lantos, chairman of the Congressional committee that would later investigate Pierce and HUD, wrote, "When…a list is compiled of the most ill-advised ventures in the 1980s, on the top of the list of lemons, high above the introduction of the 'New Coca-Cola' and the making of the film *Heaven's Gate*, will be HUD's coinsuring loans."

"I CAN STOMP ON YOU"

Deborah Gore Dean, as even her boss Samuel Pierce later said, "liked power. She liked the idea that 'I can call the shots, I can get this for you if I want, I can stomp on you, I can kill you.'" And as executive assistant to a man who spent his afternoons watching soap operas, she had plenty of power to burn. As Welfeld writes, "She was the de facto boss of HUD. She operated the secretary's autopen." Although quite young—she was only 29 in 1984, when she became Pierce's assistant—she wielded an iron, if not ethical, hand, even requiring subordinates to clean and paint her apartment during office hours. She came from a distinguished family. Her father, Gordon Dean, was a Nazi war crimes prosecutor and former Atomic Energy Commission chairman, and she is related to Democratic Vice President Al Gore.

After earning a political science degree from Georgetown, she bounced around to different jobs in Washington, tending bar and writing for a Washington society magazine. In 1982, she got a clerical job at HUD, but quickly rose to become Pierce's assistant. (In 1987, she nearly became an assistant secretary of HUD, but a Democratic Senate committee refused to put forward her nomination.) The buck stopped at HUD with Dean, and everyone there knew it. This was particularly true when it came to the matter of HUD's Section 8 moderate rehabilitation program, known colloquially as "Mod-rehab."

Mod-rehab was launched in 1979 as a program meant to finance repairs of up to $5,000 to housing units that rented to low-income tenants. The program contained, when it began, a so-called "fair-share" provision, meaning that funding was apportioned to state and local public housing on the basis of data reflecting "population, poverty, housing overcrowding, housing vacancies" and the like. This was not a huge HUD initiative, like the coinsurance program, but naturally, the Reagan Administration cut this even modest program to the bone, despite the fact that almost 3,000 Public Housing Authorities (PHAs) were clamoring for assistance for repairs to their units. Not only that, but in 1984, Congress allowed HUD to waive the fair-share provision, mainly because there was so little money and so many PHAs that it made no sense to give out cash by demographics or population—this would divide up the dwindling amount of funds into tiny slivers, which would do little good.

The problem was that HUD never developed (and Congress didn't ask for) a logical formula by which to allocate these funds. Giving these funds to contractors was left totally up to the discretion of Samuel Pierce at HUD. And, of course, Pierce in turn left it totally to the discretion of Dean, who later told the *Wall Street Journal*: "[Mod-rehab] was set up and designed to be a public program....I would have to say we ran it in a political manner."

Normally, one would not think that the financial sharks would gather around pieces of pie worth only $5,000 or so, but as the program got smaller under the Reagan Administration, the number of "projects and the amount of rehabilitation" got larger, according to Irving Welfeld. No one was watching the store, so what were simply apartment building repairs often became costly conversions of other-use buildings into public housing. In Massachusetts, for example, a historical mill was converted into apartments at a cost of $80,000 per unit, all paid to a developer picked by Dean and her cohorts. The selection was obviously political. The area around Springfield-Holyoke, Massachusetts, received nine funding allocations—and was represented by Edward Boland, chairman of HUD's appropriations committee in Congress.

Even the disgraced former secretary of the interior, James Watt, came to feed at the pork barrel. Watt, of whom a congressman once said, "his only experience in the field of housing was making Bambi homeless," received more than $300,000 from HUD in mod-

A YOUNG GIRL STANDS IN FRONT OF HER RUN-DOWN HOME IN ALVISO, CALIFORNIA, IN 1980. IT WAS
JUST SUCH PROPERTIES THAT THE DEPARTMENT OF HOUSING AND URBAN DEVELOPMENT WAS TASKED TO
CHANGE INTO SAFE AND AFFORDABLE HOUSING, WHICH IS WHAT MAKES WHAT HAPPENED
DURING THE REAGAN YEARS ALL THE MORE TRAGIC.
NATIONAL GEOGRAPHIC/GETTY IMAGES

rehab funds during his post-Cabinet life as a lobbyist and political consultant. A story in the *Wall Street Journal* entitled "Favored Friends: Housing Subsidy Plan for the Poor Helped Contributors to GOP" listed mod-rehab recipients like Fred Bush, who, while not a Bush relation, had been chief of staff to Reagan Vice President George Bush; former Senator Edward Brooke of Massachusetts; and John Mitchell, the former attorney general, disgraced during the Watergate years, who just happened to be the longtime companion of Deborah Gore Dean's widowed mother.

According to the same *Wall Street Journal* article, because of mod-rehab "a trove of rent subsidies, tax credits, and consulting fees, totaling millions of dollars on each housing project, flowed to GOP faithful and their associates." And HUD itself, as the journalist Tad DeHaven has written, was now "a sort of graduate school for ethics-challenged officials to master the complexities of housing programs such as mod-rehab, and then join the private sector and use their connections at HUD to cash in."

"BREATHTAKING CYNICISM AND HYPOCRISY"

With both the press and Congress concentrating on other scandals, what was going on at HUD managed to pass unnoticed for nearly eight years. The HUD scandals really didn't erupt until Ronald Reagan was out of office and Samuel Pierce had left the department. Because of press reports, an investigation was launched by HUD Secretary Jack Kemp, who had followed Pierce into office under the newly elected President George H. W. Bush. Kemp found "a legacy of abuse and mismanagement, fraud and favoritism, in certain HUD programs." This was putting it mildly, as an independent investigator uncovered "significant problems" of fraud and influence-peddling in twenty-eight HUD programs involving 94 percent of its budget.

It was, as a *New York Times* editorial stated, "a stain on the Reagan legacy," but of course Reagan, whose indifference had caused this amount of payola to be spread among the Republican faithful, had long since ridden off into his addled sunset. Others were left behind to pay the price. In 1990 an independent counsel investigation was launched into the activities of HUD under Samuel R. Pierce. After six years of investigation, it came up with seventeen convictions, including a conviction for Deborah Gore Dean, who was sentenced to 21 months in prison on 12 counts of corruption, bribery, and perjury, although her sentence was reduced on appeal to three years' probation and six months' home confinement.

As for Samuel Pierce, Congress investigated him for months after he had resigned his post. In his testimony before a special Congressional subcommittee, Pierce denied any wrongdoing, saying: "In eight years, I'll bet you hundreds, perhaps thousands, of people—Republicans and Democrats, governors, mayors, congressmen, senators, developers, contractors, and so on—would ask me for something." He passed on these requests, he said, to his staff to decide on a merit basis only.

Friends of Silent Sam requested sympathy for him, mentioning his previous illustrious career and the fact that it was known privately that he only hung on as HUD secretary because he hoped to be appointed by Reagan to the Supreme Court. After Pierce died at the age of 78 in 2000, one friend said that taking the HUD job "was the biggest mistake that Sam Pierce ever made." Probably so. In 1990, the House Government Operations Committee wrote in its report: "At best, Secretary Pierce was less than honest and misled the subcommittee about his involvement in abuses and favoritism in the HUD funding decisions. At worst, Secretary Pierce knowingly lied and committed perjury during his testimony." Finally in 1996, to avoid being indicted by the independent counsel, Pierce signed a statement declaring that he "created an atmosphere at HUD that allowed influence-peddling to go on."

Just as Ronald Reagan created an atmosphere of neglect that allowed Samuel Pierce to thrive. HUD was not the worst of the Reagan scandals, but it was certainly one of the ugliest. As *Newsweek* wrote in 1989: "In the mix of Washington scandals HUD ranks as historically less important than the Iran-Contra and financially less costly than the [savings and loans] crisis. Yet in terms of breathtaking cynicism and hypocrisy it's hard to match. Over eight years ostensibly respectable people effectively became poverty pimps, getting rich and powerful by subverting programs intended to help the poor."

If a picture could be taken of the person most affected by the HUD scandals of the Reagan Administration, it would probably depict a homeless person on a park bench or a homeless family huddled in a shelter. These people were not homeless "by choice," as Ronald Reagan had said, but because federal programs to aid them in finding affordable housing were cut so drastically by a president who, ironically enough, is remembered by so many people as a man of enormous empathy—the Great Communicator. Yet the scandals at HUD, combined with the drastic Reagan cuts in public housing aid, turned the 1980s into the era of homelessness. There were estimates of up to 1.2 million homeless people in the United States—levels that had not been seen since the Great Depression. Disturbingly, there was a dramatic increase in the level of "family homelessness"—fathers, mothers, and their children living in cars or shelters or on the street.

All homeless "by choice?" Not likely. Forgotten by their president and exploited by the "poverty pimps," these homeless were, in a very real sense, the true legacy of the HUD scandals.

———⋆———

CHAPTER 8

Ronald Reagan and the Iran-Contra Affair:

"WE DID NOT TRADE WEAPONS OR ANYTHING ELSE FOR HOSTAGES"

———⋆———

On the evening of Thursday, November 13, 1986, Ronald Reagan sat down in a chair at his desk in the Oval Office, faced a television camera, and addressed the American people. He had been president of the United States for six years, and even those who did not like the man had to admit that his folksy and congenial manner was incredibly effective in getting his message across to the public.

Americans had chuckled when the former Hollywood actor, jousting with President Jimmy Carter in their 1980 campaign debate, genially chided the serious Georgian, "There you go again, Mr. President!" as if the two of them were leaning over a counter at the corner diner, arguing over coffee and pie. They had marveled when Reagan, seriously wounded by an assassin's bullet lodged near his heart, told his wife: "Honey, I forgot to duck!" and then exclaimed to the hovering surgeons: "I hope you're all Republicans." They had even forgiven the forgetful Ronald Reagan, the one who was prone to such misstatements as "Now we are trying to get unemployment to go up, and I think we're going to succeed."

And despite skyrocketing deficits and a stock market that was spiraling out of control, most Americans loved and—and this is especially important—trusted Ronald Reagan. So on that November evening when he looked at the camera and the country directly in the eye and said that the "rumors" they had all heard from news outlets about the Reagan Administration trading arms to Iran in return for the release of U.S. hostages in the Middle East were "wildly false," well, most people believed him. And they believed him when he said emphatically, employing his finger-wagging, schoolmaster tone: "We did not—repeat—did not trade weapons or anything else for hostages nor will we."

The only problem was that this statement was completely false and Ronald Reagan knew it. Not only that but he knew that money garnered in these shipments of arms to Iran—one of the countries that Reagan had called "an outlaw state" and "part of a new international version of Murder, Incorporated"—was being used to fund covert and illegal attacks on another outlaw state, Nicaragua, attacks that the U.S. Congress had specifically forbidden.

The American people did not know about the Nicaragua part of the equation yet, because Ronald Reagan was hoping it would not be found out. But it was found out, setting off the greatest scandal of the Reagan Administration and, arguably, one of the greatest tests of presidential power and payola in U.S. history. Yet in the end, Ronald Reagan, the Teflon President, would emerge by and large unscathed, loved, when he left office, by well over 60 percent of the population. It was quite a feat of legerdemain, and Reagan did it by playing the role he knew how to play best: He played dumb.

"THIS WAY OF FREEDOM OF OURS"

The Iran-Contra Scandal began because two seemingly disparate historical forces—the spread of Communism to Central and South Americas and the rise of radical Islam in the Middle East—collided with the presidency of Ronald Reagan.

Unlike his more moderate Republican predecessor, Gerald Ford, and certainly unlike Democrat Jimmy Carter, Ronald Reagan had been profoundly affected by the anti-Communist witch hunts of the 1940s and 1950s. During World War II, while still a matinee idol movie star for Warner Studios, he was secretly approached by the FBI to help it root out Communism in the Screen Actors Guild (of which Reagan was president). Reagan, although nominally a Democrat, took to this enthusiastically, privately providing the FBI with the names of actors he believed to be Communist sympathizers. In 1947, he testified about the Communist threat in Hollywood as a sympathetic witness in front of the House Un-American Activities Committee.

Ronald Reagan's career in movies began to wane in the 1950s, but the affable-seeming Reagan—those who knew him privately described a man with immense determination as well as a hot temper—garnered a job as the host of the popular television show, *General Electric Theater*, which brought him into the homes of millions of Americans. He parlayed that attention into a starring role as a politician, switching to the Republican Party in 1962, endorsing the conservative presidential candidacy of Barry Goldwater in 1964, and winning election as governor of California in 1967.

Thereafter, he was a force to be reckoned with on the national scene. To many Americans, during a time of civil and social unrest that coincided with the war in Vietnam, the civil rights movement, and the continuing Cold War, Reagan was an articulate symbol of an older and safer United States, a country with moral guideposts that were clearly marked. Reagan was seen as the leader of New Conservatism, a movement that was anti-big government (and big government social welfare programs), anti-taxes (which went to pay for such programs), and anti-Communist. A speech that Reagan gave while campaigning for Barry Goldwater in 1964 was cited over and over again by the New Conservatives. In it, speaking of Soviet Russia, he said, "We are at war with the most dangerous enemy that has ever faced mankind in his long climb from the swamp to the stars, and it has been said that if we lose this war, and in so doing lose this way of freedom of ours, history will record with the greatest astonishment that those who had the most to lose did the least to prevent its happening."

A SECRET DEAL FOR HOSTAGES

In the election year of 1980, America's "Misery Index" (a measurement created by a Chicago economist combining inflation plus unemployment) was at an all-time high of 22 percent (as a point of comparison, it was at 11.72 percent in 2010). As Ronald Reagan ran for president, the

AFTER BEING HELD CAPTIVE IN IRAN FOR 444 DAYS, FREED AMERICAN HOSTAGES ARRIVE
EXUBERANTLY IN GERMANY ON JANUARY 21, 1981. THEY WERE FLOWN OUT OF IRAN SHORTLY
AFTER RONALD REAGAN TOOK THE OATH OF OFFICE AS PRESIDENT OF THE UNITED STATES,
GIVING CREDENCE TO REPORTS THAT REAGAN AND HIS STAFF HAD CONSPIRED TO KEEP THEM THERE TO
ROB JIMMY CARTER OF THE CHANCE TO FREE THEM AND SAVE HIS PRESIDENCY.

ASSOCIATED PRESS

———— ★ ————

theme of his campaign was: "Are you better off today than you were four years ago?" and the answer for most people was obviously "no." Jimmy Carter had provided little in the way of a clear vision for Americans and had presided over one of the worst downturns in recent economic history.

Even worse, he seemed powerless in the face of the fact that radical Islamic students in Iran had in November 1979 taken over the U.S. embassy in Tehran and captured fifty-three U.S. hostages. The nightly news counted down each day these men and women were held in captivity, while every effort that Carter tried to take—from diplomacy to economic sanctions to a risky helicopter rescue attempt—failed miserably. Carter's approval ratings were at 23 percent, lower than Richard Nixon's during Watergate.

———★———

RONALD REAGAN, CALLED THE CONTRAS "FREEDOM FIGHTERS." AS HE WAS LATER TO SAY, THEY WERE "THE MORAL EQUIVALENT OF OUR FOUNDING FATHERS."

———★———

Thus, it wasn't hard for Ronald Reagan to step in and assure the American people that he was tough enough in matters of foreign policy, especially when it came to dealing with radical clerics and students in Iran, never to let this happen again. He was easily elected president (by an eight million popular vote margin, winning the electoral votes of all but five states and the District of Columbia).

In the summer of 1980, Jimmy Carter redoubled his efforts to bring the hostages home from Iran, secretly negotiating with the radical Islamic clerics now in control of Tehran. According to *October Surprise: American Hostages in Iran and the Election of Ronald Reagan*, a convincing and copiously detailed book by former Carter National Security Council staffer Gary Sick, Reagan's team heard about this negotiation and worked hard to stall any possible hostage release. This was done mainly through the efforts of Reagan campaign manager William Casey, who would soon become director of the Central Intelligence Agency, and George H. W. Bush, former CIA head, and now Reagan's vice presidential running mate. Using so-called "back channels," Casey met with Iranian clerics in Spain and offered them military assistance—something Iran, about to be embroiled in its ten-year war with Iraq, desperately needed—if they would halt the release of the U.S. captives until, quite literally, the moment Ronald Reagan became president of the United States. The Ayatollah Khomeini himself approved the deal.

Later, when it looked like Iran was going to negotiate with the Carter Administration, Ronald Reagan sweetened the deal by agreeing to unfreeze Iranian assets in the United States once he became president.

On January 20, 1981—Inauguration Day—the hostages were loaded aboard a plane but forced to wait on the tarmac of Tehran Airport until the very moment of Reagan's swearing in, at which point the plane took off for West Germany. Thus, Reagan was able to greet them when they arrived home, looking like the All-American hero he made himself out to be. Except, of course, that he had—when not an elected official of the United States—secretly made a deal with a hostile foreign government to secure a domestic administration's defeat.

No one knew this about Ronald Reagan at the time—in fact, he continued to deny any involvement in the hostage release even after he left office, although interestingly it was only his own personal involvement that he denied—but this willingness

when it came to circumventing the laws of the United States to achieve his own personal ends would have a direct bearing on the worst scandal of his presidency.

"THE MORAL EQUIVALENT OF OUR FOUNDING FATHERS"

At the time Ronald Reagan took office, Central America was beginning to boil over with war. In the summer of 1979 in Nicaragua, the socialist movement known as the Sandinista National Liberation Front, whose members called themselves Sandinistas, overthrew the government of dictator Anastasio Somoza and took control of the country. At first, the administration of President Jimmy Carter was willing to work with the Sandinistas and their leader, Daniel Ortega, getting U.S. Congressional approval to send more than $100 million in humanitarian aid to the war-torn country.

However, the Sandinista government began to ally itself with the United States' longtime enemy, Fidel Castro, and started to send arms and rebels into neighboring El Salvador to overthrow the junta of Jose Napoleon Duarte. Even as liberal a thinker as Jimmy Carter expressed fear that Marxist–Leninist revolutionary movements were destabilizing the region, and thus he canceled aid to Nicaragua as one of his last acts in office.

New President Ronald Reagan had been highly critical of Carter's aid to Nicaragua during the 1980 campaign, as he claimed it supported "the Marxist Sandinista takeover of Nicaragua and the Marxist attempts to destabilize El Salvador, Guatemala, and Honduras." But following his anti-Communist rhetoric, Reagan planned on doing more than simply withholding aid to the Sandinistas. Within a few short weeks of taking office, Reagan and his administration had approved $20 million in military aid to El Salvador, a fivefold increase. He also sent U.S. advisors to train Salvadoran troops and brought hundreds of Salvadoran soldiers to the United States for more advanced training.

Central America, proclaimed Jeane Kirkpatrick, Ronald Reagan's ambassador to the United Nations, was "the most important place in the world to us." But the United States found out that military aid and money were not enough to defeat ideologically motivated armies. A government army of 17,000 in El Salvador, armed with the best guns and the most expert training the United States could provide, was having a difficult time defeating a much smaller invading force of Sandinista rebels. This was an era when people drew very different lessons from the U.S. war effort in Vietnam, which had ended in disaster only five years before. Many thought the country should stay away from all foreign wars, while others, like Ronald Reagan, sought to restore the United States' lost prestige. "I've got to win one," Reagan told friends in private.

He sought to do this by fighting a secret war against the Sandinistas, an attempt to defeat them by destabilizing the Ortega regime in Nicaragua itself. By the end of 1981, he was providing $20 million to a force of irregular soldiers training in Honduras. These were the "counterrevolutionaries," as the Sandinistas called them (*contrarrevolucionarios* in Spanish), or Contras for short.

Ronald Reagan, however, called them "freedom fighters." As he was later to say, the Contras were "the moral equivalent of our Founding Fathers."

"I AM PISSED OFF"

From the beginning, the U.S. Congress was leery about the Reagan Administration forming a force of fighters on foreign soil to interfere in the internal affairs of another government. In December 1981, in order to reassure Congress, Reagan signed a presidential "finding" that the Contras existed only to hamper the flow of Sandinista arms into El Salvador. As journalist Haynes Johnson writes in his book, *Sleepwalking Through History*, "this deception of Congress was the first of a series of lies that was to move the Reagan Administration deeper and deeper into a web of secrecy."

For, despite what administration officials told key Congressmen, the Contras were really a paramilitary force run by the CIA, intent on destabilizing the government of Nicaragua itself, through actual invasion and covert actions. Congress heard rumors of what was going on and Senators Barry Goldwater and Daniel Patrick Moynihan, chairman and vice chairman of the Senate Select Committee on Intelligence, kept "tugging at the

———★———

PREVIOUS SPREAD: CONTRA FIGHTERS LEAVE THEIR JUNGLE BASE IN NICARAGUA TO FIGHT WITH SANDINISTA FORCES. DESPITE HEAVY FUNDING FROM THE UNITED STATES, THEY WERE UNABLE TO OVERTHROW THE REGIME OF DANIEL ORTEGA.
MIKE GOLDWATER/ALAMY

CIA to tell us what was going on in Central America," Moynihan later said. In 1982, after the Democrats had swept the midterm House elections, they were emboldened to pass the Boland Amendment, after its sponsor, Massachusetts Representative Edward Boland, which restricted CIA and Department of Defense operations in Nicaragua, forbidding any covert action "for the purpose of overthrowing the government of Nicaragua."

Yet in April 1984, the *Wall Street Journal* reported that the CIA, using U.S. ships manned with U.S. crews, had mined the harbors of Nicaragua, thus endangering not only Sandinista vessels, but the ships of innocent third parties. It seemed like such a reckless act—the consequences if a Soviet ship had blown up, for instance, would have been catastrophic—that Moynihan threatened to resign from his post on the intelligence committee in protest. In the meantime, Congress learned that Ronald Reagan had personally approved the mining operation. An angry Barry Goldwater wrote an aggrieved letter to CIA Director William Casey, saying, "All this past weekend, I've been trying to figure out how I can most easily tell you about the discovery of the President having approved mining of some of the harbors of Central America. It gets down to one, little, simple phrase: I am pissed off!"

"KEEP BODY AND SOUL TOGETHER"

Congressional opposition didn't stop the Reagan Administration from pursuing the same course. The minutes of a National Security Planning Group meeting from June 25, 1984, show the president, Vice President George Bush, and numerous top aides searching for other ways to sustain the covert war in Central America. They discuss trying to get third parties to fund the CIA and its paramilitary groups. Despite the fact that Secretary of State George P. Shultz warns Reagan that White House Advisor James Baker considers getting money from third parties "an impeachable offense," Vice President Bush still wonders: "How can anyone object to the U.S. encouraging third parties to provide help to the anti-Sandinistas…?"

It is clear that Ronald Reagan felt this way, too. The old Cold Warrior thought that Communism was creeping up through the Central American corridor, from whence it would enter Mexico and then the United States, supported by the Castro regime in Cuba. And he and members of his administration saw the Boland Amendment as blatant legislative encroachment on executive branch powers, a wrongful curbing of presidential prerogatives. Around this time, Reagan firmly told his National Security Advisor Robert "Bud" McFarlane, "I want you to do whatever you have to do to help these people [the Contras] keep body and soul together."

By the summer of 1984, with the last remaining funding for the Contras about to run out and Congress unlikely to vote in more, McFarlane sought about secretly for a third party to help fund the war. He met with the Saudi Arabia ambassador to the United States,

LIEUTENANT COLONEL OLIVER NORTH'S TESTIMONY BEFORE THE IRAN–CONTRA COMMITTEE
IN 1987 MADE HIM A NATIONAL FIGURE—HERO TO SOME, SCHEMER TO OTHERS. AS AN UNKNOWN MARINE
OFFICER ON THE NATIONAL SECURITY COUNCIL STAFF, NORTH WAS THE COVERT LIAISON TO CONTRA
LEADERS—THE MAN WHO SET UP THE BANK ACCOUNTS INTO WHICH MILLIONS OF DOLLARS GARNERED
FROM THE SALE OF ARMS TO IRAN WERE POURED.

ASSOCIATED PRESS

———★———

who agreed to personally donate $1 million a month to the Contras in what McFarlane later called "a humanitarian gesture." This largesse would only last until the end of the year, but it was still quite welcome. McFarlane passed this information to his deputy, Admiral John Poindexter, who in turn passed it on to a relatively unknown marine on the National Security Council Staff, Lieutenant Colonel Oliver North, who was the covert liaison to Contra leaders. With North's help, McFarlane set up a Swiss bank account for the Contras into which the Saudis would deposit $1 million every month.

After this was accomplished, McFarlane slipped Ronald Reagan a note in his daily briefing book telling him what had happened. The president, McFarlane later said, "expressed…his satisfaction and pleasure that this had occurred."

In October 1984, without knowing anything of the secret Saudi funding but to underscore its unhappiness with the Reagan Administration, Congress passed another amendment known as Boland II, which Reagan signed into law, as he had the previous amendment. It very clearly cut off all funding for the Contras or "any military or paramilitary organizations."

After the signing, Congressman Edward Boland specifically said this law "clearly ends U.S. support for the war in Nicaragua."

"REGARDLESS OF WHAT ACTION CONGRESS TAKES"

In December 1984, Deputy Director of Intelligence Robert Gates (later President Obama's secretary of defense) wrote a secret memorandum in which he argued for an expanded war in Central America, an "open" conflict that included U.S. air strikes, because of the Monroe Doctrine: "The fact is that the Western Hemisphere is the sphere of influence of the United States…If we have decided totally to abandon the Monroe Doctrine…then we ought to save political capital in Washington, acknowledge our helplessness, and stop wasting everybody's time."

However, going about the war in Central America openly was never really an option for Ronald Reagan, because he knew he would never get Congressional funding. At first, he continued with the "private donor" route. Reagan had decided unilaterally that the Boland Amendments did not apply to members of his staff, and by his staff he meant both the National Security Council and, by extension, Oliver North. Therefore, North was free to travel around the world seeking contributions from such countries as Taiwan, Israel, Saudi Arabia (which would pledge another $32 million for 1985), the People's Republic of China, South Korea, South Africa, and Brunei. All of these countries placed funds into the Contras' Swiss bank accounts.

In essence, North was extorting money from other countries in return for the implied favor of the most powerful man on earth. North collected about $10 million this way.

Reagan became personally involved in calling Honduran President Roberto Suazo Cordova, who was threatening to shut down Contras bases in his country now that Congress was not approving funding. Robert McFarlane convinced Reagan to make the call in a memo that stated: "It is imperative…that you make clear the Executive Branch's political commitment to maintaining pressure on the Sandinistas, regardless of what action Congress takes."

Reagan made the call on April 25, 1985, and wrote in his notes of the conversation that Suazo "pledged we must continue to support the friends in Nicaragua."

"A NEAT IDEA"

At the same time, the Reagan Administration turned to a highly intractable and seemingly unrelated problem: Iran. In 1984–85, the rise of radical Islamic terrorists in the Middle East continued to plague the United States. Hezbollah terrorists—a group controlled from Iran—kidnapped CIA Middle East Station Chief William Buckley and tortured him in 1984 and executed him in 1985. By the summer of 1985, seven American and British hostages were being held captive in Lebanon. In June 1985, radical Shiite terrorists had hijacked a plane in Beirut and executed a U.S. Navy diver who happened to be a passenger on board the flight.

In response to this, President Reagan told the U.S. public: "The U.S. gives terrorists no rewards, no guarantees. We make no concessions. We make no deals."

However, with CIA information that so-called "moderate Iranians" might look favorably on arms sent to the country to help in their life-and-death struggle against Iraq, Reagan authorized the National Security Council and Oliver North to deal with the Iranians. An agreement was reached and on August 2, Reagan approved the shipment of 100 U.S. "tube-launched, optically-tracked, wire command data link, guided" (TOW) anti-tank missiles to Iran. To hide the trail, these missiles would come from Israel, which would then have its stock replenished by the United States. In September, 408 more TOWs were sent to Iran, and on September 15, the Hezbollah released an American hostage, Reverend Benjamin Weir.

By November, Israel had become wary of shipping the TOWs, thinking that the secret could not be kept forever and also fearing that the United States was not replenishing Israel's TOWs quickly enough. So Oliver North took over, using his connections to ship U.S. Hawk surface-to-air missiles. Here, even the CIA began to balk, claiming that it needed presidential approval for such direct deals with Iran, and so Reagan, in December 1985, came up with a "finding" that retroactively approved the three missile transfers, thus covering everyone's trails.

He ended the finding by writing, "Because of the extreme sensitivity of these operations, in the exercise of the President's constitutional authorities, I direct the Director of the Central Intelligence Agency not to brief the Congress of the United States...."

All was going well, it seemed, and then Oliver North came up with what he later called "a neat idea." Despite the fact that the Iranians were exchanging arms for hostages, they still weren't being given the missiles free of charge. In fact, they had paid some $30 million for what would total 1,500 missiles. But only $12 million of this money reached government bank accounts. Although some of it was given to the various shady middlemen North had used to make the deals, much of it he placed in the offshore bank accounts of the Contras.

In effect, money from one "outlaw state" was being used to bring about the downfall of another. North claimed that his immediate superior, Admiral Poindexter, now National Security Council advisor, knew about this wrinkle, and it was also his impression, although he had no direct evidence, that the president knew about it as well. And how would he not have that impression, given the president's aggressive stance on the Middle East and on Nicaragua to date?

EXPOSURE

Of course, sooner rather than later, the house of cards came tumbling down. On November 3, 1986, a Lebanese newspaper called *Al-Shiraa* carried a brief item in which it claimed that the United States had secretly shipped arms, thus resulting in the release of the latest U.S. hostage, David Jacobsen. But then U.S. journalists began to investigate and further reported the news that Robert McFarlane, who had resigned as National Security Council advisor in 1985 after a personal crisis, had secretly visited the Ayatollah Khomeini bearing gifts that included a Bible personally signed by Ronald Reagan.

It was now that Ronald Reagan went on television and personally assured the American people that "we did not—repeat—did not trade weapons or anything else for hostages nor will we." He did, however, say that in the interest of creating goodwill, "modest deliveries" of "defensive weapons and spare parts" that "could easily fit into a single cargo plane" had been delivered to Iran. But there was no quid pro quo—no arms for hostages, no dealing with terrorists.

Despite his assured manner, Reagan was in trouble and his White House advisors knew it. Many thought that when the full extent of what was going on came out, Congress would seek Reagan's impeachment. Oliver North frantically began to destroy documents in his office shredder.

Finally, however, Attorney General Edwin Meese stepped in. He told Ronald Reagan that there were too many conflicting accounts of what happened flying around and that he wanted to take a weekend to collect all the stories and then present to the president a story

RONALD REAGAN HOLDS THE REPORT OF THE TOWER COMMISSION IN FEBRUARY 1987.
THE TOWER COMMISSION CLAIMED THAT THERE WAS NO PROOF REAGAN HAD PRIOR KNOWLEDGE
OF THE SCANDAL, BUT CRITICIZED HIM FOR LAX OVERSIGHT OF HIS STAFF. IN RETROSPECT, IT SEEMS
LIKELY THAT IF PRESIDENT REAGAN DID NOT KNOW ABOUT THE IRAN-CONTRA AFFAIR, IT WAS BECAUSE
HE DELIBERATELY TURNED A BLIND EYE TO IT.

TIME & LIFE PICTURES/GETTY IMAGES

————★————

of just what had happened. This was a way of telling Reagan that he would provide the president with a "best version" of events, and Reagan grabbed at it.

On Tuesday morning, November 25, 1986, Ronald Reagan and Edwin Meese met Congressional leaders at the White House. A grim-looking Reagan told the congressmen that he had just learned some startling news from Meese, and then he gestured for the attorney general to speak. Meese told the assembled that not only had arms been sold to Iran, but that funds from the sale of these arms had been diverted to help pay for Contras fighting in Nicaragua. Then both he and Reagan went on television to announce that they had "discovered" this terrible attempt to circumvent the will of Congress and the American people.

The legislative leaders and the American public were taken aback by the extent of the covert activities going on in an administration that seemed, on the surface, as American as apple pie. Instead, it had fostered the worst political scandal since Watergate.

Immediately, of course, the men around Reagan began to fall on their swords. John Poindexter resigned and Oliver North was fired, although not before both men had undertaken what North called "shredding parties" in their offices, consigning much of the records of what was now being known as Iran-Contra to papery dust.

"A CABAL OF ZEALOTS"

As with Watergate, what followed was an attempt by Congress to find out what the president knew and when he really knew it, but Ronald Reagan proved far too wily. A blue ribbon commission, headed by former U.S. Senator John Tower, was appointed by Ronald Reagan to investigate the affair, while Congress launched its own investigation, as it considered the possibility of impeachment. But as Haynes Johnson points out, "the calendar favored the president. When the investigation began, Reagan was entering the last phase of his second full term in office....By the time the congressional investigation and hearings were finished, another presidential election cycle would have begun. Thus, everyone involved in the investigation felt a need to complete the task quickly. If there was an impeachment proceeding, it would come at the very end of [Reagan's] presidential tenure."

The Tower Commission issued its report quickly, in February 1987, stating that there was no proof that Reagan had any knowledge of the scandal, but criticized him for his lack of knowledge in general as to what was going on around him in the White House. The commission's report mainly came down hard on those around Reagan, especially John Poindexter and Oliver North, but also including Bud McFarlane and William Casey.

This 1987 Herbert Block cartoon shows the popular perception of Ronald Reagan as a befuddled president who simply could not, quite, get the story straight on what he knew about Iran-Contra.

The Congressional hearings, which began following the Tower Commission report, held the United States spellbound. Ramrod straight Oliver North became a hero for many in the nation (and his beautiful assistant Fawn Hall, who had helped him do his shredding, became a heroine), while Admiral John Poindexter was admired as a straight shooter. Unfortunately, after 250 hours of highly complex testimony from May to August of 1987, most Americans were thoroughly confused on the topic of what Ronald Reagan knew and when he knew it. The consensus became that he had bumbled somewhat, allowing others to take advantage of his steadfast anti-Communist stance to break the law. In the November 1987 report issued by Congress, Reagan was assigned personal blame (although his White House had "ultimate responsibility"), but "a cabal of zealots" had "undermined the power of Congress as a co-equal branch and subverted the Constitution."

★

UNFORTUNATELY, AFTER 250 HOURS OF HIGHLY COMPLEX TESTIMONY FROM MAY TO AUGUST OF 1987, MOST AMERICANS WERE THOROUGHLY CONFUSED ON THE TOPIC OF WHAT RONALD REAGAN KNEW AND WHEN HE KNEW IT.

★

Naturally, this "cabal" would need to be prosecuted, and after the Congressional hearings, Special Prosecutor Lawrence Walsh tried mightily to bring charges against the culpable, but his task was made much harder by the fact that Congress had granted immunity to Poindexter and North, and that William Casey, who may have known more than anyone else about the affair, had died of a brain tumor just after the hearings began. Ultimately, eleven conspirators were convicted, but only CIA operative Thomas Clines actually went to jail—for falsifying income tax records. Poindexter and North were convicted, but had their convictions tossed out of court because of their Congressional immunity. Bud McFarlane was found guilty, but pardoned by new President George H. W. Bush.

Walsh published his final report on the Iran-Contra affair in 1993, seven years after the scandal became public knowledge. In it he said that both Ronald Reagan and George Bush knew of the arms-for-hostage deal and payments to the Contras, "or at least acquiesced" in the subsequent cover-up. But Iran-Contra seemed a long time ago to many Americans, the boom Clinton years were beginning, and it was all mostly forgotten.

ON NOVEMBER 20, 1980, PRESIDENT-ELECT RONALD REAGAN AND HIS WIFE NANCY VISITED PRESIDENT JIMMY CARTER AND FIRST LADY ROSALYNN CARTER AT THE WHITE HOUSE. DURING THIS SAME PERIOD, REAGAN WAS WORKING SECRETLY TO KEEP AMERICAN HOSTAGES IN IRAN UNTIL HIS INAUGURATION, SO AS TO ROB CARTER OF THE CREDIT FOR THEIR RELEASE.

ASSOCIATED PRESS

———— ★ ————

"TELL ME WHAT REALLY HAPPENED"

Ronald Reagan was to say a lot of different things about the Iran-Contra affair. In his 1990 autobiography, he wrote:

> To this day I still believe that the Iran initiative was not an effort to swap arms for hostages. But I knew that it may not look that way to some people. Unfortunately, an initiative meant to develop a relationship with moderate Iranians and get our hostages home took on a new shape I never expected and was never told about….If I could do it over again, I would bring both of them [John Poindexter and Oliver North] into the Oval Office and say, "OK, John and Ollie, level with me. Tell me what really happened and what it is that you have been hiding from me. Tell me everything." If I had done that, at least I wouldn't be sitting here writing this book still ignorant of some of the things that went on during the Iran-Contra affair.

This is an astonishing statement for a president of the United States to make. "In effect," as Haynes Johnson writes, "Reagan pleaded ignorance in front of the American people…. His reputation of *not* being in charge saved him." While it is true that, on a number of occasions, Reagan seemed to have much less knowledge than many presidents about what was going on in his administration, the complete ignorance he professed about the Iran-Contra affair—the role of the easygoing dupe whom he chose to play—rings false. His was an administration that began with an obstruction of U.S. policy that bordered on treason—keeping the American captives in Iran hostage until Reagan's political goals were achieved.

Secrecy was thus second nature to Reagan and those around him.

And not only secrecy. While so much of the attention surrounding Iran-Contra focuses on whether Reagan knew that funds were being diverted from arms sales to the Contras in Central America, the real story is the contempt Ronald Reagan showed to Congress and the letter of law in the United States. It may be debatable, just possibly, that Ronald Reagan didn't know that Oliver North was taking funds from missile sales and putting them in secret Contra bank accounts. But it is indisputable that Reagan knowingly traded arms for hostages with terrorists, against his own oft-stated beliefs—creating what even his own Secretary of State George P. Shultz called "a hostage bazaar," with more U.S. hostages quickly being taken by Hezbollah to replace the ones ransomed.

———★———

CHAPTER 9

Bill Clinton and the Selling of the White House:

"THE BEST CANDY STORE IN TOWN"

———★———

Abraham Lincoln never actually slept in the large, second-floor White House room known as the Lincoln Bedroom. Instead he used it as his private office and Cabinet meeting room, as did all the presidents between 1830 and 1902. During the Civil War, the walls of the room were covered with situation maps, and newspapers and dispatches cluttered every surface. Lincoln signed the Emancipation Proclamation there in 1863. In 1945, during Harry Truman's renovation of the White House, furniture from the Civil War era was brought in—including a replica of the rocking chair Lincoln was sitting in when he was shot at Ford's Theater by John Wilkes Booth, four chairs used by Lincoln Cabinet members, and a desk that Lincoln himself used.

While Lincoln never slept in the 8-foot by 6-foot rosewood bed that dominates the room, his son Willie did, unfortunately dying in it at the age of 11 in 1862. The room feels permeated with sorrow and history. Theodore Roosevelt and Dwight Eisenhower both claimed they had felt a strong mystical sense of Lincoln's presence. Supposedly a visiting Winston Churchill saw Lincoln's ghost. Ronald Reagan's dog Rex used to bark outside the room, refusing to enter, and Reagan's daughter Maureen said she saw mysterious apparitions there. President Bill Clinton's social secretary Capricia Marshall once told a reporter, "A high percentage of people who work here won't go in the Lincoln Bedroom."

Well, maybe the people who worked in the White House wouldn't enter the room, but there were plenty of others during the Clinton Administration who would—938 of them, to be exact, which works out to be a guest every three days or so. Although there were a host of Hollywood stars and visiting dignitaries who stayed in the room—people including Barbra Streisand, Tom Hanks, Madeleine Albright, and Neil Simon—most of the guests had names such as Frieda Furman, Roy Furman, John Garamendi, Patti Garamendi, Joe Geller, Charles Gervais, Felicia Gervais, Marie Gray, Dorothea Green, Steven Green, Fred Hochberg, and Ruth Hunter.

Recognize any of them? No reason why you should. Bill Clinton didn't know many of them either, even though they were his personal guests. These people were staying in the Lincoln Bedroom and sleeping in the enormous bed because they had money—money to give to Bill Clinton's campaign coffers in return for a brush with history.

"I FEEL YOUR PAIN"

When Bill Clinton came roaring out of Arkansas to secure the Democratic Party nomination for president in 1992, he gave hope to people for whom twelve years of Ronald Reagan and George H. W. Bush hadn't amounted to much. True, there had been an explosion of wealth in the top one percent of the U.S. population, but one in ten Americans was living on food stamps and one in eight lived below the poverty level.

Unlike Reagan and Bush, however, Bill Clinton seemed a man of the people. He had been born dirt-poor in the you-couldn't-have-named-it-better-for-a-movie town of Hope, Arkansas. His father died before he was born, his stepfather was an abusive alcoholic, and yet Clinton had raised himself up by his bootstraps to become a Rhodes Scholar, a Yale-educated lawyer, and the governor of Arkansas in 1978, when he was only 32 years old.

Clinton was six-foot-two, handsome, and empathetic. "I feel your pain" was an expression he used in talking to people about the misery in their lives, and although it became a gag line for comedians, he really seemed to mean it. Yet at the same time, he was also brilliant, a policy wonk who could recite chapter and verse on all manner of obscure issues, without once consulting a note card.

After Clinton won the 1992 election, easily besting President George Bush and third-party candidate H. Ross Perot, he became the youngest president (at age 46) since John F. Kennedy, and many seemed ready to immediately anoint him with mythic Kennedy qualities. But like JFK, Clinton turned out to have some very real flaws. There was his womanizing, to begin with. During the New Hampshire primaries, the story of his alleged relationship with Arkansas state employee Gennifer Flowers (of whom he supposedly said: "She could suck a tennis ball through a garden hose") was broken by Flowers herself to the *Star* tabloid. Just as his candidacy seemed in the tank, Clinton went on the show *60 Minutes* with his wife Hillary Rodham Clinton, apologized vaguely for having caused "pain in my marriage," and miraculously emerged relatively unscathed, coming in an unexpected second in New Hampshire and styling himself, memorably, as the "Comeback Kid."

He managed to dodge another bullet when his answer to whether he had smoked marijuana in college—he said that he did, but that he didn't inhale—was widely ridiculed (although friends from the period claim that it was literally true—try as he might, Clinton just couldn't learn to inhale). Same when he was called a draft dodger by Republicans who had already termed him "Slick Willie." So by the time Bill Clinton and Hillary and their daughter Chelsea and their cat Socks came to live in the White House, it might have seemed the worst was behind them. But, of course, it was only beginning.

"THE MEANING OF THE WORD IS"

The Clintons seemed scandal-prone. Whether because of their own behavior or because of a "vast right-wing conspiracy," as Hillary would put it, or because of a combination of both, they were assaulted by political embarrassments from nearly the moment of Clinton's inauguration. There was Travelgate, for instance, which occurred in the spring of 1993, when White House Associate Counsel William Kennedy III fired seven employees from the White House travel office for malfeasance and incompetence. An independent counsel investigation showed that Hillary Clinton was behind the firings, although she came perilously close to perjury in

THIS PHOTOGRAPH BY BRUCE WHITE CAPTURES THE SOMBER BEAUTY OF THE BED IN

THE LINCOLN BEDROOM. IT WAS PURCHASED BY MARY LINCOLN IN 1861 FOR THE WHITE HOUSE'S

PRINCIPAL GUEST ROOM. ITS MAGNIFICENT HEADBOARD IS CARVED WITH EXOTIC BIRDS, GRAPEVINES,

AND CLUSTERS OF GRAPES. LINCOLN DID NOT SLEEP IN THE BED, BUT HIS SON WILLIE,

ILL WITH WHAT WAS PROBABLY TYPHOID FEVER, DIED IN IT IN 1862.

PHOTO BY BRUCE WHITE/© WHITE HOUSE HISTORICAL ASSOCIATION

———★———

IN 1999, DEMOCRATIC FUNDRAISER JOHNNY CHUNG TESTIFIED AT A HOUSE GOVERNMENT REFORM
AND OVERSIGHT COMMITTEE HEARING ON FUNDRAISING IRREGULARITIES IN THE 1996 CLINTON–GORE
CAMPAIGN. CHUNG, WHO LATER PLEADED GUILTY TO FRAUD, ADMITTED THAT THE $50,000 HE HAD TRIED
TO DONATE TO THE CLINTON CAMPAIGN HAD COME FROM THE CHINESE MILITARY.

NY DAILY NEWS VIA GETTY IMAGES

———★———

testifying under oath that she was not. Firing the employees was her prerogative—lying about the firing was the problem. (Once again, as with at least half of all presidential scandals, the cover-up caused far more problems than the actions themselves.)

Then there was Whitewater, a long, deeply murky, ultimately inconclusive scandal that lasted throughout the eight years of the Clinton presidency, centering on a failed land deal made by the Clintons back in Arkansas and whether they had unduly used Governor Bill Clinton's influence to help shore up a friend who owned a failing bank. It was the scandal no one could understand, investigated endlessly by two special prosecutors, and although no indictments resulted, it cast a long shadow over the Clinton presidency.

Of course, the mega-scandal of all, one that led to Bill Clinton's impeachment in 1998, was the Monica Lewinsky story. Bill Clinton brought this all on himself, by returning the affections of a starstruck intern and consummating (or nearly consummating, depending on your point of view) a tawdry affair right in the Oval Office itself. There was the embarrassment of the stains on Monica's blue dress, the denials ("I did not have sex with that woman, Miss Lewinsky!"), and the parsing of words as Clinton strove to avoid telling the truth before a grand jury ("It depends on what the meaning of the word *is* is").

Clinton finally admitted in a national television address on August 18, 1998, that he had had a relationship with Lewinsky that was "not appropriate." Clinton was subsequently impeached, but acquitted of all charges, and although his personal popularity remained high, the Lewinsky affair was a major blot on his legacy and the work his administration had done.

And yet there is the sense that Clinton's relationship with Lewinsky was not a major character flaw, but the reaching out of an isolated man who felt underloved and unappreciated. And it is true that Clinton's Republican enemies—many of them, it turned out, engaged in extramarital affairs of their own—made cynical and hypocritical use of the president's indiscretion in an attempt to destroy him for political purposes.

The story of Bill Clinton's selling of the Lincoln Bedroom to rich Democratic political donors, while less publicized than the Lewinsky or Whitewater affairs, points to something possibly more disturbing—a systematic attempt to use one of the most sacred symbols of the U.S. democracy to raise millions of dollars for a partisan political cause.

"EVERYTHING I THOUGHT WAS RIGHT WAS WRONG"

The problem began with the issues preceding Bill Clinton's run for his second term in office in 1996. Scandals aside, many of Clinton's initiatives had failed during his first term. His move toward universal health care, helmed by Hillary, was shot down in defeat and he was pilloried for focusing on equality for gays in the military and signing the North American Free Trade Agreement. In 1993, Clinton Attorney General Janet Reno authorized an attack on the Waco, Texas, compound of Branch Davidian leader David Koresh, which resulted in the deaths of four federal agents and the incineration of seventy-five members of Koresh's sect, including at least twenty-five children. And on a more personal level, Paula Jones, a twenty-seven-year-old Arkansas state employee, accused Clinton of sexual harassment during a news conference in February 1994. It was one thing for candidate Clinton to be accused of sexual malfeasance, quite another when the president of the United States appeared in danger of being forced to defend himself in a tawdry court case.

The midterm elections of 1994 were a horror for Clinton—a "disaster," as Democratic pollster Stan Greenburg wrote in a memo to the president. Democrats lost eight Senate seats and with them their majority. In the House, they lost an astonishing fifty-four seats, which gave Republicans control of that legislative body for the first time in nearly forty years. Republicans, led by the incoming Speaker of the House Newt Gingrich, were gleeful. Democrats echoed the sentiments of Hillary Clinton, who told advisor Dick Morris: "I don't know which direction is up or down. Everything I thought was right was wrong."

During the next year, Bill Clinton, with the advice of Dick Morris, would move steadily to the center on U.S. issues, thus preempting the Republican Party's traditional issues and positioning himself for a presidential run in 1996. But there was still great concern among Democrats as to whether Clinton could beat a viable Republican candidate—after all, there had not been a Democrat elected to more than one term since Franklin Roosevelt.

Raising campaign money was therefore key—not just money to reelect the president, but money that could be given to the Democratic National Committee (DNC) to help in Democratic races for the House and Senate and for state governorships. "In 1995 and 1996," writes journalist John F. Harris in his book *The Survivor: Bill Clinton in the White House*, "Clinton had been a desperate man. The pursuit of campaign cash had been a matter of survival. In this urgent atmosphere, the procedures and restraints that would have saved later embarrassment came tumbling down—and all manner of unsavory figures came waltzing in."

Strange characters began to make their appearance in the White House. One of them was Johnny Chung, a Chinese-American businessman and fund-raiser whom Bill and Hillary Clinton's close advisors warned was a "hustler." Still the Clintons let him visit the White House forty-nine times (half of the visits authorized by Hillary's office). On March 9, 1995, he handed a check for $50,000 to Hillary's Chief of Staff Maggie Williams, saying in fractured English: "You take! You take!" Hillary's staffers gave the check to the

FORMER PRESIDENT BILL CLINTON AND FORMER DEMOCRATIC NATIONAL COMMITTEE
CHAIRMAN TERRY MCAULIFFE ENJOY AN NCAA BASKETBALL GAME IN MARCH 2010.
MCAULIFFE WAS CLINTON'S FUNDRAISING ADVISOR IN 1996, WHO FAMOUSLY TOLD THE PRESIDENT:
"WE NEED TO GIVE [POTENTIAL CONTRIBUTORS] MAGIC," AND WHOSE ADVICE LED TO THE USE
OF THE LINCOLN BEDROOM AS A WAY OF RAISING FUND FOR CLINTON'S RE-ELECTION.

ASSOCIATED PRESS

———★———

DNC (it turned out to be money from an executive in a Chinese aerospace firm hoping the Clinton Administration would look kindly on them). As a near-term response to the generous check, two days later Chung and six Chinese businessmen were allowed to watch Bill Clinton give his Saturday morning radio address.

Ultimately, the DNC was forced to return $360,000 that came through Chung because it was raised unlawfully from foreign sources. Chung pleaded guilty to fraud and admitted in court that $100,000 of the money donated to the DNC came from the Chinese military.

"YOU RAISE THE MOST, YOU DESERVE TO WIN"

Chung was only one of the "hustlers" who began to surround the Clintons at the time—others included Mochtar Riady and his son James, billionaire Indonesians who donated up to $500,000 to Clinton's first campaign and met with him twice in the Oval Office, urging him to establish formal relations with Vietnam and renew the most-favored-nation trading status with China. (James Riady would in 2001 plead guilty to fraud and violation of U.S. election law and pay a whopping fine of $8.6 million.)

Unseemly as all of this was, it was happening at a time when Bill Clinton felt desperate. His newest fund-raising advisor was Terry McAuliffe, the former finance chairman of the Democratic Party, an upbeat thirty-seven year old who cheered Clinton with his certainty that the president, and the Democratic Party, could win in 1996.

"You raise the most, you deserve to win," he told Clinton. He also said that he could raise $37 million for Clinton within the first six months of 1995. This would have the effect not only of throwing cold water on the Republicans, but also of discouraging any Democratic candidates who might decide to run against Clinton.

What McAuliffe wanted to do, he said, was employ the legendary Clinton charm and charisma to good advantage. He wanted Clinton to use the White House to meet and greet potential campaign contributors, to give them something to take back to their hometowns and talk about.

"We need to give 'em the magic," McAuliffe told Clinton, according to Sally Bedell Smith in her book *For Love of Politics: Bill and Hillary Clinton: The White House Years*. "[We need] to get 'em to feel good about the reelection."

This was old-fashioned politics, the kind that Bill Clinton of Hope, Arkansas, could relate to and understand. As long as there was something as concrete before him as a contributor's outstretched hand, he would know what to do. A week after their meeting, McAuliffe sent Clinton a note in which he itemized ways rich potential benefactors could be wooed with "promises of meals, rounds of golf, coffees, morning jogs, and overnights in the residence."

Clinton was clearly pleased. Writing on the back of the note, he said: "Get other names at $100,000 or more, $50,000 or more. Ready to start overnights right away."

The first thing McAuliffe did was set up numerous coffee dates or meetings in the White House, which soon became, according to Sally Bedell Smith, "assembly-line meet-and-greets for virtually anyone with a fat bank account." These were held in the Map Room on the ground floor. Within 18 months, beginning in the spring of 1995, there would be more than 100 such coffees where donors were brought together to meet the President and Mrs. Clinton, or sometimes Vice President Al Gore and his wife, Tipper. Alarmed by this, White House Legal Counsel Abner Mikva sent out a memo in late April saying that the federal criminal code specifically states:

> It shall be unlawful for any person to solicit or receive a donation of money or other thing of value in connection with a Federal, State, or local election from a person who is located in a room or building occupied in the discharge of official duties by an officer or employee of the United States.

Abner went on to say that "fund-raising events may not be held in the White House; also, no fund-raising phone calls or mail may emanate from the White House."

But he was ignored and Clinton and other members of his administration later claimed that no money was solicited at these coffee dates. Typically what would happen would be that a prospective donor would be served coffee and sweet rolls and spend about an hour with President Clinton. Then, a few days later, a representative of the DNC would call and put the bite on the donor for a campaign contribution. The indiscriminate nature of these coffees put the president into some potentially awkward and even ethically compromising positions. Once he spent an hour with a convicted New Jersey stock swindler with ties to the Gambino mob family. He had four different coffees with Roger Tamraz, a Lebanese-American businessman trying to win administration backing for a pipeline he wanted to build under the Caspian Sea. Tamraz ended up donating $300,000.

The following year, Tamraz found himself testifying in front of the U.S. Senate Governmental Affairs Committee, which was seeking information on quid pro quo fund-raising efforts in the Clinton White House. He was asked by Senator Susan Collins (R-Maine):

> Do you believe that you would have been able to have the conversations, however brief they might have been, with the President of the United States about your pipeline project, a project in which you believed deeply, without having contributed hundreds of thousands of dollars to the DNC?

THE UNREPENTANT AND BLUNT INTERNATIONAL OILMAN ROGER TAMRAZ PREPARES TO TESTIFY AT A
U.S. SENATE GOVERNMENT AFFAIRS COMMITTEE HEARING ON CAMPAIGN FINANCE IN 1997. TAMRAZ
DONATED $300,000 TO THE CLINTON CAMPAIGN IN THE FRANK EXPECTATION THAT HE WOULD RECEIVE
ADMINISTRATION BACKING FOR AN OIL PIPELINE HE WANTED TO BUILD UNDER THE CASPIAN SEA.

AFP/GETTY IMAGES

———————★———————

To which Tamraz replied: "Honestly? No."

President Clinton had listened to Tamraz on the subject of the pipeline but was noncommittal. This, to Tamraz, was a victory. As Senator Robert Bennett (R-Utah) told a reporter at the time:

> What [Tamraz] was after, as he indicated, was not a change in policy. What he was after was government neutrality on the issue of the pipeline. If the government didn't say, "we really hate this idea," then he was prepared to sell it to other people as saying that the United States has no objection to my pipeline. And he said that in his testimony: "All I want is no objection."

"DONOR MAINTENANCE"

At around the same time, the overnights began—eventually, 938 people would stay in the Lincoln Bedroom. Not all of then were potential donors—some were friends of the Clintons from back in Arkansas, some were Chelsea Clinton's classmates from her Quaker Sidwell Friends School, and some were foreign dignitaries whom the Clintons were hosting.

But the bulk of the overnight visitors were people who the Clintons wanted to donate money to the Democratic National Committee. They got the full treatment—what Clinton's staff called "donor maintenance." One such wealthy couple (who had only briefly met the Clintons) arrived at the White House to be met by the Clinton's personal aide Carolyn Huber. They were led to the solarium and sat down at 7 p.m. for a dinner of pork chops, seemingly by themselves, but then Bill Clinton walked in and sat down with them. He didn't eat dinner, or even ask them anything about themselves, but instead launched into a nearly hourlong monologue about the current arms-embargo talks in Congress.

The next day, they again had breakfast in the solarium and Clinton joined them for coffee, once again falling into a monologue about some political issue. After he left, they were pretty much given free access to go anywhere they wanted in the White House. They ran on the White House track near the driveway of the South Lawn and went swimming in the White House pool. Hillary showed up near the end of their stay and made polite conversation with them, but didn't seem terribly interested in them either.

Still the couple was so impressed that they contributed $100,000 to the DNC.

Other guests felt the same way. One such couple was Curt and Charlotte Bradbury. Bradbury was a Little Rock, Arkansas, investment banker whose bank had extended a $3.5 million line of credit to Clinton's first presidential campaign. "I would like to be in a position to think I could call on the President of the United States and give him my views," Bradbury told a reporter. He was certainly able to do this in the Lincoln Bedroom, where he and his wife were thrilled by the history that had transpired.

IN APRIL 1996, AL GORE ATTENDED A FUNDRAISER AT A BUDDHIST TEMPLE OUTSIDE OF LOS ANGELES,
WHERE $140,000 IN CAMPAIGN CONTRIBUTIONS WAS RAISED. HIS STAFF CALLED IT A "COMMUNITY
OUTREACH LUNCHEON," BUT GORE LATER HAD A LOT OF EXPLAINING TO DO ABOUT HIS APPEARANCE
THERE. WHEN ADDED TO THE CLINTON LINCOLN BEDROOM SCANDAL, IT CONTRIBUTED TO THE FEELING
THAT BOTH CLINTON AND GORE WERE ACTIVELY USING THEIR OFFICES TO HUCKSTER FOR MONEY.

ASSOCIATED PRESS

———★———

"There is a handwritten Gettysburg Address [currently a holographic version] so it's like being in a museum," Bradbury told the Center for Public Integrity, the nonprofit organization that first exposed the coffees and Lincoln Bedroom visits. "The night JFK was shot, his brother Bobby spent the night here. They say you could hear him weeping. If you don't feel like you're absorbing history, you're missing the point."

The potential benefactors certainly didn't miss another point, which was that all this history came with a price tag. According to Sally Bedell Smith, one-third of Clinton's overnight visitors made donations to the DNC totaling $10 million. And of everyone who attended the coffees or another part of the "donor maintenance" programs, 92 percent contributed a total of $26.4 million dollars to the DNC. An important thing to remember is that this was not the so-called "hard" money that the law limited to $1,000 per donor and $20,000 to a party, but unregulated "soft" money, which can be used for the purpose of "party building,"—e.g., advertising that can go all out to attack another candidate, as long as it doesn't suggest that a citizen vote for a specific candidate.

Soft money was highly important to both parties and Bill Clinton's White House became a center for collecting it.

"FAT CAT HOTEL"

All of these coffees and overnights were an open secret in Washington and during the 1996 presidential campaign came to the attention of the media. In June 1996, *Forbes* magazine wrote that the DNC was using overnight stays to detach wealthy donors from their money, and soon after that ABC picked up the story and reported it on David Brinkley's Sunday morning television show.

Immediately thereafter came the denials.

"This has become an urban myth, like the alligators in the sewers of New York," said the DNC press secretary. "It's just not true."

But in August of that same summer, the respected Center for Public Integrity released an article by Margaret Ebrahim about a letter the DNC sent to potential donors and fundraisers with a "menu" of rewards. For instance, $100,000 would get a donor two meals with President Clinton, two meals with Vice President Gore, and a chance to be on a notoriously boondoggled "foreign trade mission," with a DNC staffer to act as their personal assistant. A Democratic lobbyist said an evening in the White House was like having access to "the best candy store in town."

The Center for Public Integrity article, entitled "Fat Cat Hotel," documented the stories of numerous wealthy benefactors who donated hundreds of thousands of dollars after spending a night in the Lincoln Bedroom, in the embrace of history, and dining with Bill Clinton. One of them said with some disingenuousness: "It was really special—a thrill. I don't know exactly

THIS HERBERT BLOCK CARTOON FROM 1997 PARODIES BILL CLINTON'S FAMOUS LINE THAT HE "DIDN'T INHALE" MARIJUANA WHEN HE TRIED IT DURING HIS COLLEGE DAYS. IT SHOWS THE COMMON PERCEPTION THAT CLINTON WAS A MASTER OF THE FINE ART OF RATIONALIZING AWAY QUESTIONABLE BEHAVIOR.

★

what gets you an invitation. I don't know why I got invited, but it's a damn nice honor." Most people whom the Center attempted to interview, however, did not respond to their inquiries.

The furor of the selling of the White House built slowly. As it turned out, Bill Clinton was running against Senator Bob Dole, a less-than-formidable opponent, and ended up beating him handily, taking thirty-one states to Dole's nineteen. But once again, a Clinton term in office was to be tarnished by scandal. In early 1997, more news reports, this time focusing on the foreign taint to some of the money collected by Bill Clinton in the White House, came to the fore and editorials began appearing in major newspapers calling for Janet Reno to appoint an independent counsel to investigate. There was also a probe begun by a twenty-five-member Department of Justice task force. Clinton's "ready to start overnights right away" reply to McAuliffe's memo was released to the public, and the coffees and Lincoln overnights received even more widespread attention.

---★---

A DEMOCRATIC LOBBYIST SAID AN EVENING IN THE WHITE HOUSE WAS LIKE HAVING ACCESS TO "THE BEST CANDY STORE IN TOWN."

---★---

At the same time, Vice President Al Gore who had for years attempted, and mainly with success, to stay above Clintonian scandals, was dragged into the muck with the revelation that he had attended a luncheon the previous year at a Buddhist temple where $140,000 was raised (supposedly most of it coming from Buddhist monks and nuns!). The Democratic National Committee returned the money, but it was now revealed that Gore had made fund-raising calls from his White House office, something that was technically against the law, although some lawyers claimed that this did not apply to Clinton and Gore because, after all, they lived and worked in government buildings—where else were they to do their fund-raising?

Most people did not buy this argument, however, and most other legal authorities thought that a case might be made for a violation of the law against fund-raising on federal property. Gore tried to smooth things over by giving an ill-advised press conference in which he claimed there was no "controlling legal authority" that prohibited his calls. He repeated this phrase seven times in 24 minutes. Watching this performance on television in the Oval Office, Clinton turned aghast to an aide: "What is he saying? This is horrible, this is horrible!"

However, Bill Clinton wasn't much better when it came to explaining away the Lincoln overnights. He said the press was to blame for "one more false story we had to endure.... The Lincoln Bedroom was never sold." He claimed he had overnight guests simply because "the only time I had to visit with people in an informal way was late at night." He said that there was "never a single case where I raised money because of this practice."

Yet videotapes of some of the White House coffees show one or two donors actually reaching for checkbooks, before White House aides tell them to put them away. The DNC's own internal documents show that guests were asked for a minimum of $25,000. With caustic articles and television sketches building—the White House was being called "Motel 1600"—Clinton sent the usual cadre of staff members out to deny any wrongdoing. Lanny Davis, White House special counsel, listened as a PBS interviewer said that 938 people were a lot of "friends" to have for sleepovers. Then he replied that, in fact, "the President of the United States gets to know a lot of people. Eight hundred of those nine hundred are in categories of people from Arkansas and people who he's known for many years. A hundred or so are people who are political supporters, people who have contributed money as friends and as supporters."

He was saying that only one out of nine of the overnighters was a political contributor, when in fact the ratio was more like one out of three.

"YOU WEIGH THINGS ON VERY DIFFERENT SCALES"

In late 1997, Janet Reno finally rejected, once and for all, calls for her to name an independent counsel to investigate the White House coffees and Lincoln Bedroom overnights. She said that there simply wasn't enough evidence of wrongdoing to support such an action. Soon this particular Clinton scandal would fade away under the much longer shadow of the news about Clinton's affair with Monica Lewinsky. However, the story of the Lincoln overnights was one, even more than Monica, which caused many people to lose faith in Bill Clinton.

Journalist Robert Kittle, of the *San Diego Union-Tribune*, stated it succinctly to an interviewer:

It is simply incredibly naive for anyone to expect that a person who gives $50,000 or $100,000 after sleeping over at the White House does so for no other reason than the pleasure of sleeping at the White House and being a friend of the President's. You know, only inside the Washington beltway is this myth perpetuated that there's no connection between large campaign contributions and buying influence and buying favors. The American people don't buy it. It just won't wash, I'm sorry. It's just not believable. We understand that money is the mother's milk of politics, and unfortunately, a lot of people are very cynical about that. But the reality is that the President was using the White House in a very tawdry way as a kind of very profitable Motel 6 to raise money for the Democratic Party to help himself to get reelected.

Kittle was a journalist for a newspaper known to lean to the right and Bill Clinton probably didn't give his criticism a second thought. But Sally Bedell Smith tells a story in which Bill Clinton did react to criticism as he was preparing to leave office in January 2001. A column by a man named Douglas Eakeley, an old friend and Yale classmate of Clinton's, appeared in the local newspaper of Bernardsville, New Jersey. It began: "My wife and I stayed in the Lincoln Bedroom in 1994, before it went on sale." It then went on to describe Eakeley's aching disappointment with Clinton, because of the fund-raising scandal, the Monica Lewinsky affair, and numerous other problems. Although the Clinton Administration had been "some ride," Eakeley speculated that "I know he [Clinton] would have liked the opportunity to do it all over again, applying the lessons he learned from his mistakes."

---★---

CLINTON WAS STRANGELY BLIND TO HIS OWN SHORTCOMINGS, AND WAS ABLE TO CONVINCE HIMSELF THAT NO WRONGDOING HAD OCCURRED.

---★---

Somewhat to his surprise, Eakeley received a handwritten letter from Clinton two weeks later, on January 18, two days before he was to leave the Oval Office for good. Referring to what his old friend had said about Monica Lewinsky, Clinton wrote: "I have no quarrel with what you said about personal misconduct." But he took serious issue with any hint that he had sold the Lincoln Bedroom. "There was never a quid pro quo," Clinton wrote firmly, "and the evidence shows it." If Eakeley didn't believe that, then "you weigh things on very different scales than I do."

The use of the scales imagery summons forth Lady Justice, an ancient symbol from Roman times, blindfolded, holding up her sword and scales, and one can guess that Bill Clinton would not do well to be weighed on her impartial scales. But Clinton was strangely blind to his own shortcomings, and as can be seen in his letter to Eakeley, was able to convince himself that no wrongdoing had occurred. In this sense, he was not lying—it was his truth and he was going to stick to it.

Bill Clinton left the White House with a 68 percent approval rating, higher even than Ronald Reagan's, but he squandered it right away when news of his last-minute pardons to shady financiers broke, as well as the story that he and Hillary were walking away from the presidency with nearly $200,000 in furniture, art, and other gifts they received. The Clintons were forced to reimburse those who gave them the gifts and then they moved on, Hillary to an immensely successful career as a U.S. senator and then as secretary of state under President Obama, Bill to a distinguished post-presidency.

But the tawdriness Robert Kittle spoke of lingers, more so than with any other living president, and possibly any president in U.S. history. As President Gerald Ford once said in another context: "If Abraham Lincoln was alive today, he would roll over in his grave."

CHAPTER 10

Bill Clinton and the Pardoning of Marc Rich:

"THERE IS NO EXCUSE FOR PARDONING A FUGITIVE FROM JUSTICE"

In a city accustomed to glitzy events, the 2000 Angel Ball in New York was an especially glamorous event. Organized by Denise Rich, the multimillionaire ex-wife of the fugitive billionaire commodities trader, Marc Rich, the ball was an annual benefit for the G&P Foundation for Cancer Research, a charity the Riches founded in honor of their daughter, Gabrielle, who died of leukemia at age 27.

By 6:30 p.m. the limousines began pulling up in front of the Marriott Marquis in Times Square and some of the wealthiest, most powerful, most famous celebrities in the United States stepped quickly across the pavement and into the lobby. President Bill Clinton was honorary chairman of the event. Larry King had been lined up as master of ceremonies. Queen Noor of Jordan, Mikhail Gorbachev, and Paul McCartney—all of whom had lost a spouse to cancer—were the evening's honorees. And Michael Jackson was slated to receive a special award. For entertainment, Rich had lined up Natalie Cole, Sister Sledge, and 'N Sync.

During the awards portion of the evening, Denise Rich took the stage and invited President Clinton to join her in the spotlight. When the president reached the podium Rich presented him with a gold saxophone.

Holding the lavish gift Clinton said, "Thank you, Denise. Thank you for everything you have done to make it possible for me and Hillary to serve."

Less than two months later, on his last day in office, Clinton would grant a pardon to Marc Rich.

A CLIENT LIST OF ROGUE NATIONS

At the time he received the pardon from President Clinton, Marc Rich was on the lam, living in Switzerland, which had been his home since 1983 when a federal court indicted him on fifty-one counts of tax fraud, including evading $48 million in taxes, and doing business illegally with Iran during the notorious hostage crisis.

Marc Rich and his future wife Denise Eisenberg had both come to the United States as children, Jewish refugees from Nazi-occupied Europe. While studying at New York University, the nineteen-year-old Rich took an apprenticeship at Philipp Brothers, the largest metals and commodities firm in the world. Aggressive and ambitious, he would later start his own commodities firm. In 1977 he diversified his business by purchasing a 50 percent stake in Twentieth Century Fox studios, a business move that delighted his wife, Denise (they had married in 1966), who loved hobnobbing with Hollywood stars.

As a businessman Rich was ruthless. He pursued deals—and by extension the profits he expected to derive from them—with absolute single-mindedness, never taking into account either the ethics or the legal implications of the transaction. In 1979 Iranian militants occupied the U.S. Embassy in Tehran and took the embassy staff and

AT THE 2000 ANGEL BALL, A CHARITY EVENT, DENISE RICH, MARC RICH'S EX-WIFE, PRESENTED PRESIDENT CLINTON WITH A GOLD SAXOPHONE. IT IS BELIEVED THAT DENISE RICH, WHO IS A CLOSE FRIEND OF THE CLINTONS AND HAS DONATED GENEROUSLY TO THE CLINTON'S POLITICAL CAMPAIGNS AND THE CLINTON LIBRARY, WAS THE DRIVING FORCE BEHIND THE MARC RICH PARDON.

ASSOCIATED PRESS

———★———

employees hostage, holding them for 444 days. As part of its response to the crisis, the U.S. government declared that any U.S. corporation that did business with Iran would be liable to criminal prosecution. Rich and business partner Pincus Green quietly defied the law and continued to trade with the regime of Ayatollah Khomeini, paying for shipments of oil with rockets and automatic rifles, which weapons-hungry Iran used in its war against Iraq.

Another of Rich's clients was Libya. After Libyan terrorists blew up Pan Am Flight 103 over Lockerbie, Scotland, in 1988, the U.S. government placed an embargo on selling certain goods to Libya, including barley and soybeans. Rich sold shipments of both to the pariah nation.

Following Iraq's invasion of Kuwait in 1990, the international community placed an embargo on the importation of Iraqi oil. Yet Rich tried to cut a deal to buy oil from Iraq, in spite of the sanctions.

Between 1979 and 1990, Rich purchased oil from Nigeria—11 million tons of the stuff—and sold it to the white supremacist government of South Africa. Nigerian government officials, citing international economic sanctions against the apartheid state, objected. These objections faded away after Rich presented certain influential Nigerian officials with a "gift" of $1 million.

According to Morris "Sandy" Weinberg, who would prosecute Rich for tax fraud, in 1980 and 1981 alone Rich's company made $70 million by buying oil from one rogue nation and selling it to another.

Biographer Daniel Ammann says that before he was indicted, "Rich was almost completely unknown to the public at large, although he was already the world's largest independent oil trader and one of the richest men in America. Outside the close-knit community of commodity traders, almost no one knew his name. Up until 1981 not a single article on either Rich or his company had ever been published outside of the trade journals."

THE STEAMER TRUNK AFFAIR

In 1981 the U.S. government began assembling its case against Marc Rich. The FBI had been tipped off by two oil traders who were each serving a fourteen-month sentence in the state penitentiary in Big Spring, Texas; they hoped they could reduce their jail time by telling the feds that Marc Rich was trying to evade paying taxes by concealing massive sums in foreign companies and bank accounts. Weinberg, an attorney for the Southern District of New York, was put in charge of the team of prosecutors who eventually would file fifty-one charges against Rich.

Morris Weinberg graduated from Princeton and received his law degree from Vanderbilt University Law School and was only thirty years old when he was assigned to the Marc Rich case.

When he learned about the informants—David Ratliff and John Troland—Weinberg arranged for them to be released on furlough to see what the men knew and whether they could back it up. Ratliff and Troland took Weinberg to their office in Abilene where they produced documents that revealed Rich had diverted the $70 million he had made in 1980 and 1981 to his company in Switzerland. As Weinberg described the case to Ammann, "The man made a whole bunch of money that was illegal….He didn't want to give it up, so he had to get it out of the country some way. He devised a scheme to launder the money outside of the United States by creating…phony oil transactions."

Representing Marc Rich was Edward Bennett Williams, an attorney renowned for winning acquittals for his celebrity clients. Over the years Williams had represented the founder of the Playboy empire, Hugh Hefner, financier Robert Vesco, and crime boss Frank Costello. In his first meeting with Weinberg, Williams said that his client was prepared to pay all taxes owed to the federal government and a substantial fine. Weinberg rejected the offer. Even when Williams raised the settlement to $100 million, Weinberg refused to settle. He wanted Rich to do jail time, and the number Weinberg had in mind was twenty-five years.

In addition to Williams, Rich hired legal teams in Washington, D.C., and Switzerland, as well as experienced criminal defense attorneys such as Michael Tigar, who had defended the Chicago Seven. But the RICO Act statutes (Racketeer Influenced and Corrupt Organizations Act) threatened to make Rich's life in the United States particularly miserable: all of his assets could be frozen, and if he was convicted of an RICO violation the twenty-five year sentence Weinberg wanted was not out of the question.

As the investigation progressed, a grand jury began to subpoena documents from Marc Rich's companies and from U.S. companies that had done business with him. Rich's companies stonewalled. Judge Leonard Sand responded by fining Rich $50,000 a day until the documents were produced. Rich refused to pay. The standoff dragged on from June until August 1983, when Judge Sand invited prosecutors and members of Rich's defense team to negotiate a settlement in neutral territory—his apartment. In the small hours of the morning, Rich's lawyers agreed that he would pay $1.35 million of the $50,000-per-day fine and surrender the subpoenaed documents.

At the time the deal was made Rich was not in town, or even in the country. In June 1983 Rich, his wife Denise, and their children had fled to Switzerland. In an attempt to dodge U.S. law, in July 1983 Rich became a citizen of Israel. He had already renounced his U.S. citizenship when he became a citizen of Spain in 1982, but the U.S. State Department refused to recognize Rich's transfer of allegiance as it had never approved his Certificate of Loss of Nationality.

IN 1983, RATHER THAN FACE ACCUSATIONS THAT HE HAD FAILED TO PAY MORE THAN $48 MILLION
IN TAXES, MARC RICH FLED TO SWITZERLAND. FIFTEEN YEARS LATER, WHEN THIS PHOTO WAS TAKEN,
RICH WAS STILL LIVING IN LUXURY IN THE ALPS.

AFP/GETTY IMAGES

————★————

Four days after the agreement in Judge Sand's apartment, Weinberg received a tip that Rich's defense team would try to smuggle some of the subpoenaed documents out of the country. The informant even revealed the flight number of the Swissair jet that would carry the documents beyond the reach of the U. S. government.

Minutes before Swissair flight SR 111 was scheduled to take off from John F. Kennedy International Airport, it was stopped by government agents and New York City police officers who removed two steamer trunks full of documents from the Boeing jet's luggage compartment.

At the time the U.S. attorney for the Southern District of New York was Rudolph Giuliani, a brash, aggressive prosecutor who loved to be in the spotlight. He called his contacts in the media and displayed the steamer trunks to them in Judge Sand's courtroom. Marc Rich, who had spent years trying to remain anonymous, was becoming internationally notorious.

"WE SHUT 'EM DOWN"

A few weeks after the steamer trunk affair, Rudolph Giuliani invited the media to another press conference, this time in the library of the U.S. attorney's office. There he read out the indictment against Marc Rich and Pincus Green, which Giuliani characterized as "the largest tax evasion indictment ever." That Rich and Green and their associates had attempted to hide more than $100 million of income from the federal government was breathtaking, but Giuliani saved the most damning charge for last.

During the Iran hostage crisis, in spite of a trade embargo imposed against Iran by the U.S. government, Rich and Green had personally "negotiated from the offices of Marc Rich International in New York…the sale of approximately 6,250,000 barrels of Iranian crude oil for approximately $202,806,291."

Immediately after the indictment the U.S. government hit Rich hard. It froze all of his personal bank accounts in the United States, as well as those of his U.S. companies. His stocks and other investment accounts were likewise frozen, and the IRS informed all companies doing business with Marc Rich that the government could seize any payments they received from Rich or one of his companies.

Morris Weinberg told Daniel Ammann, "We shut 'em down completely. We shut the company down for a year. They couldn't operate in the U.S. It cost them dearly. I assume it cost them probably a billion dollars."

With his businesses collapsing around him, Rich settled with the United States, paying approximately $200 million in fines and court costs. That took care of the government's charges against Rich's businesses, but not the charges against him personally. Giuliani and

Weinberg still wanted Rich to serve a stiff prison sentence, but they could not try him until he returned to U.S. soil. And Marc Rich never returned to U.S. soil.

Yet Marc Rich was not suffering. His company in Zug, Switzerland, was unaffected by the U.S. shutdown; it is believed that in the year 2000 alone Rich's Swiss company took in $7 billion. He maintained luxurious homes in St. Moritz, Switzerland, and Marbella, Spain. He traveled aboard his personal jet. He collected works of art. His life was not hard.

"WRONGLY PROSECUTED"

In 2000, as President Bill Clinton's term of office was winding down, two men, one an American, the other an Israeli, floated the idea of seeking a presidential pardon for Marc Rich. Avner Azulay, a former officer of Israel's intelligence service, the Mossad, and a close friend and employee of Rich, teamed up with Jack Quinn, Al Gore's former chief of staff and Clinton's former White House counsel who was now representing Rich and Pincus Green, to assemble a foolproof pardon application and present it directly to President Clinton.

Going straight to the president was a bold move. The U.S. Department of Justice had a standard procedure for presidential pardons, which required applicants to submit their petition for review to a designated attorney at the Department of Justice. If the petition passed this initial examination it was submitted to the associate attorney general. If the application survived the associate attorney general's scrutiny, it was passed to the attorney general who made a recommendation to the president whether or not he should grant the pardon.

Azulay feared that if the application went through the usual channels the story would be leaked to the press, and the public outcry against Rich would scuttle any chance of a pardon.

In preparing the applications the two men divvied up the work. Quinn presented the legal argument why Rich deserved a pardon, while Azulay assembled testimonials regarding Rich's excellent character and philanthropic spirit. In his part of the application Quinn argued that Rich had been "wrongly prosecuted," and that the case should have been heard in a civil court rather than a criminal court. Azulay's portion of the application included documentation on the $100 million Rich had contributed to "charitable, cultural, and civic organizations." According to Barbara Olson, an author and former U.S. Department of Justice prosecutor, the Rich Foundation in Tel Aviv had given $5 million to Taglit-Birthright Israel, an organization that sponsors first-time trips to Israel for Jews ages 18 to 26, and $2.6 million to the Tel Aviv Museum of Art. He also was a contributor to the Israel Philharmonic Orchestra and had donated to a fund to help Ethiopian Jews immigrate to Israel. Olson noted that the Rich Foundation pledged $100,000 to the Anti-Defamation League in the United States: The organization's director, Abraham Foxman, was among those who wrote to President Clinton in support of a pardon for Marc Rich.

JACK QUINN, MARC RICH'S ATTORNEY, AND MORRIS "SANDY" WEINBERG JR. WHO PROSECUTED
RICH FOR TAX FRAUD, ARE SHOWN HERE BEING SWORN IN AS WITNESSES BEFORE
THE HOUSE COMMITTEE ON GOVERNMENT REFORM, WHICH MET IN 2001 TO INVESTIGATE
PRESIDENT CLINTON'S PARDON OF MARC RICH.

ASSOCIATED PRESS

DENISE RICH STRUCK AN IMMUNITY DEAL WITH THE U.S. DISTRICT PROSECUTOR
WHO WAS INVESTIGATING THE CLINTON PARDONS. UNDER THE TERMS OF THE DEAL,
NOTHING RICH TOLD INVESTIGATORS COULD BE USED AGAINST HER IN COURT.

AFP/GETTY IMAGES

———————★———————

Azulay also assembled a stack of personal appeals to President Clinton from Israeli Prime Minister Ehud Barak, Nobel laureate Shimon Peres, the Chairman of the U.S. Holocaust Memorial Museum Council Rabbi Irving Greenberg, the Mayor of Jerusalem (and future prime minister of Israel) Ehud Olmert, and former Director General of the Mossad Shabtai Shavit. Even King Juan Carlos of Spain urged Clinton to pardon Marc Rich.

The application was delivered to the White House on December 11, 2000, and that same day Ehud Barak phoned Clinton about Rich. "I just wanted to let you know," Barak said, "that here [in Israel] he is highly appreciated for his support of so many philanthropic institutions and funds, and that if I can, I would like to make my recommendation to consider his case." Later that same day Shimon Peres called Clinton, urging him to pardon Rich. In the next four weeks Barak would call Clinton at least two more times on Rich's behalf.

"HE OWES ME MONEY"

In the United States Marc Rich's greatest champion was his ex-wife Denise. She was a generous contributor to Democratic Party candidates. Between 1992 and 2000 she had written checks totaling $1.1 million for the campaigns of Senators Teddy Kennedy of Massachusetts, Barbara Boxer of California, Chuck Schumer of New York, and Barbara Mikulski of Maryland. In 2000 Denise Rich had donated $450,000 to the Clinton Presidential Library, then under construction in Little Rock, Arkansas, and $100,000 to the Democratic National Committee. She contributed $109,000 to Hillary Clinton's senatorial campaign. She wrote a check for $10,000 for Bill Clinton's legal defense fund. She paid the $40,000 tab for the entertainment at Hillary's birthday party in 2000. As the Clintons prepared to move out of the White House, Denise gave them $7,000 worth of furniture for their new home. And during the debacle following the presidential election of 2000, Denise contributed $25,000 to the Gore/Lieberman Recount Committee.

President Clinton described Denise as one of his "closest friends." During the Monica Lewinsky scandal, when Clinton tried to keep a low profile, one of the few invitations he accepted was a gala at Denise's New York penthouse overlooking Fifth Avenue.

According to Rich's biographer Daniel Ammann, initially Denise Rich was not willing to help her ex-husband in his pardon appeal. Several years earlier he had promised to contribute $40 million to the Riches' foundation for cancer research, but he never sent the check. Nonetheless, given Denise's close ties to the Clintons, it was crucial to the Rich pardon team to have her on their side. If she decided to use her influence against her ex-husband's petition the result very likely would be disastrous. So Azulay flew from

Switzerland to New York to win Denise over. Their initial meeting did not go well: Denise flat-out refused to support Marc's petition for a pardon. And she told Azulay her reasons. "He screwed me," she said. "He owes me money."

Azulay realized that they could not afford to have an angry, hostile, vindictive Denise Rich opposing them, so he volunteered to act as a mediator, arranging a settlement by which Rich and Green agreed to make an annual gift to the foundation of $500,000 each. More or less satisfied by the contribution and feeling pressured by her children to help their father, Denise promised to use her influence with President Clinton to win a pardon for Rich.

On December 6 Denise Rich sent Clinton a personal appeal to pardon her ex-husband. On December 20, at a dinner honoring winners of the National Medal of Arts and the National Humanities Medal, Denise had a quiet moment with Clinton to make her case in person. Barbara Olson said that at the time the president was chatting with Barbra Streisand—how Denise managed to separate Clinton from "one of his most vocal—and clinging—Hollywood supporters…must have been a sight to see."

But Azulay was not the only member of the team who recognized the importance of appealing to the president's emotions in the pardon petition. Jack Quinn knew that President Clinton believed he had been the victim of overzealous prosecutors and that he would never forgive Kenneth Starr's investigation into the Monica Lewinsky and Paula Jones scandals, which led to Clinton's humiliating impeachment and trial before the U.S. Senate. In the pardon application Quinn wrote as if he were addressing Clinton personally; in describing the Rich case he used phrases such as "grossly overprosecuted," which Quinn believed would strike a deep emotional chord with the president.

TAKING THE FIFTH

In January 2001 Denise Rich was at her home in Aspen, visiting with Beth Dozoretz, a former chief fund-raiser of the Democratic National Committee and a prominent FOB (Friend of Bill). Between 1994 and 1999 she brought $5 million in contributions. Dozoretz was famous for having raised $1 million in a single evening at a party held in her Washington home. More recently, in May 2000 Dozoretz had personally contributed $1 million to the fund for the Clinton Library.

Beth Dozoretz and her husband Ron had hosted fund-raising events for Democratic candidates since 1993, and Bill and Hillary Clinton were frequent attendees at these posh events. The Dozoretzes and the Clintons became close friends and the two couples often vacationed together. In 1998 the Dozoretzes asked the president to be godfather to their daughter. The Dozoretzes remained loyal to President Clinton during the Monica Lewinsky scandal, and Beth raised money for the president's legal defense fund.

In November 2000 Jack Quinn, also a friend of Beth Dozoretz, told her that he would be filing a pardon application for Marc Rich and asked Dozoretz "to help me be sure that the president himself was aware of the fact that the application had been filed with the White House Counsel's office."

Dozoretz became an active ally of Quinn. In 2001 in testimony before the House Committee on Government Reform, which investigated the Marc Rich pardon, Quinn estimated that in December 2000 and January 2001 he and Dozoretz spoke between five and ten times about the pardon. When she learned that the president had granted Rich a pardon, Dozoretz was in Beverly Hills with her husband; she called the White House to thank President Clinton.

The degree of Dozoretz's involvement in securing the pardon, how often she was in touch with Clinton, and what they talked about is unknown, because when Beth Dozoretz was called before the Congressional investigating committee, she exercised her right to protect herself against self-incrimination and took the Fifth Amendment. When she appeared before the committee, Denise Rich would do the same.

THE FAX

Early in the evening of January 19, 2001, President Clinton met with his White House staff in the Oval Office to discuss the final pardons. To his staff's surprise, he brought up the name of Marc Rich. The staff had thought the Rich pardon had been scratched, but Clinton told of yet another phone call he had received that afternoon from Israeli Prime Minister Ehud Barak who once again asked the president to consider a pardon for Rich.

White House Counsel Beth Nolan, Deputy White House Counsel Bruce Lindsey, White House lawyer Meredith Cabe, and Associate Counsel Eric Angel all declared themselves to be against granting Rich a pardon; they based their opposition on Rich's flight from justice. At the end of the discussion, Clinton called Jack Quinn. In a conversation that lasted about twenty minutes, the president expressed his willingness to grant a pardon, but only on the condition that within an hour he receive by fax a letter from Quinn stating that Rich and Green understood that their pardons did not apply to civil penalties. Quinn agreed, and had one of his attorneys write and fax the letter to Clinton. It read, in part, "My clients, Marc Rich and Pincus Green, waive any and all defenses which could be raised to the lawful imposition of civil fines or penalties in connection with the actions and transactions alleged against them pending in the Southern District of New York."

After the phone conversation with Quinn, Clinton informed Bruce Lindsey and Beth Nolan of his decision to pardon Rich and Green.

The pardon of Marc Rich caused a public outcry. *New York Times* columnist William Safire denounced it as "the most flagrant abuse of the presidential pardon in U.S. history." The *National Review* damned the pardon as "one of the most disgraceful chapters in the history of the Justice Department. Not the *modern* history, the *entire* history."

CNN ONCE DESCRIBED BETH DOZORETZ, ONE OF THE DEMOCRATIC PARTY'S MOST ENERGETIC
FUNDRAISERS, AS THE "DOYENNE OF THE DOLLARS." SHE ALSO BECAME A VERY CLOSE FRIEND OF
THE CLINTONS. DOZORETZ USED HER FRIENDSHIP WITH THE PRESIDENT TO LOBBY FOR A PARDON FOR
MARC RICH, AND WHEN IT WAS GRANTED, SHE CALLED THE WHITE HOUSE TO THANK THE PRESIDENT.
DOZORETZ IS SHOWN HERE WITH HER ATTORNEY, THOMAS GREEN BEFORE THE HOUSE GOVERNMENT
REFORM COMMITTEE. ASKED ABOUT HER INVOLVEMENT IN PRESIDENT CLINTON'S LAST-MINUTE PARDON
OF MARC RICH, DOZORETZ TOOK THE FIFTH AMENDMENT.

ROLL CALL/GETTY IMAGES

———————★———————

The *Washington Post* asked, "What conceivable justification could there be for former president Clinton, on his last morning in office, to have pardoned fugitive financiers Marc Rich and Pincus Green?"

Former President Jimmy Carter, speaking at Georgia Southwestern State University, said, "I think President Clinton made one of his most serious mistakes in the way he handled the pardon situation in the last few hours he was in office.... I don't think there is any doubt that some of the factors in his pardon [of Marc Rich] were attributable to his large gifts. In my opinion, that was disgraceful."

———★———

THE PARDON OF MARC RICH CAUSED A PUBLIC OUTCRY. *NEW YORK TIMES* COLUMNIST WILLIAM SAFIRE DENOUNCED IT AS "THE MOST FLAGRANT ABUSE OF THE PRESIDENTIAL PARDON IN U.S. HISTORY."

———★———

When an aide brought word of the pardon to Rudolph Giuliani, who had prosecuted Rich, Giuliani told his aide that he was confused, it was probably Michael Milken who had been pardoned. The aide went back, confirmed the information, and returned to Giuliani. "Impossible," Giuliani declared. "The president would never pardon a fugitive, especially Marc Rich. It cannot have happened."

Amid the outcry Clinton published an op-ed piece in the *New York Times* on February 18, 2001, entitled "My Reasons for the Pardons." It was a detailed, lawyerly defense, and he concluded by declaring that "foreign policy considerations and the legal arguments" persuaded him to grant Rich and Green pardons. But Clinton did not stop there. "The suggestion that I granted the pardons because Mr. Rich's former wife, Denise, made political contributions and contributed to the Clinton Library Foundation is utterly false," he wrote. "There was absolutely no quid pro quo."

Every member of Clinton's own party, individuals who stood by him during all the scandals that plagued the Clinton White House, and defended him during the impeachment and Senate trial, let it be known what they thought of the Rich pardon and of the man who gave it to him. New York Senator Charles Schumer, a prominent Democrat, when asked whether former President Clinton's op-ed piece was convincing, replied, "No. To me there is no excuse for pardoning a fugitive from justice. You can't let somebody opt out of the system by running away, and opt into the system by being pardoned. Doesn't matter how weak the case might have been, doesn't matter how much charitable work the man did after he fled the country. He should be tried by the rules and play by the rules."

Another prominent Democrat, Senator Pat Leahy of Vermont, told syndicated columnist E. J. Dionne, "It was a terrible pardon. It was inexcusable. It was outrageous....Here was a man who was involved in a huge swindle and has shown absolutely no remorse."

In Washington, D.C., a street vendor named Avdal A. Dosky made a living photographing tourists as they stood beside life-sized cardboard cutouts of various U.S. presidents. After the pardon scandal, tourists who asked to be photographed with the Clinton cutout dropped to almost nil. Dosky removed Clinton from his lineup. As R. Emmett Tyrrell put it in his book, *The Clinton Crack-Up*, "Some corporations might still be willing to fork over $100,000 to hear the disgraced president talk, but tourists would not give Mr. Dosky $6 to be seen with Clinton in public."

Ultimately, the fallout from Pardongate, as it was known at the time, was short-lived. The aftermath of the Bush-Gore recount dominated the news, distracting the country from the Marc Rich pardon. Bill Clinton went on to create a new persona for himself as a bipartisan humanitarian, working with former President George H. W. Bush to funnel donations to rebuild the Gulf Coast after Hurricane Katrina, and then working with former President George W. Bush to bring relief to Haiti after the earthquake of 2010. Nonetheless, there is reason to believe that Clinton has lost his clout among Democrats, exhibit A being his wife's failure to win the party's nomination for president in 2008.

Marc Rich never returned to the United States. Switzerland remains his primary country of residence, although he now lives in a villa on the shores of Lake Lucerne. He is still active with charitable causes in Israel, including Bar-Ilan University and the Chaim Sheba Medical Center outside Tel Aviv. In 2006, *Forbes* magazine listed Rich as the 242nd wealthiest American, with an estimated net worth of $1.5 billion.

---⭐---

CHAPTER II

George W. Bush, Dick Cheney, and Halliburton:

"DEEP IN THE HEART OF THE WHITE HOUSE—AND IRAQ"

---⭐---

Texas has always prided itself on being big, in terms of size—it is nearly 262,000 square miles—and economic clout. It has more than 14,000 square miles of railroad tracks and is a nexus of the trucking industry, especially since the 1992 North American Free Trade Agreement (NAFTA) made the state's borders with Mexico a huge asset. The port of Houston is the sixth largest port in the world, bringing in imports (especially oil) from all over the world.

Some of the United States' largest companies are headquartered in Texas, including three of the country's seven biggest airlines. The amount of money in the state makes it a major political power. For years it has dominated the U.S. Congress, with Texas politicians receiving plum committee jobs. Thus empowered, they can do right by their districts and the rich businessmen who sent them to Capitol Hill in the first place. According to Robert Bryce, author of *Cronies: Oil, the Bushes and the Rise of Texas, America's Superstate*, former Texas Senator Phil Gramm used to brag: "I'm carrying so much pork, I'm beginning to get trichinosis."

Texas also has had, as it turns out, a cozy relationship with the executive branch of the U.S. government. In the forty-four years between 1960 and 2004, twenty-four U.S. presidents or vice presidents have been from Texas—the vice presidents picked mainly as ticket balancers by Northeasterners concerned about the perils of ignoring the Lone Star State. This practice started well before 1960, in fact, when "Cactus Jack" Garner became Franklin Delano Roosevelt's vice president—at least until Roosevelt dumped him for his habit of "winning" amounts as high as $200,000 from rich Texas oilmen while playing poker.

But at no time has Texas ever had a cozier relationship with the White House than during the administration of George W. Bush. Of course, Bush is from Texas, and his father before him (while not actually *from* Texas) adopted the Lone Star State as his second home, so it is natural that Texas influence might be big in his administration. But, more than that, George Bush's Vice President Dick Cheney and Cheney's notoriously close and, some would say, corrupting relationship with a company called Halliburton symbolizes much that went wrong in the Oval Office from the years 2000–08.

"A FAMILY BUSINESS"

Halliburton is the world's second largest oil field services firm operating in more than seventy countries. From meager beginnings in the Texas hill country of the 1920s, it has grown to a monolith with more than $18 billion in revenue per year. The company's main line of work is providing technical products and services for petroleum and natural gas exploration and production, but through its subsidiary Kellogg, Brown & Root (KBR) it also provides construction as well as logistics support for other large firms, but in particular for the U.S. military. Actually KBR should be classified as a former subsidiary of Halliburton, because the company divested itself of KBR in 2007 amid a great deal of controversy. However, during the years when it worked hand in glove with the Bush Administration, Halliburton/ KBR garnered highly lucrative contracts.

How lucrative? Through its former CEO and Bush Vice President Dick Cheney, Halliburton received federal contracts worth $7 billion to rebuild Iraq's oil fields after the U.S. attacks began in March 2003. Under a 10-year contract with the Pentagon called the Logistics Civilian Augmentation Program (LOGCAP), KBR itself has received more than $25 billion (beginning in 2001) to supply U.S. troops in combat situations with food, shelter, and comfort. The huge bases built in Kuwait and Iraq established at the beginning of the Iraq War are not staffed by soldiers, but by KBR employees, most of them East Asians making substandard wages. This was undoubtedly beneficial to the American military. No longer did U.S. soldiers pull KP duty as of old, peeling potatoes and scrubbing mess tents. Without the massive numbers supplied by the old draft, the military simply doesn't have the personnel to perform these tasks.

KBR frees soldiers to fight wars, something they are trained to do. In the meantime, it serves meals (720 million by 2008, the company estimates in a press release), provides water (12 billion gallons), and staffs "mini malls" within rear area bases where U.S. soldiers can get everything from lattes to Big Macs.

There is no reason why U.S. fighting men and women should not have as many comforts as possible before going back out to face hardship and danger. The problem comes when one begins to examine the close relationship of Halliburton/KBR to the Bush White House. Halliburton received its lucrative contracts shortly after 9/11 in a "no-bids" situation, atypical of the federal government's mandated way of doing business, which is to collect any number of bids from different contractors. Also the Halliburton contract was known in government jargon as a "cost-plus-award-fee, indefinite-delivery, indefinite-quantity service."

Even the uninitiated can glean from this gobbledygook that Halliburton's contract was vague and open-ended. The key phrase is "cost-plus," which means that Halliburton's profit was a fixed percentage of what it cost to do business. Therefore, hypothetically speaking, if it had cost Halliburton $4 to serve one soldier one meal, and the plus factor is 10 percent, then it made a profit of 40 cents per meal.

It doesn't take a genius to figure out that the more Halliburton's services cost, the more money it made.

The people who were so pivotal in awarding Halliburton a no-bid sweetheart deal worth billions were, of course, Vice President Dick Cheney and President George W. Bush. Cheney resigned as CEO of Halliburton when he became vice president and was immediately given a retirement package worth $33.7 million, which was to be paid out in installments over a period of years. He also retained unexercised stock options.

And George W. Bush's committee to reelect the president received well over $1 million from Halliburton in 2004. A conflict of interest? Many people think so. "The Bush-Cheney team has turned the United States into a family business," wrote Harvey Wasserman, author of *The Last Energy War*, in 2003. "Have they no grace, no shame, no common sense?"

"I HAVE SOME MONEY"

To be fair, when it comes to Halliburton, it is not just Texan Republican politicos without grace, shame, or common sense—Texan Democrats, namely Lyndon Baines Johnson, have been just as bad.

In 1919, George Brown and Herman Brown, two brothers from central Texas, started a construction business they called Brown & Root (the name Root came from their brother-in-law, who invested money in the business). They got a contract building roads through rural Texas, but continued to struggle (even turning for a brief time to raising pigs) before they understood that the way to get ahead in Texas was to grease the palms of politicians. They were particularly good at the art of the low bid—underbidding everyone else to get a public project, but then increasing costs during construction so that they would make a good deal more money than their initial bid.

In 1937, when the Brown brothers heard that a young man named Lyndon Johnson was running for Congress, they sat down with him at dinner and promised him backing and financial support in return for his promise to award them a federal dam-building project if elected. He won the election and they won the bid to build the Marshall Ford Dam on the lower Colorado River, making a profit of $1.5 million, according to Johnson's biographer Robert Caro, more than they'd made in twenty years of business. As World War II began, more federal contracts followed—a shipyard in Houston, the Naval Air Station in Corpus Christi (Brown & Root bid $24 million to build the latter; it ended up costing $125 million).

And it was all, as one politician said, because George and Herman were "friends of Lyndon." In return, George and Herman contributed what one biographer has called literally "bags of cash, envelopes stuffed with hundred dollar bills" to LBJ's unsuccessful Senate run in 1941 and they also helped him out enormously during his successful Senate bid in 1948—more hundreds, and this time company airplanes to ferry him around the state as he campaigned.

By the time Lyndon Johnson made it to the White House, as JFK's ticket-balancing vice president, and then as president after the Kennedy assassination in November 1963, Brown & Root were firmly established in the executive branch. Telephone conversations recorded between Lyndon Johnson and George Brown in 1960 bear this out: "I have some money that I want to know what to do with," Brown is heard telling Johnson. "I was wondering…just who should be getting it."

This cartoon portraying Dick Cheney as a warrior fighting for Halliburton, Inc. captures the cozy relationship Cheney had with the company. Before becoming George W. Bush's vice-president, he was Halliburton's CEO and instrumental in earning Halliburton billions during the Bush Administration.

Library of Congress

———— ★ ————

"BURN & LOOT"

Around the same time as the Brown Brothers were beginning their business, oil was booming in Texas and a young man named Erle Palmer Halliburton was seeking a way to profit from the black gold spouting out of the ground. He wasn't a driller, but he had learned the technique of oil well cementing, a way to lessen the possibility of underground explosions by pumping wet cement slurry into the gap between the wall of the hole and the oil pipe itself.

Halliburton's company grew over the years and branched out into other areas, becoming immensely profitable during the war, so much so that in the 1950s, Erle Halliburton was one of the ten richest people in the United States. In 1962, after Herman Brown died, Halliburton acquired Brown & Root. Within a few short years, the Vietnam War would begin in earnest, with Lyndon Johnson committing hundreds of thousands of U.S. troops to what would become his, and his country's, quagmire. Vietnam did not have the infrastructure to support these troops—and, naturally, Lyndon Johnson turned to his old friends, Brown & Root, to build it for him, with sweetheart government deals worth, in the end, $1.9 billion.

The company became known by cynics as "Burn & Loot," because of the swathes of destruction its bulldozers laid over the countryside and because of its obvious war profiteering. One young Republican congressman in particular—his name just happened to be Donald Rumsfeld—was enraged. He told Congress that the LBJ Administration had signed contracts that were "illegal by statute." He wanted an investigation into the "thirty-year association—personal and political—between LBJ as congressman, senator, vice president and president" and George Brown. Rumsfeld was especially upset because the government's General Accounting Office (GAO) had discovered that Halliburton had essentially "lost accounting control" of about $120 million—the money had simply vanished from the books.

No matter how much Rumsfeld complained, no investigation was ever launched into Lyndon Johnson's relationship with Halliburton or Brown & Root. Which, from the point of view of Rumsfeld's later career, would turn out to be quite a good thing.

THE RISE OF RUMSFELD AND CHENEY

In 1968, Donald Rumsfeld was offered a chance under President Richard Nixon to run the Office of Economic Opportunity (OEO) and he resigned from his Congressional position to do so. The OEO was a part of Lyndon Johnson's War on Poverty and was supposed to provide grants for community-based programs, but under Rumsfeld's tenure nearly the opposite occurred—with Nixon's approval Rumsfeld used the office to choke off aid to any program that contained so-called radicals who were against the Vietnam War, of which there were many.

A Saudi investor walks by the Halliburton display stand during a regional energy conference in Saudi Arabia in 2007. Halliburton had become so entrenched in the Middle East by this time that CEO David Lezar announced that he was moving the company's headquarters to Dubai.

AFP/Getty Images

———— ★ ————

Needing a liaison with Congress, Rumsfeld hired a twenty-nine-year-old Nebraskan named Richard Cheney, which was the beginning of a long and beautiful relationship. Cheney followed Rumsfeld to a new agency called the Cost of Living Council whose job was to impose wage and price controls to help stem inflation. Both men believed in a free market and abhorred government controls, but they did their job well and were rewarded. After Nixon resigned, Rumsfeld went on to become Gerald Ford's White House chief of staff and brought Cheney along as a special consultant.

★

WHAT IN FACT HALLIBURTON WAS REALLY BUYING WAS CHENEY'S ACCESS—ACCESS TO LUCRATIVE DEFENSE CONTRACTS AND ACCESS TO THE POWERFUL TEXAS DYNASTY OF THE BUSHES.

★

When Jimmy Carter defeated Ford in 1976, both men were out of a job, but with valuable experience and connections. Cheney moved back to Wyoming, where he had made his home since getting out of college, and became a U. S. congressman, while Donald Rumsfeld made millions working as CEO of Searle Pharmaceuticals. Rumsfeld kept his hand in politics, taking jobs and becoming a special envoy to Iraq for Ronald Reagan. Dick Cheney rose in the House of Representatives during the 1980s to become minority whip and, importantly, was the ranking Republican on the Congressional committee that investigated the Iran-Contra scandal. The minority report that Cheney helped prepare at that time indicated that he thought that Congress was trying to usurp President Ronald Reagan's prerogatives on national security and foreign policy for "hysterical" political purposes. This made Cheney even more popular in Republican circles—and when George H.W. Bush took over as president in 1988, Cheney became his secretary of defense.

In the meantime, he became friends and fishing buddies with Thomas Cruikshank, the soon-to-be retiring chief executive officer (CEO) of Halliburton. Halliburton had grown even richer in the years following the Vietnam War, gaining lucrative government contracts in Kuwait, in the wake of the first Iraq War, and later on in Kosovo. It would acquire a competitor, Kellogg Industries, which it merged with Brown & Root to form Kellogg, Brown & Root (KBR) in 1998. After George H. W. Bush was voted out of office in 1992 and the years of the Clinton Administration began, Dick Cheney was casting around for a job when Cruikshank, in 1995, decided to offer him the post of CEO of Halliburton.

On some levels, this was an odd choice, because Cheney had never worked for a private corporation in his life. Cruikshank tried to explain the decision by saying that "a lot of the things that [Cheney] was overseeing as secretary of defense would be similar to the things he would be overseeing at Halliburton. Long-range planning. Logistics planning. Budgeting. Personnel management. Technology management."

Perhaps. But what in fact Halliburton was really buying was Cheney's access—access to lucrative defense contracts and access to the powerful Texas dynasty of the Bushes.

THE KINDNESS OF RICH MEN

When George W. Bush ran for president in 2000, it was almost entirely because of the influence and power of his father, George Herbert Walker Bush. The senior Bush was a New England preppie who had successfully transplanted himself to Texas, gotten rich via the oil business, and parlayed his web of connections into the presidency. His son George had nothing of New England about him, but was a Texan through and through, first a hard-drinking, hard-cussing one who once called a *Wall Street Journal* columnist (in the presence of the man's wife and young child) a "fucking son of a bitch" and then he became an abstemious, born-again Christian.

But one thing that was constant throughout George W. Bush's life pre-White House were his business failures. He failed at oil exploration. His Arbusto Energy/Bush Oil Exploration Company ("Arbusto" means "Bush" in Spanish) lost millions, as did another oil company, Spectrum 7. Yet he sat on the board of successful companies like Harken Energy Corporation and Caterair (an airlines catering company) doing little but telling off-color jokes. Richard Cohen, an investigative reporter for the *Washington Post*, wrote: "Bush's entire business career was built on little more than the kindness rich men often bestow on the children of powerful politicians." In his only successful business venture, his ownership of the Texas Rangers baseball team, Bush received a sweetheart deal from the state of Texas, after the city of Arlington and the state put up most of the money for a new stadium. This included condemning the land around the stadium so Bush and his group could develop it.

By the time Bush ran for president, it was pretty well accepted that, as the conservative *American Spectator* magazine put it, "his rise in business coincides with his father's rise to the highest level of government." When George W. Bush ran for president in 2000, his father knew that the public perception of his son was that of a callow, inexperienced leader. Therefore, he urged George to name his former secretary of defense, Dick Cheney, as his vice presidential candidate. This would provide Bush fils with the foreign policy seasoning he appeared to need.

Cheney, of course, was the CEO and chairman of the board of Halliburton and would remain so until August 2000, when he was nominated for vice president at the Republican National Convention. Cheney had done well for Halliburton since being named to lead the company in 1995, giving it "a level of access [to government contracts] that no one else in the oil sector could duplicate," as one senior Halliburton executive has said. Cheney led Halliburton to find oil all over the world, doing business with Iran, Iraq, Saudi Arabia, and Azerbaijan. Interestingly enough, Halliburton under Cheney's watch did a great deal of oil business with none other than Saddam Hussein. Cheney also befriended the notorious dictator of Azerbaijan, Heydar Aliyev, whose civil rights abuses against his country's Armenian minority were enough to get the United States under Clinton to declare an aid embargo to the country.

However, there had been certain problems for Halliburton during Cheney's tenure as CEO, problems that showed that Halliburton/KBR was continuing with the same kind of business practices that had been a part of its corporate culture going all the way back to its Texas oil days. The General Accounting Office (GAO) showed that, while working for the U.S. Army in the Balkans, KBR had charged the U.S. taxpayers $86 for sheets of plywood worth $14. A few years later, the GAO declared that Halliburton had incurred massive cost overruns in Kosovo.

POLITICAL FAVORS

When Cheney left Halliburton in August to become George W. Bush's running mate, it was unexpected, because the nomination process had taken place in great secrecy. Instead of being upset, Halliburton decided that Cheney was not "resigning"—he was taking "early retirement." The company gave Cheney his multimillion dollar golden parachute, which he lied about to reporters during the campaign. (Once he became vice president, he also lied about the fact that Halliburton continued to pay him as much as $200,000 a year in deferred compensation.) In fact, Halliburton also provided an airplane the Bush campaign used during the Florida recount after the extremely close election of November of that year.

This was the smartest move Halliburton could possibly have made—it wasn't losing a CEO, it was gaining a president. When George W. Bush became president, Halliburton's power grew exponentially. Halliburton had for years kept lobbying offices in Washington, D.C., on 15th Street between L and M avenues, right in the heart of the so-called "Golden Triangle" business district where many big firms kept their own lobbyists. But after Bush's election, according to Pratap Chatterjee, an investigative journalist and author of *Halliburton's Army*, Halliburton's lobbying budget plummeted from $600,000 to $300,000, except when Congress was investigating Halliburton in 2004.

Why the sudden plummet? Because Halliburton simply didn't need lobbyists as much any more—the vice president of the United States was doing all of its lobbying for the company, and with the most powerful figure in the United States: President George Bush.

PRESIDENT GEORGE W. BUSH APPEARS AT A JANUARY 2005 PRESS CONFERENCE, WITH VICE PRESIDENT
DICK CHENEY TO HIS LEFT AND DEFENSE SECRETARY DONALD H. RUMSFELD TO HIS RIGHT. RUMSFELD
AND CHENEY, TWO PRIMARY ARCHITECTS OF THE IRAQ WAR AND HALLIBURTON'S PART IN IT, HAD A
RELATIONSHIP GOING BACK TO 1968, WHEN RUMSFELD HIRED CHENEY TO SERVE UNDER HIM AT RICHARD
NIXON'S OFFICE OF ECONOMIC OPPORTUNITY.

ASSOCIATED PRESS

———★———

NADER SULTAN, LEFT, CHAIRMAN OF IKARUS PETROLEUM INDUSTRIES, AND RAY HUNT, CHAIRMAN AND
CEO OF HUNT CONSOLIDATED INDUSTRIES, ATTEND A CONFERENCE IN KUWAIT CITY IN 2010. AS WELL
AS BEING CEO OF HIS OWN OIL COMPANY, HUNT WAS ON THE BOARD OF HALLIBURTON, INC., AND ALSO
APPOINTED BY BUSH TO THE PRESIDENT'S FOREIGN INTELLIGENCE ADVISORY BOARD, WHICH ADVISES THE
PRESIDENT ON THE PERFORMANCE OF THE UNITED STATES' VARIOUS INTELLIGENCE AGENCIES.

AFP/GETTY IMAGES

———— ★ ————

And Dick Cheney and Halliburton had another powerful figure on their side—none other then Donald Rumsfeld, who had left the private sector and now become Bush's secretary of defense, the job that Dick Cheney had once held. "Rummy," as he was known, was determined to clean house at the Department of Defense (DOD). He claimed that the DOD was wasting as much as $3 billion a year by not outsourcing such tasks as cutting checks for its employees, running warehouses, and collecting garbage. Rumsfeld, like Cheney, was a believer in outsourcing—and, steered by Cheney, most of the Pentagon outsourcing went to Halliburton.

Halliburton and DOD fit together nicely, in part because so many retired army generals and navy admirals had gone to work for Halliburton or KBR. Admiral Joseph Lopez became head of KBR, while General Charles Dominy retired from the army after decades of service to become Halliburton's chief lobbyist. This type of thing, of course, is not uncommon in the lobbying industry. Lobbying firms are stocked with former army brass or congressmen, all of whom are supposed to know the ins and outs of their former organizations.

The question is whether Halliburton's extremely close ties to the DOD, the vice president's office, and the Oval Office constituted undue influence and whether Halliburton was paying for these enormous favors by helping George W. Bush out politically.

"THE BEST-CONNECTED"

As a neophyte president who had little governing experience and who continued to dodge rumors of a feckless youth, allegations that he was insubstantial, and the doubts of at least half the American people that he should even be sitting in the Oval Office, George W. Bush needed to surround himself with experienced figures. This was why Dick Cheney was such an inspired choice for vice president. Not only had Cheney been secretary of defense during the administration of George W. Bush's father (whose failings had been by and large forgotten and was now a revered ex-president), but Cheney had powerful connections on Capitol Hill and also—very appealingly—did not have a long-term political agenda. The victim of four heart attacks (the last during the election recount in Florida in November 2000), he had avowed numerous times that once George Bush left the White House, he was leaving, too.

Grateful to Dick Cheney (although he would later come to resent him) George Bush listened to his vice president and Donald Rumsfeld at DOD and allowed Halliburton/KBR to become the chief contractor and outsourcer for the DOD and the U.S. military. This is despite the fact that Cheney was already under suspicion for his lies when it came to his tenure as CEO of Halliburton. In a television interview during the 2000 campaign, reporter Sam Donaldson asked Cheney: "I'm told, and correct me if I'm wrong, that Halliburton, through subsidiary companies, was actually trying to do business in Iraq?"

And Cheney replied. "No. No, I had a firm policy that we wouldn't do anything in Iraq."

In fact, according to the *New York Times*, Halliburton did more business with Saddam Hussein's outlaw regime then anyone else—about $30 million worth of business, which included, according to *New York Times* columnist Nicholas Kristof, "selling more equipment to Iraq than any other company did."

Despite this, in October 2001, George Bush appointed Halliburton board member Ray Hunt to the President's Foreign Intelligence Advisory Board (PFIAB), which advises the president on the performance of various intelligence agencies of the United States. The board, according to a 2005 article in *Salon.com*, represents the "who's who of the Halliburton-Texas Rangers-oil business crony club that made Bush into a millionaire and helped propel him into the White House."

Ray Hunt was the man who determined that Cheney's departure from Halliburton would be an "early retirement" rather than a "resignation." And Bush was giving him quite a reward. The work of the PFIAB is done in secret, and information that it discovers can help someone like Hunt—who has his own private oil company, or Halliburton, whose interests Hunt looks out for as a board member. The PFIAB position, says Steven Aftergood, who heads the Project on Government Secrecy at the Federation of American Scientists, and is quoted in the *Salon.com* article, "lends itself to exploitation for commercial and other interests." Aftergood goes on to say that the people Bush appointed or reappointed to the PFIAB board—including two others with connections to Halliburton—"are not the best and the brightest. They are the best-connected." In 2008, possibly taking advantage of his PFIAB connections and information, Ray Hunt signed an oil production deal with Iraq's Kurdistan regional government. At the time, President Bush said: "I know nothing about this deal," which many in Congress felt jeopardized negotiations with other regions in Iraq for a unified profit-sharing plan.

RIO

Halliburton's LOGCAP contract, signed on December 14, a few short months after the trauma of 9/11, outraged critics because it was a secret "no-bid" contract. The GAO occasionally signs such contracts in emergency wartime situations, under a provision known as "compelling emergency," but while the United States had attacked Afghanistan, it was still almost a year and a half away from the big war in Iraq. And even if this was a case of "compelling emergency," the Army would have needed to provide, according to testimony the GAO comptroller later gave before Congress, "a written justification to authorize work without competition."

This was never done. In fact, several army lawyers recommended against using Halliburton, because it posed a conflict of interest, and because of Halliburton's previous overcharges and "losing accounting control" of large sums of money. Yet the Halliburton deal went forward.

As the Iraq War begins in March 2003, workers from the Halliburton subsidiary
Boots and Coots International Well Control prepare to cap an oil well set ablaze
in southern Iraq. Halliburton had controversial government "no-bid" contracts covering
almost every aspect of the war, from supplying troops to rebuilding Iraq's infrastructure.

Associated Press

———★———

This quite likely indicates top-down involvement of the White House. Halliburton/KBR was also given another contact, called CONCAP (Contingency Construction Capabilities), tasking it with building new detention facilities in Guantanamo Bay, Cuba, where Al Qaeda suspects picked up in Afghanistan were being held.

But Halliburton/KBR's main job was taking place in Kuwait, where two enormous U.S. bases were being built. As 2002 began, the Bush Administration was already planning the invasion of Iraq—an invasion imagined by Donald Rumsfeld and General Tommy Franks as employing just 150,000 troops (although that would later expand to almost twice that number). To make this even remotely possible, KBR was needed to do the logistics work. But there was an even bigger and possibly more lucrative job at hand, and that concerned Saddam's threat to set fire to Iraq's southern oil fields in the event that the United States attacked. He had done this in Kuwait during the first Gulf War, his troops exploded oil wells with plastic explosives, causing fires that burned for six months that caused millions of dollars in damage. Saddam also had his troops open up valves at oil terminals, deliberately spilling vast amounts of crude oil into the Persian Gulf, which caused deeply disturbing environmental consequences that lingered for years.

The United States had U.S. Navy SEALS ready to attack and secure Mina al-Bakr, Iraq's main oil terminus for export, the minute bombs started dropping on Baghdad, but there was still a chance Saddam might fire his oil wells. Plus, Iraq's refineries were already in disrepair from years of war (with Iran and the United States) and sanctions. Therefore, there was a new contract, called Restore Iraqi Oil (RIO) just waiting for U.S. oil companies. Halliburton/KBR had already drawn up a contingency plan in case Saddam did fire his wells, for which they had billed the U.S. government $1.9 million.

Even so, there were other companies qualified and greatly interested, including Bechtel, Fluor, and Parsons. And yet, according to one Army Corps of Engineers participant, KBR representatives were allowed to attend meetings where the exact budget being apportioned for this work was discussed. Armed with this secret knowledge, they were able to make a bid that would get them the job. As it turned out, Saddam was only able to fire seven oil wells before the troops guarding his refineries were overwhelmed by U.S. forces. However, Halliburton was still under contract for nearly $5 billion to restore Iraq's oil fields, in one of its infamous "cost-plus" deals, in which Halliburton would be paid its expenses, plus 2 to 7 percent more. Once again, the higher its expenses, the more money Halliburton would make.

Despite the fact that billions of dollars worth of contracts were being given to Halliburton, the lack of oversight of the company's activities was "staggering," a 2007 report by the Center for Public Integrity (CPI) wrote. The Center found that the Defense Department was, in some cases, unable to account for what it was receiving in return for payments. Earlier, a 2004 report from the GAO focused on the fact that military officials using Halliburton's services "had received no training regarding their roles and responsibilities" and therefore had "little basis on which to judge the reasonableness of Halliburton's costs."

If those on the ground couldn't understand what they were being billed for, it is unlikely anyone higher up could either. With the Bush and Cheney war in Iraq, Halliburton had received a huge blank check, to be cashed with taxpayer dollars.

"DON'T WORRY ABOUT THE PRICE"

The Center for Public Integrity ranked Halliburton/KBR as the top earner of the U.S. government, in terms of total contract value, from 2002–04, with contracts, mainly in Iraq and Afghanistan, totaling $11,431,000,000. This is more than twice that awarded Halliburton's nearest competitor, Parsons Corp, which was awarded slightly more than $5 billion in contracts over the same period.

———★———

DESPITE THE FACT THAT BILLIONS OF DOLLARS WORTH OF CONTRACTS WERE BEING GIVEN TO HALLIBURTON, THE LACK OF OVERSIGHT OF THE COMPANY'S ACTIVITIES WAS "STAGGERING," A 2007 REPORT BY THE CENTER FOR PUBLIC INTEGRITY WROTE. THE CENTER FOUND THAT THE DEFENSE DEPARTMENT WAS, IN SOME CASES, UNABLE TO ACCOUNT FOR WHAT IT WAS RECEIVING IN RETURN FOR PAYMENTS.

———★———

During George Bush's 2004 campaign against John Kerry, Halliburton contributed more than $1 million to the Bush campaign and related Republican campaigns, and in fact had contributed more than $2 million to Republican campaigns from 1990–2004. There is nothing unusual about corporations backing candidates whom they think can provide business for them. But there has never been a higher-profile conflict of interest situation than that which existed between the Bush White House and Halliburton. Members of Congress protested from the beginning, but because of the air of heavy secrecy surrounding the Bush Administration's decisions—and because of Dick Cheney's longtime stance that Congress should have little say in the president's foreign policy decisions—it was not until 2004 that serious allegations against Halliburton were raised.

And this was mainly because of the incompetence and greed of the company itself. Auditors within the Pentagon claimed that KBR overcharged the U.S. Army for meals it had served its troops. According to a report by the Defense Contract Audit Agency (DCAA), KBR's "billed head count numbers exceed the actual meals served by 19 percent… but could be as high as 36 percent based on an ongoing DCAA analysis." In fact, said William Reed, the amount of overcharging might amount to as high as $186 million. An earlier DCAA audit had found that Halliburton/KBR had overcharged the government by as much as $61 million for gas used by its truckers in Kuwait and Iraq.

And Halliburton was doing shoddy work. It was supposed to rebuild motors and refurbish oil pumps in the Iraqi oil fields, but much of this equipment failed in under a year. The equipment installed was substandard, according to Pratap Chatterjee. Halliburton was also supposed to rebuild a vital oil pipeline network in northern Iraq, which had been destroyed by U.S. bombing. The company spent its entire $75 million budget without actually doing so, and another company had to be hired to finish the project.

Because of the type of contracts Halliburton was awarded, it was able to make money, in many instances, without actually doing much of anything. And even when it did provide services, as it did with feeding and housing U.S. troops, it had a great deal of incentive to overcharge, because the greater the company's expenses, the more money it made. As Pentagon investigators discovered, Halliburton/KBR supervisors routinely told employees: "Don't worry about the price. It's cost-plus."

Despite the allegations, Halliburton's contracts increased an amazing 600 percent in the five years from 2000–05 under the Bush-Cheney Administration. It received contracts to rebuild navy yards damaged after Hurricane Katrina, and to drill for oil and natural gas in South America. The pressure finally began to get to Halliburton, however. In 2006, as four separate Department of Justice investigations of KBR were getting under way, it decided to spin off Kellogg, Brown & Root as a separate company, with CEO David Lesar stating that the company was the victim of "vicious" political attacks. This was finally accomplished in 2007, but as late as April 2010, the Department of Justice is suing KBR because the company billed it for private armed security services it had subcontracted, which were not a part of its original contract.

TEXAS HEAVEN

George Bush and Dick Cheney are out of office now and while Dick Cheney is saying a great deal about how badly he thinks the country's Democratic leadership is running the nation, he has little more to say about Halliburton than he has already said—that the company's astonishing multibillion dollar contracts had nothing to do with his connections there, but only with how experienced and competent Halliburton was at its job. Given the investigations that have ensued, this is hard to believe.

George Bush, retired to Houston, has had little to say about the controversies surrounding KBR and Halliburton, beyond stating that if Halliburton overcharged the U.S. government, then it should repay the money. Yet Bush presided over what has become the most notorious play-for-pay operation in the history of U.S. presidents. While he did not personally profit from his and his vice president's involvement with Halliburton, his campaign coffers, and those of his fellow Republicans, were filled because of his insistence that the company be given preferential treatment when it came to hugely profitable contracts for work done in Iraq and Afghanistan and elsewhere, work which was often shoddy and corrupt.

The fact that the company was awarded sweetheart deals financed with taxpayer dollars and then provided with little or no oversight shows that it was business as usual for these Texans, business as it had been done going all the way back to the 1930s. Get the politicians on your side, low-bid or no-bid your contracts, and the rest will follow. Halliburton created a little bit of Texas heaven in Iraq, thanks to George W. Bush and Dick Cheney.

BIBLIOGRAPHY

★ ★ ★

——— ★ ———

CHAPTER 1
ABRAHAM LINCOLN

Baker, Jean H. *Mary Todd Lincoln: A Biography.* New York: W. W. Norton, 1987.

Burlingame, Michael. *Abraham Lincoln: A Life.* 2 vols. Baltimore, Md.: The Johns Hopkins University Press, 2008

Burlingame, Michael and John Hay. *At Lincoln's Side: John Hay's Civil War Correspondence and Selected Writings.* Carbondale, Ill.: Southern Illinois University Press, 2000.

Emerson, Jason. "The Lincoln Marriage." *American Heritage,* June 2006.

Emerson, Jason. *The Madness of Mary Lincoln.* Carbondale, Ill.: Southern Illinois University Press, 2007.

Turner, Justin G. and Linda Levitt Turner. *Mary Todd Lincoln: Her Life and Letters.* New York: Alfred A. Knopf, 1972.

"The Trouble with Patronage." *Lincoln Editor,* July-September, 2004.

The Lincoln Institute. "Mr. Lincoln and New York." www.mrlincolnandnewyork.org/

——— ★ ———

CHAPTER 2
ULYSSES S. GRANT AND THE WHISKEY RING

Benjamin H. Bristow. United States Department of Justice. www.justice.gov/osg/aboutosg/bristbio.html

Grant Monument Association. "Grant at Long Branch." Grant's Tomb. www.grantstomb.org/news/lb03.html

McFeely, William S. *Grant: A Biography.* New York: W. W. Norton, 1981.

Perret, Geoffrey. *Ulysses. S. Grant: Soldier & President.* New York: Random House, 1997.

Woodward, C. Vann. "The Lowest Ebb." *American Heritage*, April 1957.

———★———

CHAPTER 3
ULYSSES S. GRANT AND THE GOLD RING

Ackerman, Kenneth D. *The Gold Ring: Jim Fisk, Jay Gould, and Black Friday, 1869.* New York: Dodd, Mean & Company, 1988.

Investigation into the Causes of the Gold Panic: Report of the Majority of the Committee on Banking and Currency. Government Printing Office, 1870.

Klein, Maury. *The Life and Legend of Jay Gould.* Baltimore, Md.: The Johns Hopkins University Press, 1986.

———★———

CHAPTER 4
WARREN HARDING AND THE TEAPOT DOME SCANDAL

Dean, John W. *Warren G. Harding.* New York: Times Books, 2004.

McCartney, Laton. *The Teapot Dome Scandal: How Big Oil Bought the Harding White House and Tried to Steal the Country.* New York: Random House, 2008.

Stratton, David H. *Tempest Over Teapot Dome: The Story of Albert B. Fall.* Norman, Okla.: University of Oklahoma Press, 1998.

Trani, Eugene P. and Wilson, David L. *The Presidency of Warren G. Harding.* Lawrence, Kans.: University of Kansas Press, 1977.

——————★——————

CHAPTER 5
JOHN F. KENNEDY AND VOTE-BUYING IN WEST VIRGINIA

Casey, Shaun A. *The Making of A Catholic President: Kennedy Vs. Nixon 1960.* New York: Oxford University Press, 2009.

Haught, James. "Kennedy vs. Humphrey: 50 years ago, W.Va. made history by helping to make the JFK candidacy." *Charleston Gazette,* April 30, 2010.

Hersh, Seymour M. *The Dark Side of Camelot.* New York: Little, Brown, 1997.

Humphrey, Hubert H. *The Education of a Public Man: My Life and Politics.* Minneapolis, Minn.: University of Minnesota Press, 1991.

Porterfield, Mannix. "Catholic issue 'exaggerated' in 1960 primary?" *Register-Herald Reporter,* May 10, 2010.

Reeves, Thomas C. *A Question of Character: A Life of John F. Kennedy.* New York: The Free Press, 1991.

Rorabaugh, W. J. *The Real Making of the President: Kennedy, Nixon, and the 1960 Election.* Lawwrence, Kans.: University Press of Kansas, 2009.

Vaillancourt, Meg. "JFK campaign allegations W. Va. politician writes of buying votes for candidate in '60." *The Boston Globe,* 1994.

"Vote Buying, Bigotry Seen in Logan." *The Charleston Gazette,* May 6, 1960.

———— ★ ————

CHAPTER 6
RICHARD NIXON

Bernstein, Carl and Bob Woodward. *The Final Days.* New York: Simon & Schuster, 2005.

Herzog, Arthur. *Vesco: From Wall Street to Castro's Cuba, the Rise, Fall and Exile of the King of White-Collar Crime.* New York: Doubleday, 1987.

Rosen, James. *The Strong Man: John Mitchell and the Secrets of Watergate.* New York: Doubleday, 2008.

Summers, Anthony. *The Arrogance of Power: The Secret World of Richard Nixon.* New York: Viking Press, 2000.

———— ★ ————

CHAPTER 7
RONALD REAGAN AND THE HUD SCANDAL

Cannon, Lou. *President Reagan: The Role of a Lifetime.* New York: Simon & Schuster, 1991.

DeHaven, Tad. "HUD Scandals." *Downsizing the Federal Government.* Cato Institute. www.downsizinggovernment.org/hud/scandals.

Welfeld, Irving. *HUD Scandals: Howling Headlines and Silent Fiascoes.* New Brunswick, NJ: Transaction Publishers, 1992.

———★———

CHAPTER 8
RONALD REAGAN AND THE IRAN-CONTRA AFFAIR

Draper, Theodore. *A Very Thin Line: The Iran-Contra Affairs.* New York: HarperCollins, 1991.

Haynes, Johnson. *Sleepwalking Through History: America in the Reagan Years.* New York: W. W. Norton, 1991.

National Security Archive. "The Iran-Contra Affair 20 Years On." November 24, 2006. http://www.gwu.edu/~nsarchiv/NSAEBB/NSAEBB210/index.htm

Timberg, Robert. *The Nightingale's Song.* New York: Simon & Schuster, 1995

———★———

CHAPTER 9
BILL CLINTON AND THE SELLING
OF THE WHITE HOUSE

Bennett, William J. *The Death of Outrage: Bill Clinton and the Assault on American Ideals.* New York: The Free Press, 1998.

Ebrahim, Margaret. "Fat Cat Hotel" *Center for Public Integrity, Special Issue,* August, 1996.

Harris, John F. *The Survivor: Bill Clinton in the White House.* New York: Random House, 2005.

Smith, Sally Bedell. *For Love of Politics. Bill and Hillary Clinton: The White House Years.* New York: Random House, 2007.

———★———

CHAPTER 10
BILL CLINTON AND THE PARDONING OF MARC RICH

Ammann, Daniel. *The King of Oil: The Secret Lives of Marc Rich.* New York: St. Martin's Press, 2009.

"Benefits." *The New York Times.* November 26, 2000.

Dionne, E. J. "...And the Gifts That Keep on Giving." *The Washington Post.* February 6, 2001.

Justice Undone: Clemency Decisions in the Clinton White House. House Committee on Government Reform, 2002.

Lambro, Donald. "Carter calls Clinton's Rich pardon 'disgraceful.'" *The Washington Times.* February 22, 2001.

Olson, Barbara. *The Final Days: The Last, Desperate Abuses of Power by the Clinton White House.* Washington, D.C.: Regnery Publishing, 2001.

Reaves, Jessica. "The Marc Rich Case: A Primer." *Time,* February 13, 2001.

"Schumer Unconvinced by Clinton's Explanation of Rich Pardon." CNN. February 19, 2001.

"The G&P Foundation for Cancer Research," *Neoplasia*, 3, no. 6 (2001): 547–49. www.ncbi.nlm.nih.gov/pmc/articles/PMC1506566/

Tyrrell, R. Emmett. *The Clinton Crack-Up: The Boy President's Life after the White House.* Nashville, Tenn.: Thomas Nelson, 2008.

"Unpardonable." *The Washington Post.* January 23, 2001.

Weisskopf, Michael. "Sources: Ex-Wife of Pardoned Fugitive Gave $400,000 to Clinton Library." *Time,* February 9, 2001.

———★———

CHAPTER 11
GEORGE W. BUSH, DICK CHENEY, AND HALLIBURTON

Bryce, Robert. *Cronies: Oil, The Bushes, and the Rise of Texas, America's Superstate.* New York: Public Affairs, 2004.

Chatterjee, Pratap. *Halliburton's Army: How A Well-Connected Texas Oil Company Revolutionized the Way America Makes War.* New York: Nation Book, 2009.

Dean, John. *Worse Than Watergate: The Secret Presidency of George W. Bush.* New York: Little, Brown, Inc., 2004.

ACKNOWLEDGMENTS

★ ★ ★

My sincere thanks to my publisher, Will Kiester, and my editor Cara Connors. I am especially grateful to m friends Joseph Cummins and Cormac O'Brien. Their expertise was invaluable—I couldn't have completed this book without them.

ABOUT THE AUTHOR

★ ★ ★

THOMAS J. CRAUGHWELL is the author of more than a dozen books, including *Failures of the Presidents*, *Stealing Lincoln's Body*, and *The Rise and Fall of the Second Largest Empire in History*. He has written articles on history, religion, politics, and popular culture for the *Wall Street Journal*, the *American Spectato*r, and *U.S. News & World Report*. He lives in Bethel, Connecticut.

INDEX

★ ★ ★